CAVOUR

PROFILES IN POWER

General Editor: Keith Robbins

ELIZABETH I
Christopher Haigh

RICHELIEU
R.J. Knecht

GUSTAVUS ADOLPHUS
Michael Roberts

OLIVER CROMWELL
Barry Coward

JOSEPH II
T.C.W. Blanning

ALEXANDER I
Janet M. Hartley

CAVOUR
Harry Hearder

JUÁREZ
Brian Hamnett

NAPOLEON III
James F. McMillan

ATATÜRK
A.L. Macfie

LLOYD GEORGE
Martin Pugh

HITLER
Ian Kershaw

CHURCHILL
Keith Robbins

NASSER
Peter Woodward

DE GAULLE
Andrew Shennan

FRANCO
Sheelagh Ellwood

MACMILLAN
John Turner

CASTRO
Sebastian Balfour

. . . . .

CAVOUR

Harry Hearder

LONGMAN
London and New York

Longman Group UK Limited
Longman House, Burnt Mill,
Harlow, Essex CM20 2JE, England
and Associated Companies throughout the world.

*Published in the United States of America
by Longman Publishing, New York*

First published 1994

ISBN 0 582 01899 4 CSD
ISBN 0 582 01903 6 PPR

British Library Cataloguing-in-Publication Data

A catalogue record for this book is
available from the British Library

Library of Congress Cataloging-in-Publication Data

Hearder, Harry
Cavour/Harry Hearder.
p. cm. — (Profiles in power)
Includes bibliographical references and index.
ISBN 0–582–01899–4
1. Cavour, Camillo Benso, conte di, 1810–1861.   2. Statesmen—
Italy—Biography.   3. Italy—History—1815–1870.   I.Title.
II.   Series:Profiles in power (London, England)
DG552.8.C3H42 1994
945'.083'092—dc20
[B]   93–38424
                                               CIP

**Transferred to digital print on demand 2001.
Printed & Bound by Antony Rowe Ltd, Eastbourne.**

CONTENTS

PREFACE

A study of Cavour must be the study not so much of a
man who held power, as of one who created a position of
power which had not existed when his career began. The
first prime minister of Italy, he was to hold that position
for only a few months before his premature death, though
as prime minister of Piedmont he had been making a major
contribution to the formation of an independent Italy. He
deserves a place, then, in a series on people in power in a
rather special sense. Not only did he hold power: he himself
created it.

Recent generations of historians have been inclined to
argue that Cavour was more concerned with increasing
the power of Piedmont than with the unification of Italy.
It is an argument which will be carefully examined in this
book. It is true that while he knew Geneva, Paris and
London, he never set foot in Rome or Naples, and visited
Florence only on one brief occasion. In that sense he was
Piedmontese, or European, rather than Italian. But so far
as his personality went, he did not conform to the stereotype
of the Piedmontese, who like to think of themselves as
correct in their manner, self-controlled, even rather silent
and introvert, in contrast with the garrulous and expansive
people elsewhere in the peninsula. The Piedmontese may be
silent by Italian, if not by English, standards, but Cavour was
not silent by any standard. He was not correct in behaviour,
being given to outbursts of violent, uncontrollable rage.
He was extremely convivial, but also selfish, often ruthless.
His personality was partly redeemed by his good humour,
his total lack of pomposity, and his amused tolerance of
pretentiousness in others. He was not a tyrant, but he was far

from being a saint. His virtues, like his vices, were essentially human ones. It is this which makes a study of his life, his career, his beliefs and his motives, such an agreeable one.

I would like to thank Professor Keith Robbins for inviting me to write a book in his series. I would also like to thank Dr Robert Oresko and Professor Derek Beales: I read a version of Chapter 8 'Cavour and the Historians' to Dr Oresko's seminar on Italian History at the Institute of Historical Research of the University of London, and to Professor Beales's seminar on Modern European History at Sidney Sussex College, Cambridge. I hope that that longish chapter will not be regarded simply as a bibliographical essay, but will add depth to the picture of Cavour that I have tried to present.

Cavour was often called by his admirers 'the architect of Italy'. In so far as an architect plans a construction from scratch, the term was inappropriate for Cavour, who might better be termed 'the master-builder'. I am dedicating this book to my son, Alex, who is training to be an actual architect.

Harry Hearder
May 1993

ABBREVIATIONS

Cavour-Nigra	*Il Carteggio Cavour-Nigra dal 1858 al 1861* (Zanichelli, Bologna, 1926)
Chiala	Count Cavour, *Lettere edite ed inedite*, edited by Luigi Chiala, 6 vols., (Roux e Favale, Turin, 1883–1887)
Clarendon	The Clarendon Papers in the Bodleian Library
Di Nolfo	Ennio di Nolfo, *Europa e Italia nel 1855–1856* (Rome, 1967)
Epistolario	C. Pischedda, N. Nada and R. Roccia, editors, *Camillo Cavour Epistolario* (Olschki, Florence, 1962–1992)
Mack Smith	Denis Mack Smith, *The Making of Italy 1796–1866* (Macmillan, London, 1968; revised edition 1988)
Rome	Archivio di Stato, Ministero degli Affari Esteri, Rome
Romeo	Rosario Romeo, *Cavour e il suo tempo*, 3 vols., (Laterza, Bari, 1969–1984)
Ruffini	Francesco Ruffini, *La giovinezza del Conte di Cavour* (Bocca, Turin, 1912)
Turin	Archivio di Stato, Turin

FOR MY SON, ALEXANDER

Chapter 1

ORIGINS, BOYHOOD AND YOUTH, 1810–30

Cavour was born on 10 August 1810. His father was the Marquis Michele Antonio Benso di Cavour, an able and successful Piedmontese landowner. His mother, Adèle de Sellon, came from a French Huguenot family, who had been settled in Switzerland for several generations, and had subsequently become Catholics. Cavour's godparents were French rulers of Napoleonic Italy. His godfather was Prince Camillo Borghese, governor general of the Transalpine departments of the French Empire, and his godmother was the Princess Paolina Bonaparte, sister of the great Emperor. He was thus christened Camillo. There is no record that it was ever considered naming him Napoleon.

The family name was thus Benso, and the Bensos had been an enterprising people. They claimed to have come to Italy with Frederick Barbarossa, but what could be known historically was that they had been bankers and merchants in the province of Chieri in the late middle ages. A Goffredo Benso was trading with Brazil as early as 1542. Later in that century the family moved to Turin to take posts in the court of the House of Savoy. Carlo Ottavio Benso, who died in 1724, was made Count of Santena, and built the castle which still stands in Santena today. Carlo Benso's male line died out in 1753, but the line of the family from which Camillo Cavour was to come had already, in 1649, acquired the title of Marquis de Cavour for 20,000 lire. Cavour is a small town some thirty miles to the south-west of Turin.

The future of the family was by no means assured by the title of Cavour, but after many changes of fortune a Filippo di Cavour, in 1781, married Filippina, of the rich Savoyard family of the De Sales, of which St Francis de

Sales had been a member. Filippo was Cavour's paternal grandfather, and died only three years before Cavour's birth. Filippina, Cavour's paternal grandmother, lived until 1847, dying at the age of eighty-seven, too early to see her grandson become prime minister of Piedmont. With the wealth acquired by Fillipo's fortunate marriage the Cavours purchased considerable lands and the palace in Turin where Cavour was to be born and to die. The street is called today, inevitably, Via Cavour, having had three previous names.

Cavour's father, the Marquis Michele, was born in 1781, and was to live until 1850, sadly, like his own mother, dying before his son had achieved success. The family went through a bad spell after the Napoleonic invasion of 1796, losing a great deal of property. But they quickly accepted service under the French, and then for some years changed sides with a rapidity that would have done credit to the Vicar of Bray. They hastened to re-establish their loyalty to the restored legitimate Piedmontese regime when the Austro-Russian offensive under General Suvarov drove the French out of Italy in 1799. But after Napoleon's victory at Marengo in 1800 the Marquis Michele secured a reconciliation with the French, and was given a post at court under the new rulers. He then built up another fortune by the purchase of Church land dispossessed by the French. In 1814 he was adroit enough to secure, once again, the favour of the restored House of Savoy.

Cavour's father has often been contrasted unfavourably with his famous son, rather as Bismarck has been contrasted with the slow, thick-headed Junker who was his father. But the Marquis Michele's dexterity at changing sides at least suggests that he was not slow-witted. The difference between Michele and Camillo was primarily one between generations. Michele believed that Piedmont should remain an agricultural country under a paternalistic absolutist monarch. Camillo, as we shall see, believed passionately in gradual social and economic change, industrialization, and a limited constitutional monarchy. Relations between father and son were often strained, though an early author on the youth of Cavour, Francesco Ruffini, claimed that the most important revelation of his book, which was a serious and well written work, was that Michele was adored by all his relatives, close and distant, and that he was an excellent

2

paterfamilias. He was, according to Ruffini, only a little severe with strangers.[1]

The family of Cavour's mother, Adèle de Sellon, was cultured as well as rich. Adèle was one of three daughters. Michele di Cavour tried unsuccessfully to marry the eldest of the three, but had to settle for the second, Adèle, and they were married in 1805. Adèle had been well educated and had been taken on a long trip to Italy in 1790, seeing Rome and Naples, and staying in Florence from the end of 1792 to the summer of 1794. Like all her side of Cavour's family, she developed a great affection for the customs and culture of Italy. Of the man she was to marry she noted in her diary, when the De Sellon family set out for their Swiss home from Italy: '"Cavourino" was our second brother. He is likeable, gay, obliging, lively. He is the young man with whom I am most at my ease'.[2] Evidently Cavour's father, as a young man, was not unlike Cavour.

The considerable wealth of both of Cavour's parents obviously contributed to his self-confidence, not to say arrogance. The noble, patrician background in Turin, with its deep roots, formed a happy mixture with the more cosmopolitan background of his mother's many relatives in Geneva. Camillo's brother, Gustavo, was four years older but was to live until 1864 – three years beyond Cavour's death. The two boys grew up in close contact, always in a noisy and rowdy atmosphere. Gustavo was believed to be the philosophical genius of the family, while Camillo was characterized as a jolly extrovert, always seeking new ways of enjoying life. Their father was later to sum up the contrast between the two brothers by saying that Gustavo lived in the world of *noumena* and Camillo lived in the world of *phaenomena*.

Much was expected of the boys. Their mother was distressed when she could not teach Camillo the alphabet at the age of four, and when he hated book studies at the age of five. But he had great intellectual curiosity. The tutors their parents hired for the two boys praised Gustavo, but complained that Camillo lay in bed until midday, then got up, did well at his lesson, but was not very obedient. He grumbled and cried at having to study. 'He has been very naughty all day', commented the tutor. To which Camillo replied, with a precocious sense of humour, 'I cannot stand studying. What do you want me to do? It is not my fault'.[3]

Camillo as a boy was clearly high-spirited, awkward, often impossible, but also likeable and entertaining. (His brother was to have a life punctuated by tragedy. He married, but his wife died when she was young. He had three children, two boys and one girl. Of the two boys, who might have kept the Cavour line going, one remained a batchelor, and the other was killed in 1848 in the First War of Italian Independence, at the battle of Goito.) Their mother was a devoutly religious woman. Gustavo acquired her pious convictions and habits of life, which Camillo never adopted. Gustavo was not entirely a recluse, however. He was to take a seat in the Piedmontese parliament, where he was concerned only to defend the Church against the assaults of the secular state, especially assaults launched by his brother. But although their opinions and their whole attitude to life were in such sharp contrast, the two brothers retained an affection for each other.

The Benso family had for long had ties not only with the royal government and the landed nobility, but also with the Piedmontese army. Usually the eldest sons of Piedmontese noble families were trained for the army, but as Gustavo was a quiet, studious, introverted boy, whose health was believed to be poor, it was decided that the robust Camillo should have a military career. His aunt, the formidable Vittoria de Clermont-Tonnerre said he was 'born and created to be a military man'. Her judgement was not good. So, on 30 April 1820, at the age of ten, Camillo was sent to be a boarder at the Royal Military Academy in Turin. The institution was run on strictly military lines, and the teachers were army officers or N.C.O.s, sometimes rather rugged and brutal soldiers. It was a grinding curriculum of academic study, military exercises and religious practices, with no official vacations. Attendance at chapel was required twice a day. Like many spirited youths, Cavour was turned against formal Christianity by regular religious services. A savage discipline was imposed, with punishments consisting of prolonged military exercises, or long periods spent on the knees.[4]

At school Cavour was thus inevitably a rebel, receiving severe punishments for disobedience and for possessing forbidden literature. He was most successful in mathematics and mechanics. To anyone familiar with English public schools it may come as a surprise to learn that mechanics was taught in such an institution, but the traditional classical subjects were also, of course, taught. Cavour, who was never very competent in literary subjects, and who always spoke better than he wrote, did poorly in Italian language and literature. On the positive side, it must be said that the school seems to have been strong in the teaching of the sciences, both pure and applied. Several leaders of the *risorgimento* were, after all, educated there, though whether they were forward-looking as a result of their education or as a backlash against it, is open to argument.

The little Cavour's first letters home suggest that he was homesick and that he missed his 'dear mama' and his 'dear brother', thus implying that his home life, if tempestuous, had been a happy one. By 1821, when he reached his eleventh birthday, he was doing very well academically – better than his contemporaries – but was getting into trouble for offences against the discipline of the place, a discipline which he was intelligent enough to regard as mindless. Nevertheless, when the revolution of 1821 broke out in Piedmont, and some students of the Royal Academy got into trouble with the authorities, Camillo remained immune. In February 1822, however, he was found 'guilty of grave disobedience', and condemned to bread and water for three days, and in August of that year he and a friend were found guilty of 'having kept books without permission of his superiors', but apparently the books in question were simply two novels from his father's house.

That he was already eager to secure recognition in the world is indicated by a desire to be first in the class, a desire which led him to request to be moved into a lower class, where he knew he could shine. His tutor, as gently as possible, explained that it would be better for him to remain where he was, but to work harder. The letters of the young Cavour from school thus show him to have been proud, conceited, always ready to contradict his superiors and above all, disobedient and rebellious. They were characteristics which were to be of considerable service to Piedmont and Italy in the years ahead.

On 9 July 1824 Prince Carlo Alberto, the future king of Piedmont, nominated Camillo one of his pages. He had not yet reached his fourteenth birthday, and the Cavour family were delighted. A valuable pension and a brilliant career seemed to be opened to Camillo. But the young man did not share his parents' enthusiasm. 'You must realize, my dear papa', he wrote, 'that I have no wish to be a page, But since it will please you, I resign myself to it patiently'. What particularly irritated him was the quaint red livery that he had to wear, a livery which seemed to him that of a humble domestic, and the court rituals he found equally degrading.

Meanwhile at school he continued to do well in maths, which was evidently taught thoroughly because it was needed by officers in the artillery and engineering branches of the army. For Cavour the importance of mathematics lay in its role as a training of the mind. He still did less well in literary subjects, and later regretted that he had not been taught to write elegantly or fluently, although some of his parliamentary speeches and letters suggest that he exaggerated the deficiency. In physical and military exercises he was not brilliant, mainly, it seems, because he disliked taking orders, and was lazy. He preferred to study the social sciences and history, which he had to do on his own.

In 1825–26 Camillo experienced a sharp crisis with his family. He became a close friend of another, slightly older, boy – Severino Cassio, who was something of a revolutionary and an Italian nationalist. The family insisted that Camillo should break off the friendship, which he did, but only with great bitterness and distress, and, as it proved, only temporarily. He subsequently renewed relations with Severino, asking his forgiveness for having broken with him so suddenly. His relationship with his father, on the other hand, changed, as Camillo acquired maturity and psychological autonomy. However, the Marquis Michele, having threatened to send his rebellious son 'to die of hunger in America', was subsequently to be very generous to him. It is interesting to speculate what Camillo would have made of America: that he would have died of hunger seems unlikely.

There is some evidence that it was at this time – in his sixteenth year – that Cavour began to read newspapers and historical and political works, though such readings had no immediate influence. At the Academy his private war against the authorities continued. On 15 March 1826 he was excluded from horse-riding exercises for having been 'extremely negligent', and on the next day he was placed under arrest for having openly and defiantly disobeyed a superior. He was under arrest for two weeks, and on 19 April arrested again for replying arrogantly to a superior. But if they were trying to break him, they did not succeed. The Academy set forbidding final exams, which lasted for five months from March to August, 1826. Cavour's results were impressive. He secured maximum grades in all subjects, which related mostly to the application of engineering to military needs, but included differential calculus, civil architecture, history and even *elocuzione*, by which was meant literature. His name was at the top of the list of exam results, and for promotion purposes second only to a certain Marquis Scati, who, unlike Cavour, had remained a respectful page of Carlo Alberto. Cavour's disrespect and openly proclaimed contempt for the 'lackey's uniform' of the page led to his dismissal by Carlo Alberto.

Even before his sixteenth birthday, however, the young rebel had been made a second lieutenant in the Royal Engineers. When Prince Carlo Alberto asked his king, Carlo Felice, to strip Cavour of his newly acquired commission, the king was at first inclined to do so, but the commander of the engineers intervened: if Cavour were to go, the commander would resign also. So Cavour remained in the army, but the Cavour family abandoned any idea that he might have a career at court, and Cavour, for his part, kept his distance from Carlo Alberto, so soon to be king of Piedmont. Cavour did not take up his commission immediately, because of some undefined illness, from which he had evidently recovered early in 1827. In theory, he was not entirely averse to his new job in the army. When his pacifist uncle, Jean-Jacques de Sellon (of whom more in a moment), attacked armies in general, Cavour argued that the engineers might be a deterrent to warfare, and quoted Carnot, who had said that other military arms were destructive, but 'strong places' (presumably constructed by the engineers) were purely defensive.

When Cavour was at home in Turin the house was always full of relatives. Gustavo must have found it considerably more difficult than Camillo to live with this extended family of the nobility. Two of their mother's sisters, together with their husbands, came to live in the Palazzo Cavour. One of them – Vittoria de Clermont-Tonnerre – was married to a French peer and was a strongly reactionary influence on the young Cavour. Another relative on his mother's side was her brother, Count Jean-Jacques de Sellon, who was an influence in a strikingly progressive sense, whether directly, when he was living in the family house in Turin, or by correspondence. While Cavour's father's family were loyal monarchists, his mother's family tended towards republicanism and free-thinking, Adèle herself being the exception. Cavour had grown up in an atmosphere of continual debate, though evidently civilized and cultured debate. Arguments often went on until daybreak. Of all the large family Cavour seems at first to have preferred the company of his uncle, the Count de Sellon, although his own political opinions were always appreciably less advanced than De Sellon's convictions, which in their day seemed utopian.

De Sellon was proud to be called a 'philanthropist', and considered philanthropy 'the chivalry of modern times'. He had lived in his youth for four years in Italy, staying for long periods in Rome, Naples and Florence, so that this Swiss intellectual who was a first influence on Cavour actually knew Italy better than Cavour was ever to know it. It was in Florence that De Sellon found his spiritual home, partly because it was in Florence that capital punishment had been abolished by the good Grand Duke Piero Leopoldo in the eighteenth century, and the abolition of the barbarism of capital punishment was perhaps the main driving force of De Sellon's life. Another important motivation was pacifism on the international scene, and De Sellon founded in Geneva, as early as 1830, a society for establishing world peace. (If he could have lived until 1867 De Sellon would have witnessed another congress in Geneva for world peace, a congress attended by Garibaldi.) If the death sentence were ever to be abolished there would inevitably be more people confined to prison, and this thought led De Sellon to a study of the penitentiary system, an interest which would also be one of Cavour's. Even if Cavour was never to share the visionary ideas of De Sellon, he had, at least, been exposed to them.[5]

On 15 October 1828 Cavour was sent to Ventimiglia in connection with the building of fortifications. On 25 February 1829 he was moved to a different garrison at Exilles, and in May 1829 to the fortress of Lesseillon, near Modane. In these remote spots on the Alpine borders he was immensely bored. He always needed stimulating company, which he was not likely to find in the Piedmontese army. With the other young officers he could play and gamble at cards, but for intellectual satisfaction he was left to read in solitude. A rather strange publication has reproduced all Cavour's jottings – notes certainly never intended for publication. They include a variety of writings, from mathematical calculations to the poetry of Byron and Pope, carefully copied out in the original English. During his time in the army they included transcriptions, also in the original English, from Gibbon and David Hume.[6] He also read Adam Smith, Nassau Senior, David Ricardo and Malthus.

In the early autumn of 1829 Cavour spent two months in Geneva, two months during which the free and refreshing atmosphere of his mother's home town made a great impression on him. Now eighteen years old, he was expressing ideas more coherently, and in particular writing warmly of his belief in progress. It was impossible to read history, he wrote, without acquiring the belief that civilization ultimately overcame every difficulty, but that an honest person should feel an obligation to contribute to the process. On 28 November 1829 he wrote to his uncle, Jean-Jacques de Sellon, saying that he had waited to do so to give himself time to read Bentham's *Introduction to the Principles of Morals and Legislation,* or to be accurate a French translation and heavily adapted version by the Swiss writer, E. Dumont. Cavour makes the valid observation that Bentham's calculus of pleasure and pain omits the importance of 'moral and intellectual sufferings'. After a passing reference to Robespierre, Cavour comments: 'I do not believe that it is against natural law to kill a man when the well-being of society necessitates it', even though the majority of men are pained by the sufferings of their fellow-men. 'I do not believe that it is a natural law that children should blindly obey their parents as the Romans insisted', but it is socially desirable that parents should have power over their children, 'provided they exercise it within reasonable limits'. Religious sentiment can contribute towards this end and all peoples, 'and I would dare to say, all individuals' have some form of religious sentiment. These comments seemed to suggest that Cavour was aware of the limitations of Bentham's philosophy. He then adds, rather ambiguously, 'If we do not take as a basis of morality and legislation the principle of utility, then it is necessary to have recourse to natural law or to the dogmas of revelation'. And 'natural law', he says, has been appealed to as the justification for many bad laws. It is 'natural' for society to defend itself – an argument which can be taken as justifying hanging and torturing people. 'A system based *uniquely* on revealed truths or on the New Testament, it seems to me', Cavour continued, 'has very grave disadvantages, and Bentham has pointed them out with great skill'. If the teaching of Christ were observed to the letter, self defence, industry, commerce, and reciprocal bargains would be undermined. Ecclesiastical history illustrates the frightful evils which can result from certain interpretations of Christian teaching; but an interpretation according to Bentham's principle is possible without departing from a single Christian maxim. These arguments, if confused, at least illustrated the serious nature of the young man's thought. In the end, he seemed to be justifying Benthamism and his subsequent attitude to social and economic issues was to be essentially Benthamite.

In March 1830 the army posted Cavour to Genoa. In contrast to garrison posts in the mountains Genoa seemed to him a lively and intellectually stimulating place, much more so, indeed, than Turin. Two or three years later he was to confess that in Genoa in 1830 his political opinions had been 'very exaggerated' ones. In the exhilaration of that moment he had even – he remembered – dreamed that he might one day wake up to find himself prime minister of Italy. Since the very notion of Italy as a political unit was in 1830 a somewhat utopian one, the dream of this young man of twenty, the younger son of an admittedly noble family, was certainly a remarkable one. During his stay in Genoa Cavour was at his most radical. He enjoyed much democratic speculation at the salon of the Marquise Anna Giustiniani, with whom he started a long-drawn-out love affair. It was in Genoa that he heard news of the July Revolution in Paris which replaced the Bourbons by Louis-Philippe. To young radicals in France the revolution seemed to have gone off at half-cock, since one monarchical regime was replaced by another, which seemed liberal only in contrast with the Bourbons. Cavour, however, greeted the news of the Paris revolution with enthusiasm, expressing dismay only at the fact that 'Austrian bayonets' had prevented any improvement in the condition of Italy.

His open expressions of sympathy with the revolutionaries in Paris were probably the reason for the army's decision to move him from Genoa to another garrison in the mountains – Bard, in the Val d'Aosta. The boredom of his existence at Bard was more than he could stand. He asked leave to end his military career, and on 12 November 1831 the government granted his wish. Cavour was as delighted to be given an honourable discharge from an institution for which he was wholly unsuited as the army was almost certainly relieved to get rid of him. His official reason for being discharged was poor health, and more specifically deteriorating eyesight. It was true that he was short-sighted and wore glasses with powerful lenses at an early age, but the immediate reason for his release from the army – from the point of view of the establishment – was his enthusiastic reaction to the news of the fall of the French Bourbons.

At twenty-one Cavour's place in the world was a wholly undistinguished and unsuccessful one. No one could have guessed what achievements lay ahead.

· · ·

NOTES AND REFERENCES

1. Francesco Ruffini, *La giovinezza del Conte di Cavour* (Turin, Bocca, 1912), p. xxvii.
2. Rosario Romeo, *Cavour e il suo tempo*, vol. 1 (Bari, Laterza, 1969), p. 41).
3. *ibid*, p. 183.
4. *ibid*, p. 203.
5. Ruffini, *op. cit.*, has a good discussion of De Sellon on pp. 16–92.
6. *Tutti gli scritti di Camillo Cavour*, edited by Carlo Pischedda and Giuseppe Talamo (Centro Studi Piemontesi, Turin, 1976), the volume for the years 1823–1834.

Chapter 2

LOVER, FARMER AND SPECULATOR, 1830–48

Europe in 1830 seemed to be on the verge of great developments, but as so often in history the expected revolution was to prove premature. Since 1815 the dominant powers in Europe had been the Austrian empire under the Habsburg monarchy and the Russian empire of the czars. Britain's financial wealth and dominance of the seas made her influential in Europe and the Mediterranean, while France had not yet fully recovered from the disastrous defeats of 1812–15. The Austrian chancellor, Prince Clement von Metternich saw himself as the guardian of the existing political and social order, an order which he believed to be doomed, but which he felt was worth preserving for as long as possible. He regarded Italy as an Austrian sphere of influence, and until 1830 the other European powers tended to accept his claim.

. . .

ITALY IN 1830

Italy had emerged from the 1815 settlement, drawn up at Vienna by the representatives of the powers which had defeated Napoleon, without any form of political identity. Even the loose Confederation which the German peoples enjoyed (or, rather, suffered under) was lacking in Italy. The Italian peninsula consisted of the two provinces of Lombardy and Venetia, which were integral parts of the Habsburg Monarchy; the wholly independent states of the Kingdoms of Piedmont-Sardinia and Naples; the Papal States under the sovereignty of the pope; the rather smaller Grand Duchy of Tuscany; the yet smaller Duchies of Parma and Modena, and three or four minute states without political significance. For all intents and purposes, then, 'Italy' was a term for the cultural and geographical unit which consisted of six independent states and an important part of the Austrian empire.

The Austrian provinces with their historic capitals of Milan and Venice were deceptively called 'the Kingdom of Italy' by the Austrians, though the 'king' was the Habsburg emperor, Francis I. Since the emperor lived in Vienna, and visited Italy only on rare occasions, he was represented in Lombardo-Venetia by a viceroy, and the administration was in the hands of two governors in Milan and Venice, both of them Austrians. Piedmont, the state in which Cavour was born, and which he was to make the nucleus of a united Italy, was in 1830 an absolute monarchy whose king was Carlo Felice of the House of Savoy. The other genuinely independent kingdom in the peninsula, in strict diplomatic terms called the 'Kingdom of the Two Sicilies', was, and always has been, referred to as the 'Kingdom of Naples', although it included the island of Sicily, whose history has usually been very distinct, and in some ways more colourful, than that of mainland Naples. The king, Francesco I, died in 1830, and was succeeded by Ferdinando II. They were Bourbons, of the branch which had originally come from Spain, but were, by 1830, perhaps more Italian than any other prince in the peninsula, except the most Italian of them all – the pope. In that year the pro-Austrian pope, Pius VIII, died after only one year in office. At the end of 1830 his successor had not yet been elected. The pope who was elected in 1831 took the name of Gregory XVI. He was a theological scholar, not interested in politics, and determined to make no political changes. His election was greeted by revolutions.

The Papal States straddled across the peninsula, and already in the early sixteenth century Machiavelli had argued that their existence was primarily responsible for preventing the unification of Italy. Cavour was never to set eyes on Naples or Rome, but his policy was to be deeply concerned with both places. Between Piedmont and the Papal States lay the Grand Duchy of Tuscany ruled by a branch of the Habsburgs, the House of Lorraine, in the person of Leopoldo II. Tuscany, like all the other Italian

13

states, lacked any form of constitution; yet, with its capital
in Florence, it was perhaps the most free-thinking part of
Italy, since it lacked the oppressive censorship imposed
by the other regimes and by Metternich's Austria. The
two smaller duchies of Parma and Modena were both
theoretically independent states, but in practice they were
under the influence of Vienna, and liable to be occupied
by Austrian armies when the need seemed to Metternich
to arise. Cavour was never to have direct dealings with
Metternich, since the Austrian chancellor was to fall from
power in 1848 and Cavour was not to secure power until
1852, but in his old age Metternich was to identify Cavour
as the most brilliant statesman in Europe, and to regret that
he was on the side of the enemy.

In the nineteenth century Italy was to secure the political
unity which had, in spite of her cultural unity, eluded her for
centuries. By the time of Cavour's death in 1861 a Kingdom
of Italy existed. At that moment its existence was recognized
diplomatically among the great powers only by Britain, but
its diplomatic recognition by the rest of the world was to be
only a matter of time. The process of unification had, in the
event, come about with remarkable speed – far more quickly,
indeed, than Cavour himself had foreseen even in 1859, not
to mention 1830. But from 1830 to 1848 several important
developments in intellectual history took place, and although
they had an influence on Cavour's thinking it cannot be said
that he played an important part in them. He was, after all,
only twenty in 1830, and still a comparatively young man
of thirty-eight in 1848. The first important development of
those years was the Mazzinian movement.

Giuseppe Mazzini was five years older than Cavour, and
his appearance on the Italian political stage preceded
Cavour's by an even longer period. Mazzini was a native
of Genoa. As a member of the revolutionary society of the
Carbonari, he was arrested in 1831, and during a brief stay
in a Piedmontese prison he evolved an ambitious and almost
mystical programme for Italy's future. Italy, he decided,
should not simply secure independence from Austria, the
pope and the princes, but should be united into a single,
integrated republic. On his release from prison, Mazzini
went into exile in France, where he founded a secret
society, *Young Italy*, and organized revolutionary cells not

only in France and Switzerland, but all over the Italian peninsula.

There is no evidence that Cavour and Mazzini, who were to be bitter enemies, ever met, but it is at least possible that they did so in 1830, before Mazzini's arrest, when both young men were in Genoa, and frequenting republican circles, like the salon of Anna Giustiniani, who became Cavour's mistress. If they did not meet then – and neither of them recorded, or remembered, any such meeting – it is highly improbable that they met on any later occasion, since Mazzini was in exile from Italy for most of his life, and under sentence of death in Cavour's Piedmont. But it is interesting to reflect that if they had met in 1830 they might well have agreed on fundamental political issues.

The Mazzinian movement dominated the thinking of the politically conscious Italians throughout the 1830s. More than one revolutionary attempt organized by Mazzini against the Piedmontese government failed pathetically, but Mazzini's importance was as an educator of Italian nationalism, an inspired propagandist who convinced thousands of educated young Italians that the notion of 'Italy' could be turned into a political nation-state. Mazzini's achievement in intellectual terms was thus an immense one, and without it Cavour's career would never have culminated in the creation of the Kingdom of Italy. It was a paradox that Mazzini was never to recognize Cavour's creation as 'Italy', and Cavour was always to regard Mazzini as a dangerous force working against Italian interests.

In 1830, however, Cavour greeted the news of the July Revolution in Paris with great joy, as the beginning of a more progressive phase in world history. His hopes were not shared by the Piedmontese government, which was even more reactionary than Metternich in its response to developments in Paris. Initially the July Revolution of 1830 seemed like a renewal of the great French Revolution. The restoration of the Bourbons in Paris in 1814, in the person of Louis XVIII, had been deeply unpopular, primarily, perhaps, because it had been made possible only by the occupation of France by foreign armies. Initially during the July days in Paris in 1830 it had seemed that the republicans would gain control. The recognition of Louis-Philippe as king, and the passing of power to comparatively conservative men like his banker, Laffitte, could not immediately be foreseen. The Piedmontese government therefore had some reason for suspecting that a French revolutionary army would once again cross the Alps, as it had done in 1792. However, a Piedmontese attempt to weld together a coalition of the autocratic powers in Europe against a possible French attack was rebuffed by Metternich, who had already reached a less aggressive arrangement with the czar, Nicholas I. The Austrians and Russians had rejected the idea of forming a great coalition against France, and had merely decided that the two of them together would act in common if attacked by the French. Metternich realized that the existence of the July Monarchy, and the fall of the Duke of Wellington and the Tories and the coming to power in Britain of Lord Grey and the Whigs, were facts which had to be recognized. The Piedmontese government therefore found itself in a reactionary isolation, an isolation which continued after the accession of Carlo Alberto to the throne on 27 April 1831 and made the government even more abhorrent to Cavour.

For Cavour the July Revolution brought great hope. He wrote to his uncle, De Sellon, of the revolution as 'the dawn of the day which must illuminate Italian regeneration'.[1] He was outraged, though, when radicals in France demanded the death sentence for the Bourbons' ministers, and felt that if this were granted there would be a repetition of the Terror of 1792–94.

Revolutions broke out in Italy in 1831, the most important in the Papal States, or more specifically in Bologna, but also in the duchies of Parma and Modena. Provisional governments were set up, but it was clearly probable that the Austrians would intervene if the revolutionary regimes looked like becoming permanent. The new French government declared a policy of non-intervention so far as Italy was concerned. Cavour had hoped that France would come to the help of the Italian national cause, and the declaration of non-intervention came as a blow to him. Eventually the Austrians suppressed all three Italian revolutions, and the only French action was to send an expeditionary force to the Adriatic port of Ancona, from which base it did not stir.

Cavour watched the developments of 1831 with despair at the defeat of the Polish revolution by the czar in September, and at the inactivity of the French. On 4 January 1832 he wrote to a cousin:

> The state of Italy, of Europe, of my own country have been the source of great pain to me. How many hopes deceived, how many illusions which have not been realized, how many misfortunes have just fallen on our beautiful country . . . the fact is that the Revolution of July, after giving us the finest hopes, has plunged us into a state worse than before.

Nevertheless in the same letter he proclaimed his continuing faith in freedom, even though its immediate prospects were so dim.[2]

His sense of the betrayal of Italy by the July Monarchy was quickly modified, partly through the influence of Louis-Philippe's ambassador in Turin, the Baron de Barante, with whom the young Cavour formed a close attachment. Barante was a moderate, tolerant man, who had a beneficial effect on Cavour in one of his not infrequent moments of emotional crisis.

. . .

PRIVATE LIFE AND TRAVELS

Cavour had passed through the most impressionable and radical phase of his whole life. He had been in Genoa for five months when news of the French revolution of 1830 had reached him. As his relative, William de la Rive, wrote at the time: it was unlikely that 'this magnificent Genoa, this brilliant city, so Southern, opulent, hospitable, bathed in sunshine, full of light, action, stirring with business and ideas' would not 'enchant a young man, full of vigour and fire, eager for action and freedom'. Cavour was bound to respond with 'his vivacity, his grace and natural manners' which would 'open all doors and conquer all hearts'.[3] It was in Genoa, de la Rive concluded, that Cavour made his true début in the adult world.

It was in Genoa at this time that Cavour met the woman who played the most important and the most tragic role in his life. Anna Giustiniani Schiaffino, always referred to in the early writings on Cavour as *l'Incognita'*, was

born on 9 August 1807 in Paris. Her grandfather had
had a distinguished career during the First Empire, as
a Counsellor of State, and had been made a count by
Napoleon. He had survived the restoration, and had been
minister of finance under Louis XVIII from 1815 to 1820.
An efficient man, he had inherited a chaotic financial
situation, but had successfully balanced the books. Anna's
father, Giuseppe Schiaffino, had become a naturalized
Frenchman, and had been appointed Consul General at
Genoa by the French Bourbons in 1817. Anna's background
was thus more French than Italian, and, like Cavour,
she spoke French more readily than Italian. She was
an intelligent and highly educated woman, knowing also
English and German, and having sophisticated tastes in
literature and music. She was evidently beautiful, with
blonde hair and large black eyes. Unfortunately she had
a morbid attitude to life. Long before meeting Cavour she
had written: 'I suffered and was discouraged, incapable of
tasting the sweetness of life. The only prospect before
me was a short, languid and useless life which would
soon be ended.' At the age of nineteen she had married
Stefano Giustiniani, and had with him three children of
whom two survived.[4]

Cavour met Anna – or Nina, as she was called by her
intimates – when he was deeply unhappy, 'vegetating', as he
put it, 'in a state of great confusion'.[5] But she was married,
he was still in the army, and he intended the affair to be
a passing one. He certainly had no intention of becoming
embroiled in a scandal. After he left Genoa, Anna wrote
him three letters to which he did not reply. But she was
more deeply involved. A year after this first separation, in
January 1832, she wrote to him 'I dare to believe that a
link has been formed between us, and that nothing in the
world can break it now'. She was a highly excitable person,
and had passed through a phase of religious fervour in
her adolescence – not, perhaps, such a rare experience
– but had then rejected what she called 'the absurdity of
the practices of Catholicism'.[6] Anna had become a radical,
even a republican, and her influence on Cavour in a radical
direction was far from negligible.

That Cavour was still a radical in 1832, at least in the eyes
of the Austrians, is apparent from the report of the Austrian

minister in Turin, the Count Heinrich von Bombelles, who
wrote:

> This young man belongs to one of the most prominent
> families of Piedmont, and his father, the Marquis de
> Cavour, is generally well thought of, and is the first to
> suffer from the conduct and principles of his younger
> son. This young man, gifted with much talent, was in
> the military engineers. His relations and intimate liaison
> with other wrong-thinking persons and notably with a
> *gentleman attached to the French embassy*, persuaded the
> king, soon after His Majesty ascended the throne, to
> send him to the fortress of Bard, not as a prisoner, but
> as an artillery officer. This kind of exile lasted for about
> six months, after which Camille gave in his commission,
> and withdrew to his father's house. *I consider him a very
> dangerous man; and all efforts made to bring him round have
> been unsuccessful. He deserves to be carefully watched.*[7]

As a result of this despatch Cavour was excluded from the
Italian provinces of Austria.

For a few years after leaving the army Cavour lived, in
considerable frustration and unhappiness, in his father's
house in Turin, a palace full of his numerous relatives.
Also living there were his brother Gustavo and his family.
Camillo's close relationship with his brother had been
adversely affected by Gustavo's marriage. Gustavo's first
child, Augusto, had been born in 1828. The child was
a source of irritation to Camillo, and led to violent rows
between the two brothers. The second child, Giuseppina,
was born in 1831. Gustavo's wife died in December 1833,
after giving birth to a third child, Ainardo, who was to
be the last of that line of Cavours. The poor relationship
between Gustavo and his wife had perhaps explained his
increasing religious piety, which in its turn was a source
of friction with Camillo. On the death of his sister-in-law
Cavour went into print for the first time with an elegy
in the *Gazzetta Piemontese* on 4 January 1834. He wrote
it in French, but had it translated into Italian by his
friend, Silvio Pellico, who was becoming famous for his
recently published *My Prisons* – an account of his life
in Austrian prisons, which became a major classic of the
risorgimento.

The Marchese, Cavour's father, had always been a close friend of Carlo Alberto, the sad, introverted and lonely man who ruled Piedmont. The king rewarded the Marchese for his loyalty by making him one of the two mayors of Turin in 1833 and 1834. He proved an efficient and successful mayor. Cavour himself, when still only twenty-two years old, was made mayor of the little commune of Grinzane, where the family owned much of the land, and half of the medieval castle which overlooked this little estate. Cavour remained mayor of Grinzane until March 1848, but his duties were extremely light, since the commune had a population of only 350 people; there were no council offices, and the archives were kept in the Cavour half of the castle. Not often does a tiny hamlet have as its mayor a man who is to become one of the most able European statesmen of his century. Cavour was not yet interested in the agricultural world, however, and, far from cultivating the vines of Grinzane, he remained obsessed with European politics, although he could not yet play a role on that big stage. The first months of 1834 were a bleak period for Cavour. 'Everything is finished for me politically', he wrote in his diary. 'It would be ridiculous for me to retain the illusions of grandeur and glory which nursed my young years' (he was not yet twenty-four). 'Ah! If only I were English . . . but I am Piedmontese'.[8]

Cavour's first familiarity with things British, before his visit to Britain in 1835, came from a friendship with an Englishman, William Brockedon. With Brockedon he walked in Swiss mountain valleys, discussing literature and politics. His reading in English literature included Pope, Shakespeare, Bulwer-Lytton, Walter Scott, and, above all, Byron. Scott and Byron were perhaps even more highly valued on the Continent than in Britain in this age of the Romantics. In his readings of political works Cavour was at this time developing a great respect for Jeremy Bentham, and after the Reform Act of 1832 the British Whigs became his heroes, only later to be replaced in his admiration by the new Tories under Sir Robert Peel.

In 1835 Cavour travelled to Paris and Britain. He stayed in Paris for two and a half months, from the end of February to the beginning of May. He was immensely impressed by Paris, and this, of course, was the old Paris before Haussmann's rebuilding under Napoleon III – Cavour was not to live long enough to know the new Paris of the grand boulevards. Nevertheless, he was not blind to the poverty of the *faubourgs*. He went to the theatre often, and especially admired Bellini's *I Puritani*, although the debates in parliament were clearly of greater interest to him. His companion on the whole journey was an old friend, Count Pietro di Santa Rosa, who kept a fuller diary on the trip than Cavour, and provided greater detail on how the two young men passed the time. They spent most of the mornings discussing and weighing up what they had experienced the day before. Then, towards midday, they went out to visit hospitals, prisons, schools and the city's monuments. In the evening they enjoyed the night life of the Parisian upper classes: balls, the theatre, restaurants, and also political clubs. In these years after the July Revolution Paris was teeming with political life. Cavour was not entirely happy in Paris, however, feeling dissatisfied with his own position and prospects in life, and finding Santa Rosa, although a dear friend, a little narrow intellectually and unimaginative as a companion. These sentiments Camillo confided in letters home to his brother. At least Santa Rosa encouraged him in examining the minutiae of social life in Paris – the food served in the hospitals and the wages paid in the factories – although these details, Cavour confessed, often bored him.

Thinking of the future, Cavour decided that he would be prepared to manage one of his father's estates – to be precise, Leri – and to study economic and social questions with a view to improving the conditions of the lower classes. His father reacted promptly to the suggestion, writing to Camillo in Paris to promise him complete autonomy in the running of Leri.

In 1834 there had been a rising of the silk workers in Lyon. The employers had been obliged to grant reasonable working conditions and wages to the workers. When some employers reneged on their promises an armed insurrection took place and for a few days the workers were in control of Lyon. The rising was put down by royal government troops with some ferocity, and while Cavour was in Paris, trials were being held of republican and socialist leaders of the rising. Cavour clearly felt little sympathy for the republicans on trial, writing to his cousin, Paul-Emile Maurice, that they had done their cause more harm than good.

At six o'clock in the evening of 9 May 1835 Cavour and Santa Rosa left Paris on what was in those days a long journey to London. At four in the morning of the 10th they reached Rouen. On the 11th they sailed down the Seine to Le Havre. On 13th they embarked on another ship for Portsmouth, and arrived in London only on the 14th at six in the evening. (Two years later Mazzini was to make a rather shorter journey across the Channel and up the Thames to London.)

In London Cavour's friend, William Brockedon, gave him some initial instructions and arranged an invitation for him to the Royal Geographical Society. From London Cavour visited Windsor – as a tourist, not as a guest of William IV – Oxford, Cambridge and Birmingham. He saw factories in the Midlands and the North, and farms in Cheshire and East Anglia. He travelled across Wales, without, unfortunately, leaving a record of what must have been a wild country. Through Brockedon he met Murray, the publisher, and Michael Faraday. In London he visited the Inns of Court; University College, which had been founded only seven years before; Harrow School; hospitals and a lunatic asylum. He heard Peel speak in the House of Commons and was impressed by the seriousness of debates there. He noted with approval in his diary that if some point of fact was requested by a member, and was not immediately available, the matter would be referred to a later session. In London Cavour also met Edwin Chadwick, Nassau William Senior, the economist, and Alexis de Tocqueville. He had already read De Tocqueville's *Democracy in America*, and had felt considerable sympathy for the author's general conclusion that while democracy brought with it a lowering of cultural standards, it was inevitable, and the price paid was worth paying, in that it brought an increase in the simple dignity of the common man. In conversation the two men disagreed on what was likely to happen in England. De Tocqueville believed that the social divisions in England were so great, that even though political inequalities might be disappearing, there must before long be violent revolution. Cavour believed that, on the contrary, although there was without doubt a violent radical movement in Britain, its violence lay in words rather than in proposals of action. The middle class in England had too much horror of violence to countenance, or to lead, any revolutionary movement. Cavour's deep respect for the English led him to assume that they had sufficient moral and political forces to enable them to avoid the trauma of revolution. His admiration stemmed from his belief that the English always weighed up what was practically possible, and did not follow utopian dreams. They talked less, he said, than other nations, but they did more.

. . .

LANDOWNER

At the end of July, 1835, Cavour returned to Turin to find the city in the grip of the cholera. In the meantime, his father had made him superintendent of his four estates at Leri, not far north of Turin. In August he was already writing that he was adapting himself to the life of a farmer, a life of stables and heaps of manure. The main farm was a former monastery, which had been secularized during the French period. Cavour at once set to work to modernize the estates, clearing and digging irrigation canals for growing rice. He even started silk production, an industry much more intense farther east, in Austrian Lombardy. He also practised and improved the breeding of sheep from Spain and England. He imported sheep from Hungary, too, and exported them to Egypt. Although occasionally regretting that he could not play a less humble role in life, Cavour clearly found the study of agriculture interesting and challenging. His friend, Michelangelo Castelli, said that he never saw Cavour looking so happy as when he was leaving Turin for Leri, and it was he who recorded Cavour's remark that a serene and lively satisfaction could be obtained from seeing a well cultivated field, or a meadow covered with rich grass.[9]

Some insight into Cavour as landowner and farmer comes from the publication of the letters he received from Giacinto Corio, who later managed his estate at Leri in his absences. Corio kept Cavour closely informed of developments on the farm such as the death of a prize bull (evidently a major disaster) or the lameness of a cow, noting that one type of pasture blew up the stomachs of the cattle without nourishing them, while another type gave the proper nourishment. Even at this later date Cavour took a keen interest in these rustic details, and encouraged Corio to keep him fully informed. The information continued to flow at least until 1855, by which time Cavour had other preoccupations.[10]

One of the more sympathetic aspects of Cavour's personality was his freedom from pomposity. Where other aristocrats might have told Corio that they would leave the question of what gave cows bloated stomachs to him, Cavour took a keen scientific interest in such matters. In any case, the estate at Leri was a very large one, and Cavour had a material interest in ensuring that the dairy products were of a high quality, and that the production of rice and maize was kept at a maximum. Corio shared Cavour's enthusiasm for the new technical methods, which were usually opposed by the peasants. He was, moreover, more than simply a salaried estate manager. A nine-year lease, from 11 November 1849, was entrusted to a company, of which Cavour, his brother, and Corio, were the directors. Corio was thus a partner.

There is plenty of evidence that Cavour was a good landlord, who treated his peasants well. As late as 1858 he was taking an active part in the running of Leri, keeping Corio up to scratch, and at times differing emphatically with a man who was so obviously his intellectual inferior. The years 1835 to 1848 were years of waiting for Cavour. He had no intention of taking part in politics so long as Piedmont was an absolutist monarchy under its chilling and uninspiring king, Carlo Alberto. But his life as a farmer was punctuated by gambling sprees, love affairs, and political speculation. All his short life he was a gambler and a speculator, sometimes gambling with other people's lives.

After his return from France and Britain in 1835 Cavour developed an addiction to gambling in the most direct sense of playing cards and the tables in the casinos. In Paris he had frequented the *Café Flore*, and lost a considerable sum there, and in spite of firm resolutions he continued to gamble in Turin. He was therefore relieved to accept the task of travelling to Villach in Austria to buy a flock of Merino sheep, since the expedition would take him away from the gambling tables. Although he had a letter of recommendation from the Austrian minister in Turin, the Austrian authorities searched his baggage and read all his papers – an experience which enraged him. He reached

Milan in April, 1836. Although he found the city 'superb', he was still too full of resentment against the Austrians to enjoy the visit. He then travelled to Verona and visited what claimed – and still claims – to be the tomb of Romeo and Juliet. At Udine he bought two horses, which appeared to be splendid black beasts, but in the purchase of which he had been cheated, for after only a brief walk the younger of the two horses went lame. Finally he reached Villach, where he found the Merino sheep. Again he proved a poor businessman, buying sheep which were already well past the average age of such a breed. His failure on this particular expedition contrasts strangely with his efficiency in running his estate back at Leri.

Cavour's exploration of Austrian Italy continued with visits to Trieste, and then, by boat, to Venice. His attitude to the Austrian presence was ambivalent. All his adult life he had been outraged at the injustice of the Austrian occupation of cities so obviously Italian as Milan and Venice. Yet he was intellectually honest enough to recognize that the Austrians were administering North-East Italy efficiently, with commerce healthy, communications good, and the public services working well.

For several years, in between farming at Leri and gambling in Turin, Cavour went on further journeys in Western Europe – again to England, frequently to Switzerland, and three times to Paris in 1837 and 1838. In 1839 he acquired a seat on the board of directors of a railway company, which was planning to link Geneva to the Rhone Valley, mainly by rail, but also by boat. The idea in principle was sound, but was not supported by the Piedmontese government – or by Cavour's own father – and resulted in a financial disaster, which Cavour could not have sustained himself without cash backing from his father.

In 1840 another major gamble by Cavour came badly unstuck. There was a sharp international crisis which started as a phase of the Eastern Question. In a confrontation between the Ottoman Empire and the upstart naval power of Muhammed Ali in Egypt, the French government, under Adolphe Thiers, supported Egypt, while Britain, with Lord Palmerston at the Foreign Office, supported Turkey. The other great powers entered the crisis as temporary allies of Britain, with the Prussian government adopting an aggressive stance against France. For a moment it seemed that there might be a European war, a war on the Rhine and in the Mediterranean. Cavour judged it a good moment to invest in armaments. However, Louis-Philippe, the pacific French king, forced Thiers to resign, the French climbed down, and the crisis passed. Cavour lost heavily, and once again had to depend on his father for a financial rescue.

. . .

ANNA GIUSTINIANI

Cavour's loss of a fortune in 1840 must have contributed to the emotional crisis which he suffered in 1841, though a greater cause may have been the suicide of his mistress, Anna Giustiniani, which must be considered in a moment. In spite of the crisis, his life did not come to a halt in practical terms. While keeping clear of a political career, he maintained an interest in public affairs. For example, he actively joined a movement to found infant schools of a secular kind in Turin. He found light relief at this time in playing whist, at which he was very skilful, and he even founded a whist club. (He would probably have preferred the more demanding game of bridge, but bridge did not reach Western Europe until very late in the nineteenth century, when it was introduced from Turkey.) Perhaps more important than the whist club, was Cavour's founding of the Agricultural Society; and his travels continued in the early 1840s. In Paris he met distinguished literary figures, including Prosper Mérimée, who was already well known for his short stories, and who was soon to publish *Carmen*, Charles Sainte-Beuve, the great literary critic, and Alexandre Dumas, whose *Count of Monte Cristo* and *The Three Musketeers* were published in 1844 and 1845 respectively. Cavour also sat in on courses at the Sorbonne in Philosophy, and – perhaps surprisingly – Religion.

In 1841 the grim news of the suicide of Anna Giustiniani reached Cavour, and must have given him a heavy emotional weight to bear, alongside his doubts about his future, and his sense of a lost destiny. Evidence of their affair comes from her letters, and the diary which Cavour briefly kept. From these sources it is clear that Cavour wrote frequently to her, but his letters have not survived. When they met briefly again in Genoa in January 1832, they seemed to have become good friends, their affair over, and Anna reconciling herself to this situation. However, she was in poor health, and some of her relatives believed that she was mentally disturbed, although there seems to have been little evidence for their belief. For Cavour these years were perhaps years of loneliness – in spite of the crowds of people who continually surrounded him – as well as of emotional instability. As has already been suggested, the marriage of his brother, Gustavo, in 1827, had diminished the closeness of relations between the two men. Camillo confided to his diary his thoughts of suicide, but his conclusion, like Hamlet's was that the continuing a useless life was the lesser of the two evils. He declared to his diary, however, that he would welcome terminal pneumonia.

Early in 1834, after a pause of four years, Cavour renewed his relationship with Anna. They had a brief period of happiness together in Turin, in spite of attempts by Anna's husband to separate them. Paradoxically, however, it was Anna's own parents – and more particularly her mother – who condemned her relationship with Cavour, more strongly than her husband did. It seems to have been her parents who drove the young woman to despair and thoughts of suicide.

Cavour's own suffering in the affair came rather from the agonies of a bad conscience. Aristocratic society in Turin at that time would certainly not condemn a man for having an affair with a married woman, but Cavour felt guilty at the degree of passion he had roused in Anna. That he loved her from time to time is clear, but it was a far more controlled love than Anna's for him. He had at least one other fairly serious affair at this time, with another married woman, the Marchesa Clementina Guasco di Castelletto. The Marchesa Guasco was a stronger-minded, more demanding, and less pathetic woman than Anna Giustiniani, but seems to have loved Cavour quite sincerely. It may seem surprising that Cavour, who was at this time something of an unsuccessful nonentity, already growing rather fat, should have stirred passions in women who were evidently beautiful and intelligent.

Charm in conversation, high intelligence and some kind of charisma he clearly enjoyed even in the darkest moments of his life.

In the autumn of 1834 Cavour and Anna slept together again on several occasions, at Voltri, in the Giustinianis' house, Anna's husband having reconciled himself to the situation by this time. However, Cavour then went on his travels in Western Europe, and developed a passion for European politics rather stronger than any remnants of passion for Anna Giustiniani. While he travelled, Anna continued to write to him. When he was in Paris, she wrote that she liked to think of him moving around in a city where she had been so happy as a child – though the evidence seems to be that her childhood had been anything but happy. Her letters often touched the depth of despair, with references to her wish to die, and of the possibility of suicide. Why should the thought of death be so horrendous? she asks. Why should one fear 'a few moments of purely physical suffering, followed by a dreamless night?'[11] In the event the poor woman was to suffer rather more than a few moments of pain at her death. Then she wrote, suddenly, 'I am afraid that we shall never see each other again',[12] and later told how, in the middle of the night, she had taken out Cavour's portrait and found that his eyes were avoiding her, that he seemed to have a fierce and threatening look, and that she had not looked at his portrait again: not a very pleasing letter for Cavour to have received.

On the night of 23–24 April 1841 Anna Giustiniani threw herself from an upstairs window. She survived for six days, with occasional moments of consciousness, but of great pain. She was only thirty-four.

Cavour meanwhile had affairs with at least two other women, and probably several more. The affairs tended to last for only a few months. They were always with married women, who were a few years older than he was. One woman with whom he had a brief affair in 1838 was the French novelist, Mélanie Waldor, who had previously had an affair with Alexandre Dumas lasting several years. Mélanie Waldor's novel, *Alphonse et Juliette*, written in 1839, may have been partly inspired by confidences from Cavour. There is a Nina in Waldor's novel who bears a striking resemblance to the real Nina. After parting from Cavour, Mélanie wrote a passionate letter to him, one passage of which she used, with only a few changes, in her novel.

For his part, Cavour wrote Mélanie Waldor a letter which has often been quoted by his biographers. It is in reply to a suggestion from her that he should settle in Paris. His reply was that he could not leave his family or his country, since the only influence he could exercise for the good of humanity was at home. His 'unfortunate exiled and proscribed brothers' in Paris were doing nothing useful for their fellow-countrymen. 'I shall never separate my fortunes from those of Piedmont', he concluded – a resolution which he was going to keep faithfully.[13]

Some of Cavour's earliest writings were on British themes, inspired by his visit to Britain. In 1844 he wrote a long article on Ireland. Although he admired Daniel O'Connell's Irish nationalism, the article was in some respects a conservative one. It expressed respect for private property and aversion to revolution, but it also criticized the Catholic priests of Ireland for benefiting from the ignorance of the peasants. The English, however, were also blamed for their repression of Ireland. Cavour was sure that they would not give up their hold on Ireland, nor did he recommend them to do so. He did not support independence for Ireland, nor even home rule. What he recommended was a programme of social reform, and here he showed considerable knowledge of the social conditions of the Irish. Cavour believed that the basis of Ireland's troubles lay in the land question, and in this anticipated Gladstone's attitude of many years later. He pointed out the ills of absentee landlordism, and the huge scale of the English estates in Ireland. He was optimistic that Peel and his successors would continue to take measures to improve the conditions of the Irish, and, although they might move too slowly, it was by these measures, he considered, that the Irish Question would be solved. He could not, of course, in 1844, foresee the terrible tragedy of the great famine which was to devastate Ireland two or three years later. His article had a note of scholarship about it, and was favourably received in some quarters in England, notably by the economist, Nassau Senior. It was published in the *Bibliothèque Universelle* of Geneva.

In 1845 Cavour published an article which was of far greater significance for Italy. It concerned the railways, in which he had invested cash, though his investment had been in French, rather than Italian, railways. He argued now that Italy needed a railway network to link her with Northern and Central Europe. Piedmont, in particular, he believed, could be an obvious link between the 'German and the Latin races'. More immediately important, however, was a railway network in the Italian peninsula to break down the municipal identities of Italian cities and regions. Yet he seemed to be looking beyond a vague Italian nationalism to a greater, a European, sense of identity. Railways could 'Europeanize' the Italian states. When Cavour was writing, Piedmont was in fact rather behind Naples and Austrian Italy in the planning and building of railways, but this was to be rectified when he was himself in power in the 1850s.

His 1846 article was in theory simply a review, for the French journal, the *Revue nouvelle*, of a long book by Count Ilarione Pettiti, entitled *The Italian railways and an improved plan for them*, but Cavour's article showed an imaginative sweep beyond Pettiti's work. The railway, in Cavour's words was a 'marvellous conquest of the nineteenth century'. He pressed for a railway tunnel under the Alps at Mont Cenis – an idea which he would bring nearer achievement during his premiership, and which he said would be 'the most beautiful triumph of steam'.[14]

The railways were part of the industrial world for which Cavour had such high hopes. Often he was too optimistic, and anticipated the industrial world too soon, as when he invested in a small chemical industry, which went bankrupt. He could, however, claim to be one of the founders of the Bank of Italy, since he persuaded the Piedmontese government to allow the Swiss firm of De la Rue to found a bank in Genoa, which later joined another newly formed bank in Turin, with which Cavour also had connections, to form the Bank of Italy. He was not only a shareholder in the Bank, but had a seat on the governing board.

Cavour was playing with nationalist ideas in economic terms – with concepts of 'Italian' railways and banks. Meanwhile a different form of nationalism had appeared in Italy, a form which was political in nature, but far more moderate than Mazzini's republican utopianism. The first protagonist of the movement was the Piedmontese, Vincenzo Gioberti, who had been ordained a priest, but whose only clerical experience was to be briefly a chaplain to Carlo Alberto. He had resigned from this post in 1833, arrested as a revolutionary conspirator, and exiled without trial. During his years of exile Gioberti lived in Paris and Brussels, where, in 1843, he published an immensely influential work, *Concerning the Moral and Civil Primacy of the Italians*. The work was smuggled into Italy and widely read. Although it was based on somewhat academic themes of philosophy and theology, its exalting of Italian history and civilization had a profoundly political effect. For Gioberti God was the only reality from which existing things were created. God was the source of language and civilization, and thus the Church was the axis of society. Gioberti drew from this the conviction that Italy – the region in which the Italian language was spoken, and where Italian civilization had flourished – should have some form of political unity under the Church. Specifically, Gioberti recommended an Italian confederation under the presidency of the pope. His ideas were very far from those of Cavour, but the idea of the Italian states being loosely united into a confederation with the pope as president was one with which Cavour would have to grapple, and to which he would briefly have to accommodate himself, when it was adopted as the policy of the French emperor, Napoleon III. It was to remain an idea, however, and never became a fact.

In Italian history Gioberti's importance lay in his influence on the reading public. He made a vague, but exalted, version of Italian nationalism popular with classes and groups which had refused to accept the radical and democratic nationalism of Mazzini.

Slightly less influential, but more politically relevant, was a work published by another Piedmontese, Count Cesare Balbo – *Concerning the Hopes of Italy*. It appeared in 1844, and was dedicated to Gioberti. Balbo was to work closely with Cavour a few years later, and his book was far more significant for Cavour's policy of the 1850s. For Mazzini the Papal States had been a great stumbling block to the creation of a united Italy; for Gioberti the papacy had been a great asset in that struggle. Balbo was more realistic than Gioberti in that he saw Austria as the real enemy of the Italian cause. In 1843 Gioberti had been reluctant to deal with the question of the Austrian presence in Italy, yet by 1849, as prime minister of Piedmont, he was to be instrumental in involving his country in a hopeless and foolish renewal of the war against Austria. As Cavour later said of Gioberti: he would have been a great man if only he had possessed some common sense.

No one, in 1843 or 1844, was recommending war with Austria, but Balbo realized that by some means or another the Austrians must be persuaded to withdraw their troops and their administrators from Lombardy and Venetia. His proposal was that the operation should be conducted by diplomacy, rather than by the violence of revolution (which had failed so miserably in the past), or by warfare. The apparent disintegration of the Ottoman Empire offered opportunities. Since the eighteenth century there had been a firm conviction in Europe that the Ottoman Empire was cracking up. Balbo was not to know that in the event the Ottoman Empire was to survive until 1922 – longer than the Austrian or Russian Empires, and even longer than the German Empire, which had not yet been born. Outlying parts of the Turkish Empire included the provinces of Moldavia and Wallachia on the lower Danube. The Rumanian nationalist movement, which was soon to demand independence and unity for these Rumanian-speaking regions, had not yet developed. It seemed to Balbo that they could be given to Austria in return for her withdrawal from Italy. In fact Metternich, who had a powerful fascination for Italy, and no desire to advance Austrian frontiers into the Balkans, would never have considered such an idea. It was only after 1866, when Metternich and Cavour were both dead, and Austria had lost her Italian lands, that Austria turned her attention towards the East. Cavour, however, was toying with precisely this idea as late as 1856, when he was in control of Piedmontese policy. In a sense there was less excuse for Cavour than there had been for Balbo in 1844, because by 1856 a Rumanian nationalist movement had developed, and to give Moldavia and Wallachia to Austria would have offended against the 'principle of nationality', which Napoleon III was then supporting. But Balbo had anticipated a subsequent line of Cavour's thinking, and his idea was certainly no less realistic than Gioberti's hopes for papal supremacy: the pope of 1844, Gregory XVI, had not the slightest intention of leading even the most moderate Italian movement. Even so, the non-violent doctrines of Gioberti and Balbo found a sympathetic hearing in Italy, and established a movement of thought which historians have called the 'moderate' movement, though, since it involved the retention of the Papal States and the independence of the separate Italian states, it was in spirit conservative.

In 1846 Gregory XVI died, and the newly elected pope, Pius IX, surprised the world by decreeing a number of measures, which could only be described as radical. He had read Gioberti's book, and was an ardent Italian patriot, if not a nationalist. He challenged Metternich on a number of points, and some months before 1848 – the year of revolutions – had become a national hero in Italy. 'Viva Pio Nono' became a cry synonymous with revolution in Austrian eyes. For perhaps the last time in his life, Cavour felt a wave of sympathy for the papacy, writing that Pio Nono (Pius IX) had placed himself in the vanguard of civilization.

. . .

REACTIONS TO THE APPROACH OF REVOLUTION

As a wave of revolutionary sentiment swept Italy in 1847 even Carlo Alberto felt that he must do something to modify the authoritarianism of his regime. After several noisy demonstrations in Turin, it was announced that trade would be liberalized, and the press censorship eased, so that more independent journals could come into existence. It seemed the beginning of a thaw, and at last Cavour felt that he could enter public life.

His initial step was to co-operate with Cesare Balbo in founding a journal, which they called *Il Risorgimento*. Much of it Cavour was to write himself, and he was now to move in a circle of journalists, as well as of businessmen. One evening in December 1847 the business circle in Turin threw a banquet to celebrate the limited reforms Carlo Alberto had made. Cavour attended. Many speeches were made, most of them consisting of somewhat empty patriotic rhetoric.

Cavour spoke in a more practical way, considering the advantages to be gained from Carlo Alberto's commercial reforms, and especially with regard to the silk industry.

A meeting of journalists in January 1848 was also attended by Cavour, who took this opportunity to suggest that Carlo Alberto should be petitioned to grant a constitution. The other journalists were surprised at what they considered to be a radical suggestion – and surprised that it should have been made by Cavour. Some believed that the suggestion was premature. It was decided to adjourn the meeting, and reconvene on the following day, January 8. On this second occasion Cavour failed to carry the meeting with him, and it was decided that no petition should be presented to the king, since it would not have been a unanimous one.

Nevertheless Carlo Alberto's constitution was announced in February 1848, and promulgated on 4 March. It was a conservative document, apparently preserving the prerogatives of the monarch in many respects, but ambiguously worded. An electoral law published shortly afterwards gave the vote only to those literate men who paid an appreciable sum in taxes. Within this narrow compass, however, all 'Italians' could vote – which included the large number of refugees from other parts of Italy who had come to Piedmont since the revolutions of 1831.

This was the constitution within the framework of which Cavour was to operate as prime minister, and which was to be the basis of the constitution of united Italy in 1861. It was Cavour who was to turn the constitution into a more genuinely parliamentary one, by making himself indispensable, and so limiting the power of the crown. The first prime minister under the constitution was his friend, Cesare Balbo, who was, however, well to his right in his political ideas. *Il Risorgimento*, of course, applauded the appointment of Balbo.

On 17 March a civilian rising in Milan against the Austrians led to five days of bitter fighting, and the expulsion of the Austrian army from the city. Metternich had already fallen from power in Vienna, and fled to England. To the exhilarating news Cavour reacted like a full-blooded Italian nationalist. On 23 March he wrote in *Il Risorgimento*:

The supreme hour for the Sardinian [Piedmontese] monarchy has struck; the hour for strong deliberations, the hour on which depends the fates of empires, the fortunes of peoples. In the face of the events in Lombardy and Vienna, hesitation, doubt, delays are not possible; they would be the most lamentable of policies. We are cool-headed men, accustomed to listening to the dictates of reason rather than the impulses of the heart, and having pondered our every word we must now in conscience declare that there is only one path open for the Nation, for the Government, for the King. War! Immediate war without delays.[15]

On that very same afternoon Carlo Alberto and his council of ministers drew up a declaration of war.

The first elections under the constitution – always referred to simply as the *Statuto* were held in May of 1848. Cavour stood, but was not elected. However, on 26 June, in by-elections, he was elected in four constituencies: Turin, Monforte, Cogliano and Iglesias on the island of Sardinia. He chose to sit, inevitably, for Turin. The deputies immediately began to identify themselves by sitting on the right or the left of the house, according to the custom established in Paris during the Great Revolution. Cavour chose to sit on the right, with his closest friends and associates. He had finally arrived on the political scene.

.   .   .

NOTES AND REFERENCES

1. Romeo, I, p. 351.
2. *ibid*, p. 363.
3. Ruffini, pp. 101–2.
4. Paolo Pinto, *L'amore segreto di Cavour* (Camunia, Milan, 1990), pp. 27–28.
5. *ibid*, p. 59.
6. Romeo, I, p. 275.
7. Chiala, I, p. 13, and Ruffini, pp. 140–43, who makes heavy weather of the exact wording and sources of this document, but its basic significance is clear.
8. Romeo, I, p. 379.
9. Ruffini, p. xxxvi.

10. Alfredo Bogge, editor, *Lettere di Giacinto Corio a Camillo Cavour 1843–1855* (Fondazione Camillo Cavour, Santena 1980).
11. Pinto, *op. cit.*, p. 183.
12. *ibid*, p. 187.
13. Romeo, I, pp. 754–55.
14. Chiala, I, 49–56.
15. Giuseppe Massari, *Il Conte di Cavour, Ricordi Biografici* (Botta, Turin, 1873), p. 34.

Chapter 3

CAVOUR'S ECONOMIC AND POLITICAL PHILOSOPHY

. . .

THE ECONOMY

'Philosophy' may sound too grand a word to describe the ideas of a politician, but Cavour was no ordinary politician. By the age of twenty he had thought long and deeply about economic, political and sociological matters. His views were part of a single, consistent conviction in progress. He was a man of the nineteenth century in his firm belief that there was no contradiction between the values of material progress and those of moral or spiritual progress. He would not have understood how a term like 'consumerism' could come to be used, in the last years of the twentieth century, in a pejorative sense. For him industrial progress did not imply the triumph of materialism over the life of the spirit. On the contrary, industrialization represented the triumph of the human mind over the inanimate world. The need for industrialization represented a great challenge to humanity, and demanded courage and the readiness to take risks. Here Cavour, the supreme gambler, was in his element.

He thought of industrialism as being irrevocably linked to liberalism. While there may have been a naïve element in this conviction, it was considerably less naïve than the belief of the Piedmontese ruling class before 1848 that industrialization, as a revolutionary feature in economic terms must inevitably lead to revolution in political terms. The absurd belief that gas lighting or the railway was politically dangerous was only too common in the first half of the nineteenth century. In one sense Cavour accepted the argument, but only in the conviction that that particular kind of revolution was one which he would welcome.

One important aspect of the growth of industry and

37

of material progress was a belief in the need for free trade. Cavour developed his ideas when the Piedmontese government was bitterly opposed to both free trade and industrialization. He realized that it was an instinctive repugnance, a kind of complex from which the government could not free itself. There were also real agricultural interests opposed to free trade, if not always for valid reasons. For Cavour there was a strong political dimension to the question. Free trade between the countries of Europe meant better political relations, and, more specifically, for Piedmont freer trade could bring valuable allies. For these reasons he bitterly regretted the ignorance of the science of economics displayed by his government. As early as 1832 he wrote to his friend Brockedon in slightly quaint English:

> Most unhappily nowhere the true principles of eco-nomical science are so little understood as in Piedmont. The lucid theories and profound reasonings of the philosophical writers, as well as the numerous facts and evidence collected by the care of various enlightened Governments, are totally unknown here. The violent passions of the one, and the blind and selfish interest of the others, are the only arms employed, till now, in the discussion of this question of so mighty interest.[1]

At that time Brockedon argued that unilateral measures of free trade were too generous, and that governments should simply grant each other reciprocal free trade arrangements. When Cavour was in office he was to follow this policy, but as a young man of twenty-two he was convinced that the removal of customs and tariffs for one and all could only be beneficial to one and all. He went farther, and argued that the economic crisis in Britain which preceded and accompanied the Reform Bill of 1831–32 would have been less acute if the Corn Laws had been modified.

There was a generous side to Cavour's belief in free trade. Helping other countries as well as one's own did not seem to him such a negligible achievement. He looked forward to the day, he said, when 'injustice to other nations will cease to be regarded as an aspect of patriotism to be praised'. It is not too much to see in this an early form of internationalism, or, at least, a sense of identity with Europe as a whole. On the other hand, there is his conviction that European values are superior to those of other continents. 'I do not believe', he wrote, that there is a single person among educated Hindoos who would prefer to fall under the yoke of Brahmins or indigenous sovereigns, rather than under the domination of the [East India] Company'.[2]

In 1847 Cavour had the opportunity of meeting one of the high priests of free trade. Richard Cobden was lionized in Genoa, Livorno, Bologna and Naples – in Papal and Bourbon Italy, then, as well as in Piedmont, but not, of course, in Austrian Italy. He passed through Turin on his way back. Cavour spoke at a banquet given in Cobden's honour, and proposed a toast, praising him in rather extravagant terms: 'Those who are far admire you', he said, 'those who are near love you'.[3] Thus Cavour supported the idea of the unilateral abolition of tariffs before he became minister of commerce himself. On 4 April 1850 he declared in parliament that some customs could be abolished without any reciprocal arrangement, and abolished, of course, for imports from all nations. When the chamber showed its disapproval of this over-generous doctrine, Cavour explained that he was not recommending the abolition of all customs and tariffs on imports from all countries at all times. Certain tariffs could be abolished, but there should always be room for further reciprocal agreements with other countries to be negotiated by the government. Referring to France, he said that he did not imagine that the French government would be prepared to adopt a policy of totally free trade with Piedmont, although he considered that France would gain by substituting a policy of free trade generally for one of protection. What he believed at that moment was that some reduction of tariffs could be reciprocally arranged with France. However, in this speech in April 1850 he stuck to his guns in general terms, and declared that even in the case of countries like Austria or Greece, who would not offer reciprocal terms, he believed it would be to Piedmont's advantage if she voluntarily abolished taxes imposed on goods imported from those countries. The chamber was not at all convinced by Cavour's argument.

The most obvious and dramatic manifestation of industrialism was perhaps the spread of railways across Western Europe. In England in 1835 Cavour had travelled on the first passenger line in the world, the one between Liverpool and Manchester, which had been opened only in 1830. It had taken only an hour and a half to travel from one city to the other, and for Cavour this was a shining symbol of the wonders which science, freedom and industry would bring to the world. He was in Paris for the opening of the first line in France, to Saint-Germain – really rather less impressive than the one from Manchester to Liverpool, but, as Cavour said,

> a new and astonishing spectacle for the honest idlers of Paris. Yesterday there were 10,000 travellers, and there will perhaps be more today. You can say now that the forest of Saint-Germain is in Paris.
>
> The railways will produce a revolution in the physical world, for the French they will take the place of political revolutions for some time. Indeed since they have been the centre of interest Louis-Philippe has begun to walk about Paris without guards or escort, and no one thinks of assassinating him. The French need novelty, when the world of physical things provides it they have no need of novelty in the moral order of things.[4]

Here, then, was an interesting inversion of the usual argument: according to Cavour, railways made political revolution less, not more, likely.

Although Cavour accepted with enthusiasm the industrialized, capitalist society, which he saw in existence in Britain, and to a lesser extent in France, he saw the drawbacks in the capitalistic approach to agriculture which he found in Britain. He recognized that what appeared to be a rationalizing of agriculture by the creation of huge estates, had led to unhappy results in social terms. In purely economic terms British agriculture may have appeared productive and modern, but it had destroyed many small farms, and 'had transformed the soil into a meeting of vast estates, where there was only a master and workers'. There was a need, he believed, for 'a link of sympathy between those who own and those who cultivate the soil', a link which must be preserved even if it led to economic sacrifices.[5]

In 1843 Cavour wrote from London:

> The great European question at this moment is the commercial question. At least that is what all thinking people in England believe. In spite of the reaction in favour of a protectionist system which is apparent in several countries I have no doubt that the cause of freedom will make progress in enlightened minds. In England it has completely won over the intellectual world. There is no longer anyone of significance who is not, deep down, in favour of the abolition of tariffs. In this matter there is no real difference between Sir Robert Peel and Lord John Russell ... The real Tories are furious.[6]

They realized, he explained, that Peel was deceiving them, but they appreciated also that he was a natural Conservative leader, and that Wellington accepted Peel's commercial beliefs. The death of the Duke would probably lead to a rupture in the Tory party, and Peel would probably seek support from the moderate Whigs. Cavour, then, showed a good understanding of British politics, even if he assumed that the crisis in the Tory party would come with the death of Wellington, rather than the disaster of the potato famine in Ireland and the Corn Law crisis of 1846 – events which no one, of course, could foresee in 1843. From the point of view of an assessment of Cavour's political stance, it is interesting that he most emphatically refused to identify himself with 'the real Tories', rather than moderate Tories like Peel and his followers.

In this same letter from London Cavour returned to the question of the railways. 'I have always travelled on the railways', he wrote. 'What I have seen makes me more than ever want to see them established on the continent. Distances no longer exist in England. The post leaves twice a day from London in almost all directions. They sort out the letters en route'.[7]

Although he believed that the 'world of the spirit', as he called it, was more alive in the intellectual oasis of Paris than in London, he still felt that the future was being planned in England, and it was with that future that he wanted to be identified.

41

. . .

NATIONALISM

In a Western Europe open to free trade, and with her cities and regions linked by the railway, it might seem that the nineteenth-century version of nationalism, based on language, culture or history, would be outdated. At times it certainly seemed that Cavour's vision of a new world went far beyond a sense of national identity. It is therefore relevant to ask whether he was ever really concerned with 'Italy', and the process of creating an Italian nation-state, and whether he thought of himself as an 'Italian'. The question is not an easy one to answer, since there are cross-currents in his national consciousness. But if there were complexities in his personality, there were no contradictions.

When Cavour referred to 'my country' he usually meant Piedmont, but sometimes 'Italy'. There was an ancient precedent for this. When Dante, in the thirteenth century, referred to 'my country' he sometimes meant the Republic of Florence, and sometimes Italy. Or – to point at a contemporary analogy – when a Welshman in the twentieth century says 'my country' he sometimes means Wales, but sometimes Britain. A man or woman may have more than one country. In a letter to his aunt, Alessandra de Sellon, on 4 January 1832, Cavour commented that 'the state of Italy, of Europe and of my country have been the source of acute pain to me'. 'My country' here clearly meant Piedmont, though at least the statement showed his preoccupation with 'Italy' – a country which did not yet exist politically. In the next sentence he referred to 'notre belle patrie', and here he surely meant Italy.[8]

By the time of the revolutions of 1848 Cavour was, of course, fully convinced not only of the existence of 'Italy', but of an Italian Question which was distinct from the aims of Piedmontese foreign policy. Thus in a speech to parliament on 11 November 1848 he referred to the *'causa italiana'*.[9]

Earlier in his life he had already reflected another tradition of Italian nationalism. Machiavelli, Pope Julius II and other Italian figures of the Renaissance had referred to the 'barbarians' from the North. Machiavelli had been aware of the disunity and weakness of Italy, and of the contrasting strength of countries to the North. A strong state, said

Machiavelli, should have either the strength of the lion or the cunning of the fox. Since the countries to the North had the strength of the lion, it was for Italians to cultivate the cunning of the fox. It could be argued that Cavour's achievements were very much in this tradition. When a young man of twenty-three, he had written to Auguste de La Rive: 'My position in the *juste-milieu* does not prevent me from desiring as soon as possible Italy's emancipation from the barbarians who oppress her'.[10] A few months earlier he had made his much-quoted statement about one day waking up prime minister of Italy. The context of the statement was a letter to the Marchesa Giulia Falletti di Barolo, a letter written in a very humble mood, when Cavour was the simple mayor of Grinzane. He wrote of how he had once had 'illusions of vanity, of fame, of glory, of ambition', and added: 'I confess to you, at the risk of giving you a good laugh at my expense, that there was a time when I believed nothing beyond my powers, when I would have believed it quite on the cards that I would wake up one fine morning to find myself chief minister of the Kingdom of Italy'.[11] So, when he had been yet younger, and totally unknown in the world, this cadet son of a Piedmontese nobleman had considered it feasible that he would one day be prime minister of a country that did not yet exist. Even allowing for a certain exaggeration in his letter of 1832, the passage is an extraordinary one. There is too, a note of tragedy in it: this almost inconceivable achievement of becoming prime minister of Italy was to come to him only a few months before his death, and after the kind of struggle which few people attempt, and very few carry to success. In the context of this chapter the important point is that in 1832 Cavour was writing of 'Italy' as a country which would exist, and would have a prime minister.

Three years later, in 1835, the Countess Anastasia de Circourt wrote to him, suggesting that he should settle in Paris, and take up a literary career. He replied in melodramatic terms, saying that 'the political troubles which have desolated Italy have forced her noblest sons' into exile – 'the most distinguished in all fields' had left 'my country', but he would never abandon her. Here then 'my country' meant Italy. But later in the same letter he wrote: 'I shall never separate my lot from those of the Piedmontese'.[12] The fortunes of Italy and Piedmont were inextricably linked in his mind.

Cavour's nationalism, like all his policy, was pragmatic, and this was illustrated by his attitude to Irish nationalism, which has already been considered in Chapter 2. In the case of Ireland he did not consider the creation of an independent nation-state a priority, nor did he, when in power, show much sympathy for the creation of an independent Rumania.

One element which is lacking in Cavour is any trace of chauvinism. He did not share the hatred of the French which both Gioberti and Mazzini displayed at different times, and although he planned a war against Austria, he never expressed any antipathy for German-speaking people. But if Cavour thought of himself essentially as a European, there is little doubt that he also considered himself an Italian. What constitutes a person's sense of identity is often the language he or she speaks, but it can also be the cultural background, which is often, though not always dependent on language. In Cavour's case his first language was French, but it would be absurd to argue from that fact that he was in any sense a Frenchman.

Cavour was less concerned with the nationalist movements of other peoples than, for example, Napoleon III was. He had no enthusiasm for the creation of an independent Ireland. Rumania or Poland. He was prepared to work with Hungarians against the Habsburgs, but that was clearly from self-interest. Yet there is enough evidence to consider applying the term 'Italian nationalist' to Cavour. After all, he and Cesare Balbo settled on the name *Risorgimento* for their journal – the term which had first been used by Vittorio Alfieri at the beginning of the century, when he foretold a movement of Italian spiritual revival. In April, 1848, when Cavour had failed to obtain a seat in parliament, he wrote to the Baron Enrico Vicario di San'Agabio that he would have 'to work only with the pen on the great work of the Italian *risorgimento*'.[13] A little later another letter confirms his acceptance of the fact that Italy was already united in spirit. He was invited, in July, 1851, by the Marchese Cosimo Ridolfi, to become a member of the famous society of economists in Florence, the Accademia dei Georgofili. He modestly and gratefully accepted the invitation, and added that he could see in it 'a shining proof of the sympathy which my country and the men who govern it inspire in the most distinguished and generous Italians of sister provinces'. Here, then, in one sentence are two concepts: Piedmont is 'my country' ('*il mio paese*'), but Tuscany is a 'sister province'. In international law, of course, Piedmont and Tuscany were independent sovereign states, but there were ties of sentiment which belied this arid fact, and as early as July, 1832, Cavour had referred to the inhabitants of the Papal Romagna as '*nos compatriotes*'.[14]

Yet Cavour was not a fully fledged 'nationalist' in the sense that Mazzini was. He had not read Johann Gottfried Herder's recommendations of respect for cultural nationalism, as Mazzini had. Indeed, he had not read Mazzini's own writings, as so many of his contemporaries – noblemen or commoners, Piedmontese, Tuscans, Lombards, Romans or Neapolitans – had done.

If the definition of Cavour as an 'Italian nationalist' rings slightly false, it is not because of his inadequate control of the Italian language. That he spoke and wrote French more easily than Italian is certain, but the point has been made rather too emphatically in the past. Thus Nassau William Senior, in an entry made in his diary in Turin in 1850, quoted the Marchesa Arconati as saying: 'Cavour is naturally a good speaker, but in Italian he is embarrassed. You see that he is translating; so is Azeglio'.[15] The Marchesa was talking nonsense so far as Azeglio was concerned. Azeglio had lived in Milan, Florence and Rome, as well as Turin, for long periods, and it is inconceivable that he did not speak Italian fluently. In talking to Senior the Marchesa was doing what many Italians have done ever since, when talking to Englishmen: she was trying to make Italy seem interesting by implying that it was full of people speaking all kinds of different languages. Although she was wrong about Azeglio, the situation regarding Cavour was more complicated. Cavour had not had a literary education, and was the first to lament the fact. If he did not write Italian, or speak it in parliament, with ease, it was also true that he did not write French with grammatical precision. He made many errors in writing French. He would spell a word differently in the same letter. Thus he sometimes wrote '*tems*', but sometimes '*temps*', sometimes '*sentimens*', but sometimes '*sentiments*', and sometimes '*fésant*', but sometimes '*faisants*'. A Piedmontese friend called De Buttet had his name rendered as 'Debuté. Cavour would even occasionally spell his own estate of Leri 'Lery'.[16] These variations of French spelling were often, of course, simply indecisions between a slightly archaic, or a rather more modern, style. Nevertheless, Cavour's inconsistencies suggest that he did not have a strong control of the French language.

The somewhat negative conclusion must therefore be reached that Cavour may not have been an Italian nationalist in the Mazzinian sense, but to suggest that he was not a nationalist in any sense is clearly absurd.

. . .

HIS VIEWS ON DEMOCRACY

Cavour's commitment to free trade was only one aspect of his belief in the need for a free society generally. In mid-nineteenth century Italy such a belief involved a consideration of the role of the Church. Catholic Christianity, to which the overwhelming majority of Italians adhered, dictated an acceptance of a spiritual authority which would inevitably limit the freedom of the individual. But the Church, too, could claim its right to freedom from the State. This clash of two different kinds of freedom was to lead Cavour ultimately to his formula of 'a free Church in a free State'. He realized, however, that the concept would allow ecclesiastical practices of which he would not approve. Long before he had coined his famous phrase, during discussions in the Piedmontese parliament of the secularizing measures of 1851, he recognized that allowing the Church to have its own schools would have certain dangers as regards what was likely to be taught in them. There was little doubt that in Catholic schools the secular state and the liberal regime of which Cavour approved would be denounced. Nevertheless, to deny the Church the right to have its own schools would be an infringement of another form of freedom. The only solution was to allow the Church to retain a certain autonomy, provided it did not usurp the legitimate rights of the liberal state. When it did so – in a free society – everyone had the right to attack it, and Cavour was not over-delicate in his attacks on right-wing clerics or ultramontanes. Thus in a letter to Auguste de la Rive in 1844 he expressed strong sentiments against the ultramontane party in France and the Swiss cantons, saying that they were behaving in a totally unreasonable and absurd manner. 'This party is a greater scourge of humanity than communism', Cavour wrote, employing an early use of the term 'communism'.[17]

In 1852, before he arranged the *connubio*, and became prime minister, he still saw what he called 'the reactionary-clerical faction' as his greatest domestic enemies, and as the most dangerous opposition to constitutionalism and liberalism in Western Europe as a whole. He wrote to Alfonso Lamarmora in July 1852:

> The violence of the Catholic party does not astonish me. This Court has renounced methods of conciliation and leniency, to fight with the most murderous arms. In Italy, in Belgium, in England, Rome pursues the same end, the conquest of civil society. The methods vary, the form changes, but in the end the same principle is dominant: a struggle to the death against the independence of the civil power. Provided she reaches her aims, Rome does not bother about means. If in our country she is allied to the most unbridled reactionaries, in Belgium she seeks foreign influence, and in Great Britain she employs the language of the most exalted demagogues. If you read the pastoral messages of the Irish bishops regarding the elections, you will find radical declamations, besides which the speeches of Brofferio and Valerio would appear moderate.
>
> The Roman question is at this moment a European question. Rome has decided that it can profit from the reactionary movement which all Europe is experiencing to reassert its influence as in the middle ages.[18]

He added, more optimistically, that Rome's success would be short-lived, as there would be a 'terrible reaction' against clerical policies. Already the reaction against Catholic pretensions in England was being felt. Cavour showed himself well-informed on the point, because in Britain there was indeed a reaction against what was described as the 'Papal Aggression' of 1851, when the Catholic hierarchy had been re-established.

For the Jesuits Cavour felt a special animosity. Some years before, in a letter probably written in 1844, to Anastasia de Circourt, he had written of the Jesuits that they had learnt nothing and forgotten nothing.[19]

There was a sharp distinction between Cavour's attitude to the political influence of the Catholic Church, and his convictions concerning the historic role of Christianity in a more general and profound sense. In 1833 he read the two works of the French philosopher, Théodore Jouffroy, *How dogmas end*, and *Of the problem of human destiny*, and copied passages of the latter into his diary. Jouffroy pointed out that a purely religious, Christian, doctrine had served European civilization for many centuries, but that in more recent centuries a philosophical doctrine was demanded by thinking people and 'a great war had broken out in Europe between human reason on the one side and the imperfections' of religious doctrine on the other, and this had led the educated classes to abandon the traditional faith. There was then a need for a rigorous new philosophy which would have greater depth than that of Voltaire, and in which Christianity would still have a part to play. However, the role of Christianity, though still important, had now become a transitional one, and once that role had been played out Christianity, the last religion of which mankind had need, must withdraw. Cavour accepted much of this doctrine, while believing that the immediate role of Christianity was more vital than Jouffroy seemed to suggest. The great achievement of Christianity, Cavour believed, had been its ability to adapt, unlike 'the immobility which destroyed the Judaic law'.[20] Consequently Christianity remained historically the most advanced religion. So far as the different forms of Christianity went, it seems likely that Cavour felt more sympathy for Swiss Protestantism than for Italian Catholicism, though he never, of course, joined any Protestant communion. Formal religious observance did not appeal to his enquiring mind.

Cavour's political convictions started with the firm belief that autocracies were doomed. 'The nobility is crumbling on all sides, the princes, like the peoples, tend equally to destroy them'.[21] He was not opposed to monarchy, though, only to its feudal trappings. He felt a supreme contempt for the life of the courtier, with its mixture of luxury and deference.

His contempt was partly the result of his early experience as a page, but was also part of his rejection of the absolutism of Carlo Alberto. The censorship which Carlo Alberto's regime imposed before 1847 prevented Piedmontese writers from dealing with political subjects, and there was even a law forbidding them from publishing abroad, a law which was inevitably largely ignored. Cavour regarded the censorship practices of Carlo Alberto as 'highly absurd'.[22]

His demands for a constitution in 1847 and early in 1848 were thus not only sincere, but passionately felt. On 7 February 1848 his journal, *Il Risorgimento*, contained an article by Cavour recommending a constitution to Carlo Alberto in terms aimed, not at antagonizing the king, but rather at converting him to Cavour's own convictions. He argued that the reforms already introduced by the king formed a sure base for the grant of a constitution, which would bring Piedmont in line with the most civilized countries of Europe. In the same article he advocated the creation of a civic guard – a citizens' armed body to protect the achievements already made by reforms, and to prevent them from 'degenerating into licence'. Cavour's basic suggestion was for a constitution, though, and he waxed loud in praise of the constitution which the King of Naples had already granted to his people, pointing out that on the whole in Europe the assumption was that Piedmont was better prepared for a constitution than Naples.

Cavour's distaste for autocracy was balanced by his fear of democracy. In 1845, however, he believed that a democratic revolution would be unlikely to succeed in Italy, because it would have little following with the masses, who – apart from a few urban groups – were attached to the traditional institutions of the country. Radical democratic ideas were held only by the middle, or upper middle, classes, and even they had many interests they would want to defend. Fortunately in Italy property did not belong exclusively to one class. Professed republicans would probably rally to the conservative cause if the social order was really threatened. The events of 1848–49 made Cavour less sure that Italy was safe from extreme democracy. He would no longer have repeated what had, in fact, been his shrewd analysis of 1845. He said in parliament in 1851:

You cannot forget the tremendous effect produced on European public opinion by the extravagances, disorders, exaggerations which followed the upheaval of 1848 in France . . . I remember having seen, leaving Turin in the winter of 1848, men who were considered far more liberal than me, and then seeing them return infinitely more conservative than I was. I believe that even the most convinced members sitting on the other side [of the chamber], if they had witnessed the disorders of Lyon, or the June Days in Paris, would not have so complete or so absolute a faith in the ideas of indefinite progress.[23]

It was unusual for Cavour to query the nineteenth-century idea of progress, but his hatred of the radicalism of Paris in 1848 had given him pause. The young Cavour of 1835 had written: 'We cannot deceive ourselves. Society marches with great strides towards democracy; it is perhaps impossible to foresee the forms it will take, but in the end there can be no doubt of its goal . . .'[24] Then followed the passage about the crumbling of aristocracy which has already been quoted.

Cavour's hatred of despotism and fear of democracy had led him to faith in a middle way – le juste-milieu – as the true vehicle for political and social progress. Already in 1833 he had expounded his conviction in an honest and introspective letter to his cousin, Auguste de La Rive. It had seemed to him then that the revolutions of 1830–31 had forced many people into positions of extreme reaction or extreme republicanism. But he continued:

As for me I have been for a long time undecided in the midst of these movements. Reason pushed me towards moderation; an extreme desire to make our reactionaries march forward threw me into the movement; finally, after numerous and violent agitations and oscillations, I ended by fixing myself, like a pendulum, in the juste-milieu. Thus I assure you that I am an honest juste-milieu, desiring, hoping, working for social progress, but determined not to buy it at the price of a general political and social upheaval.[25]

By 1847 he was still a defender of the juste-milieu, and in a letter, again to De La Rive, he wrote:

This poor *juste-milieu* is not in favour with young people, but experience and reason become stronger than the imagination and passion, and a man of good faith decides in the end that if he need not yield to fashion, which is leading society towards unknown regions, it is equally unreasonable to move backwards.[26]

Cavour's passionate belief in the *juste-milieu* was partly the result, and partly the cause, of his admiration for Guizot in Paris and Robert Peel in London, both of whom he had heard debate in parliament. He respected – and perhaps exaggerated – the intellectual weight of Guizot's language, and he recognized the clarity and honesty of Peel's argument. But he never fully realized that what is the middle way at one moment of time may, in the same place, have become a reactionary stance in a changing situation. While Guizot represented the *juste-milieu* at the start of his career, few historians would today consider him a moderate on the eve of the February revolution of 1848. Cavour was not altogether prepared to admit that a liberal could become a reactionary. He never abandoned his admiration for Guizot and the July Monarchy, but he was also, in a sense, generous to political radicals – for example, he believed that revolutionary German students in 1848 might have the future on their side, although they were dangerous at that moment. His admiration for British institutions sometimes makes him sound conservative today, but on specific points he would imply criticism of those institutions. His respect for elected legislative bodies, rather than ones appointed by a monarch or the executive, clearly gave him doubts about the role of the House of Lords in Britain. He certainly insisted that it would be a mistake for Piedmont blindly to copy the British House of Lords, a body appointed by the executive government, and by definition containing only members of the nobility. Yet he would never have called himself a 'democrat', and he was opposed to much that would be considered natural features of 'democracy' in the twentieth century. One example of such a feature was the secret ballot. Electors, he believed, should be able to give reasons for their choice of deputies: if they merely put a cross against a name in secret, they would do so in an inarticulate and irresponsible manner. (It must be remembered, however, that the secret ballot was introduced in British elections only in 1872.) More basic was his fear of universal suffrage, and his belief that the vote should be given only to the educated: literacy alone was not enough.

Cavour's encounter with Tocqueville in England, which was mentioned in Chapter 2, encouraged him in his praise of the *juste-milieu*. His attitude, though, was appreciably different from that of Tocqueville, who believed that there was an inevitable progression towards democracy, a progression which would bring a lowering of cultural standards, and mediocrity in intellectual life, but would create a more egalitarian society, which would have some positive, if humble, characteristics. Cavour accepted this broad belief, but was a politician at heart, even before he had begun his political career, and so was concerned with the more immediate prospects of society. Tocqueville's grand prophecies were interesting, but for Cavour what was important was how today's politics should react to the immediate clash of parties and aims. It was as a present necessity that the middle way in politics had to be adopted – the way which would lead to 'moderation, wise progress and useful reforms'.[27]

. . .

SOCIAL REFORM AND SOCIALISM

Cavour was in no doubt that political leaders pursuing the *juste-milieu* had to carry through large programmes of social reform. He believed, like Tocqueville, that in Britain the ruling class would have to accept a more equitable distribution of land if they were to avoid social revolution: the enormous estates, owned by a small aristocracy, would have to be diminished before they became politically dangerous as a provocation to the dispossessed. He did not accept Nassau Senior's argument that in an industrial society the workers were not interested in the ownership of land. In a sense, though, Senior was right, since the industrial workers in Britain hated the mill-owners and the mine-owners more than the landowners, who were usually remote from their lives; Captain Swing and his agricultural revolutionaries belonged to an earlier phase of English social history. It is understandable that Cavour should be surprised to find so few indications of a class war in Britain, in view of the unequal class system he found there. There was, of course, plenty of social protest in the 1830s, and the striking social inequalities suggested to Cavour that political democracy was advancing too quickly for the comfort and safety of the property-owning classes. Still, he applauded Lord Grey and the Whig Reform Act of 1832, and he believed that British trade unions were less dangerous to social stability than they were thought to be by observers on the Continent. He approved of the workhouses, which were just being introduced on his first visit to Britain, under the New Poor Law Act of 1834. Dickens was not to publish *Oliver Twist* until 1837–38, and the movement against the New Poor Law had barely begun. Cavour's assessment of the new workhouses was based on a very superficial knowledge of them. Still, for what it was worth, his judgement was that the English workhouses were less demanding on their inmates than Catholic charitable establishments in France, or at home in Piedmont.

While believing that governments should carry through basic social reforms, Cavour rejected what he understood as 'socialism'. In a debate in the Piedmontese parliament on 21 January 1851, he made one of his more profound statements. Modern history, he declared, demonstrated that the development of society was one of progress, but that even the wisest philosophers and statesmen had so far failed to define the rules of that progress. However, one thing was certain: that progress was in two spheres, the political and the economic. In the political sphere progress implied the modification of institutions in such a way that an increasing number of citizens would share political power. In the economic sphere progress implied 'an improvement for the lower classes, and a better distribution of the products of the land and of capital'. There were two methods of securing economic progress. One was 'according to the principle of liberty, the principle of free co-operation, the free development of moral and intellectual humanity'. This method, he considered, was that of what he called the 'economic school', which today would perhaps be called that of the 'classical economists'. The statesmen ruling England, he said, followed this school. The other method involved restraining more and more individual action, and increasing central control. 'This', he said, 'gentlemen, is the socialist school'. Although its politics had led to 'dismal and sometimes atrocious' results, it could not be denied that there was something in its principles which 'generous and elevated spirits' found seductive. Therefore socialist ideas must be fought on the intellectual plane; 'cannon and bayonets' may keep order for a while, but in the end they alone could not succeed.

Cavour then put forward an argument, which must have surprised many of his listeners, since he was taking them beyond the usual span of their intellectual ability. A great ally of socialism, he said, was protectionism. The protectionists, like the socialists, believed that governments had the right, and thus the duty, to intervene in the employment and distribution of wealth. They believed that governments were more enlightened than the free will of individuals. However, if the protectionists, like the socialists, believed thus, the workers could argue that governments should in that case intervene also to organize labour and protect wages. Logically, Cavour argued, a defence of protectionism led to a defence of socialism.[28]

Original and penetrating although Cavour's speech was, it was inevitably tied to the time and circumstance in which it was delivered. Europe's experience of socialism in action in 1851 was extremely limited: indeed, it might be said to have consisted only of the steps taken by the French Second Republic from February to June 1848. Cavour felt vaguely that those steps had been mistaken, and had had 'dismal and atrocious' results. But his real concern was to attack protectionism, and to defend what in the late twentieth century would be called 'a market economy'.

The positive feature of Cavour's political philosophy was his belief in progress, and in this he was a quintessential figure of his age. And the progress in which he believed was one towards universal prosperity and peace. Although he planned one major war, he passionately wanted, ultimately, eternal peace between the nations.[29] He did not share the conviction, later common to fascists, but already expressed by Joseph de Maistre, that war was an expression of the will of God. Cavour would not have agreed with Bismarck, who said of warfare that 'there is no other means in this present century by which the clock of development can be made to show the correct time'.[30]

Whatever may be thought of Cavour's political, economic and social creed, it must be concluded that he was on the side of rationalism, and in that sense, if in no other, was an heir to the eighteenth-century Enlightenment. The year 1829 may not seem in retrospect to have shown much advance of the human spirit, but in writing its obituary, on 16 January 1830, the young Cavour commented to Sellon:

> I have read recently with much pleasure accounts of the progress of the human spirit in the year of grace 1829: the human spirit is on the march, and in spite of the vain efforts of the ignorant and the wicked it continues to advance with a sure step. I have a great hope and desire that this year may be as fruitful as the last. Many causes are in conflict. Please God let reason and enlightenment triumph.[31]

. . .

NOTES AND REFERENCES

1. Romeo, I, pp. 567–68.
2. *ibid*, p. 569.
3. Giuseppe Massari, *Il Conte di Cavour Ricordi Biografici* (Botta, Turin, 1873), p. 26.
4. Chiala, I, p. 315.
5. Romeo, I, p. 571.
6. Chiala, I, pp. 326–27.
7. *ibid*, p. 327.
8. *ibid*, p. 278.
9. *ibid*, p. 114.
10. *ibid*, p. 283. Letter dated 13 May 1833.
11. *ibid*, p. 283.
12. *ibid*, p. 289.
13. *ibid*, p. 401.
14. Ruffini, p. 136.
15. Nassau William Senior, *Journals kept in France and Italy from 1848 to 1852*, 1871, vol. I, pp. 291–92.
16. Ruffini, p. xlvi.
17. Chiala, I, p. 344.
18. *ibid*, pp. 524–25.
19. *ibid*, p. 353.
20. Romeo, I, pp. 593–95.

21. Ruffini, p. 322.
22. *ibid*, p. 194.
23. Chiala, I, p. 175.
24. *ibid*, p. 287.
25. *ibid*, p. 283.
26. *ibid*, p. 383.
27. Romeo, I, p. 329.
28. Chiala, I, pp. 191–93.
29. Ruffini, p. 69.
30. Quoted in William Carr, *The Origins of the Wars of German Unification* (Longman, Harlow, 1991), p. x.
31. Ruffini, p. 94.

Chapter 4

POWER AND THE FIRST TASTE OF EUROPEAN POLITICS, 1848–56

In the battle of Goito, at the end of May 1848 an event of great personal concern had a profound emotional effect on Cavour. His brother's son, the Marquis Augusto Cavour, who was only twenty-one, was killed. It seems probable that Augusto had been closer to Cavour than he had ever been to his own father. He was without doubt the closest thing to a son Cavour ever had. Michelangelo Castelli, whose personal impressions of Cavour are so vivid, went to console him, but found him inconsolable. in fact – according to Castelli – weeping and rolling on the floor in uncontrollable grief. Cavour had his nephew's bloodstained uniform placed in a cupboard in his own room, where it remained until Cavour himself died.

Cavour's first speech in parliament was made on 4 July 1848, when Piedmont was at war with Austria, and twenty days before the overwhelming Austrian defeat of the Piedmontese at the battle of Custozza. By 4 July Milan had been liberated and was still free, and a revolutionary parliament in Venice had voted for union with Piedmont. The Piedmontese parliament to which Cavour delivered his maiden speech was debating a law uniting Lombardy and Venice to Piedmont. He spoke badly, and was booed from the gallery – an experience with which he was to become only too familiar – but he was his own most severe critic. He believed that his performance suffered from an inadequate literary and classical education, the kind of education which had been enjoyed by the British aristocracy whose parliamentary eloquence he so much admired. It was not likely, though, that Cavour would be deterred by an initial failure in oratory. Within three years he was to acquire a total dominance of the parliamentary scene. So far as the content of his speech on this first occasion went, he supported the government of Cesare Balbo, considered by the vocal public to be a government of the Right.

The Piedmontese defeat at Custozza was followed by an armistice. Carlo Alberto wanted the right-wing Count Ottavio di Revel to form a government with the immensely popular Vincenzo Gioberti, but such a combination of men from opposite sides of the house was impossible. Revel became prime minister, with Gioberti heading the opposition. The parliamentary session reopened in October 1848, with Cavour supporting a government that was even more right-wing than Balbo's had been. He spoke now with greater strength and conviction, but was still whistled at from the public gallery. At the end of the year of revolutions he was at last playing a role on the public stage, but was bitterly unpopular with the liberals in parliament.

In December 1848 Gioberti formed a new government, with the intention of renewing the war against Austria. Before taking such a step he dissolved the chamber, and in the elections Cavour lost his seat. Inevitably he felt bitter, but he was rightly convinced that Gioberti's government was about to make a gross blunder. With reference to Piedmontese domestic politics and his own position, he wrote to Michelangelo Castelli in January 1849:

I beg you to believe that the deplorable result of the last elections has neither surprised nor discouraged me . . . To tell the truth, if I allowed myself the true inclinations of my character, what has happened would amuse me enormously, because the spectacle which we have before our eyes is singularly ridiculous . . . There is not even a little chemist, or a wretched village priest, who, armed with his *Gazetta del Popolo*, would not believe that he could treat us – you and me and those who read the *Risorgimento* – as narrow and limited spirits, or stupid retrogrades. In the last elections my friends did not dare to pronounce my name, such is the immense unpopularity which my name enjoys in the politics of the countryside.

This result, not very flattering to my self-esteem, is far from disgusting me as regards the life of politics:

I consider it as an inevitable episode which must be endured without weakness or bad temper. So far as I am concerned I have no intention of abandoning the *Risorgimento*.[1]

In March 1849 the Piedmontese were defeated in their second war against Austria. Carlo Alberto abdicated, and his son, Vittorio Emanuele II became king. In May Massimo d'Azeglio formed a government. Cavour, who was soon to be back in parliament, agreed with the new king and Azeglio that to attempt to renew the war with Austria would be foolish and would mean the loss of the Piedmontese constitution. Azeglio persuaded the king to dissolve the assembly. On 20 November the king issued the Moncalieri proclamation (Moncalieri was one of his chateaux), encouraging the Piedmontese to elect moderate deputies who would not vote for war. It was an unconstitutional proclamation, but in the circumstances a wise one. In December 1849 the voters followed Vittorio Emanuele's advice and elected an assembly which gave an overwhelming vote for peace, Cavour, who had been re-elected, agreeing with the majority.

. . .

CAVOUR IN OFFICE

He rapidly established himself as the most dynamic figure in the ruling party. In October 1850 he was made minister for trade and agriculture, and shortly afterwards also for the navy. He was already aiming at the premiership, but he saw as his path to that goal the efficient administration of the departments for which he was responsible. Taking over the navy, he intended to make it as large and effective as the Neapolitan one. He could not, of course, pretend to any maritime experience: his longest ride at sea had been on a cross-channel boat to England. Cavour found the Piedmontese navy undisciplined. There had been a mutiny in 1849, inspired by Mazzinian ideas. On the other hand, the senior officers were reactionary in every sense, even resisting the introduction of steam navigation. Two important changes were taking place in the navies of the developed nations – a switch from sail to steam, and from wooden ships to ironclad ones. Cavour, of course, was on the side of the future, and impatient with naval officers who resisted change. Two such officers were charged with insubordination and court martialled, but charges were dropped when friends at court intervened. It was typical of Cavour that he should find himself in conflict, during his brief period in charge of the Piedmontese navy, with the old forces of privilege and royal prerogative.

On 26 February 1851 Cavour was appointed to the much more important post of minister of finance. The three ministries he already held were scrapped or incorporated in the ministry of finance. He was now the most important member of the government after the prime minister. His rise to power had been as rapid as it had been belated.

As minister of finance he took his first steps towards drawing Piedmont closer to France. The occasion was the renewal of a commercial treaty of 1843. Writing in April 1851 to the French minister in Turin, after the treaty had been discussed in parliament, he said that he was motivated by political, as well as economic, factors, since 'France is the nation with which we desire the most intimate and the most extended relations'. Nevertheless, he still wanted to strike a good bargain with the French, and reminded the French minister that the Piedmontese cabinet had had to make it an issue of basic foreign policy to get parliament to agree. The French, too, pressed a hard bargain, and he had to point out that the Belgians and the British were prepared to grant more favourable terms to Piedmont than the French were offering. In the end he secured treaties with France as well as Belgium and Britain on terms that were not unfavourable, though, so far as the Franco-Piedmontese treaty went, France obtained marginally the better deal.

The Piedmontese government desperately needed cash, primarily to pay off the indemnity imposed on the country by the Austrians after the defeats of 1848 and 1849. To secure a loan Cavour now despatched to London a man who was subsequently to lead the Right in parliament against him – the Count Ottavio de Revel. Cavour seems to have had full confidence in him. Previous loans, negotiated by Cavour's predecessors, had placed Piedmont heavily in debt to the House of Rothschild, and dependence on the most powerful banking family in Europe made Cavour feel uncomfortable.

Overtures to the Bank of Baring had been unsuccessful, and Cavour was now counting on getting a loan from the smaller Bank of Hambro, who had the patronage of the Danish court. He had all the detailed financial knowledge at his finger-tips, and could give Revel the most clear and precise instructions.

The first payment secured from Hambro had to be paid to Austria to keep the terms of the peace treaty of 1849. It was typical of Cavour that, although he wanted to free Piedmont from too tight a stranglehold at the hands of Rothschild, he did not want to antagonize so powerful a banking house needlessly. He therefore arranged with Baron James Rothschild for their Paris bank to handle the payment to Austria. He already felt, however, that the loan from Hambro had been secured only just in time, since there was an anonymous article in *The Times*, inspired, Cavour believed, by James Rothschild, announcing that the Piedmontese government was nearing bankruptcy. Cavour referred to the Rothschilds as 'our enemies'. There may have been a touch of paranoia in his attitude to the Rothschilds, but one thing is certain: anti-semitism is not a prejudice which would ever have entered his consciousness.

Cavour was still responsible for the navy and suggested while Revel was still in England that he should consult Lord Minto on naval matters. As Minto, Cavour said, had been first lord of the admiralty 'for a long time' (in fact since 1835) he must know all about the British navy. Here Cavour was perhaps giving greater respect to the British ministerial system than it deserved, but he was at least aware of the need, not so much to increase the Piedmontese navy, as to modernize it by scrapping old ships and building new ones. As it happened, the Piedmontese fleet was not needed in the 1859 war against Austria. The disastrous performance of the Italian navy in 1866 – five years after Cavour's death – could hardly be blamed on him.

Almost immediately on paying off the war indemnity to Austria, Cavour negotiated with his recent enemy for a commercial treaty, and on 1 August 1851, could announce that the negotiations were going well, and depended only on the suppression of smuggling on the Austro-Piedmontese frontier – which meant in effect the shores of Lake Maggiore, and the banks of the River Ticino. This problem was evidently overcome, and the treaty was signed.

. . .

THE *CONNUBIO*

The prime minister in 1851, Massimo d'Azeglio, was, as a person, an exact contrast to Cavour. Azeglio was easy-going, relaxed, inclined to be lazy, but on the positive side knew Italy in a way that Cavour was never to know her. He had lived in Milan, Florence and Rome as well as Turin. He had lived a Bohemian life as an artist in Rome, and had painted melodramatic pictures, and written melodramatic novels, usually with tongue in cheek. The fame from his writings in the 1840s was responsible for his climb to the premiership. Although an intelligent man, he did not prove an efficient politician. He was too obviously bored by the minutiae of politics, which Cavour could master so completely. With his broad cultural interests, Azeglio seemed not to take politics too seriously, Ministers reported to him as he lay in bed and there was always the possibility that things would happen without his knowledge. However, the periods when he was ill in bed, instead of attending debates in parliament, were caused by genuine illness. He had fought in the 1848 war, and had been wounded at the battle of Vicenza. His colleagues and political opponents tended to believe that he used his wound as an excuse for indolence, but this was only partly true. The wound had been a serious one: in 1852 there was still a question of having a leg amputated.

One of the less attractive illustrations of Cavour's character was his ungenerous attitude towards Azeglio. Cavour wrote from England to his colleague, Lamarmora, on 23 July 1852, saying that Azeglio was an 'enigma', and he could not decide if he was 'the simplest or the most cunning of men'. Two or three weeks later he wrote again from England, saying that Azeglio could not be opposed because he was so popular abroad, especially in England, but that he (Cavour) did not believe Azeglio indispensable; on the contrary he believed him more harmful than useful: if Azeglio resigned it would be a blessing for the country.[2]

The issue which was mainly preoccupying Azeglio and the Piedmontese government in 1851 was the dispute between

Church and State, a dispute quite as bitter as the *Kulturkampf* which Bismarck was to fight against the Catholic Church some twenty years later. The social control exerted by the Catholic Church made Piedmont still in some ways a medieval country. The Church still had its own law courts; criminals could still claim sanctuary from the law in ecclesiastical buildings; there was no civil marriage; and the Church still had a strong hold on education. When laws were introduced into parliament to reduce the power of the Church in these matters, the Piedmontese bishops put up a strong resistance, threatening with excommunication anyone who voted for, or obeyed, any such laws. The Archbishop of Turin, Monsignor Fransoni, refused the sacraments to Cavour's friend, Pietro di Santa Rosa, when it was believed that he was dying, on the grounds that Santa Rosa had supported the anticlerical legislation. While the Archbishop's refusal may have been correct and logical in ecclesiastical terms, it was a mistake in human terms, and antagonized most politically conscious people in Piedmont. Cavour himself felt bitter animosity towards the Catholic prelates, but was going to handle the crisis with careful diplomacy. He was perhaps less anticlerical than Azeglio, who had been educated by Jesuits, but had reacted against the papacy during his young days in Rome.

A new session of parliament opened on 4 March 1851. Cavour had made the extraordinary decision to conduct government policy on a basic issue without reference to the prime minister. Azeglio's government of the Centre Right had depended on the support of people further to its right, like Balbo and Revel. The Far Right had lost much sympathy in the country because of the militant policy of the Church. Cavour now decided to break with the people of the more extreme Right, and to seek the support for the government – Azeglio's government – of the Centre Left, which was led by the lawyer, Urbano Rattazzi. Cavour's policy was to succeed, and was to be known as the *connubio*, or 'marriage'.

The first step in the *connubio* was for Cavour to announce that the government no longer counted on the support of the extreme Right. He made the announcement without even informing Azeglio, who was not present in the chamber, and was understandably astonished when he heard what had happened. A few weeks later Cavour completed the *connubio* by persuading the house to elect Rattazzi as President, the president being something between the Speaker and the Leader of the British House of Commons.

Cavour was counting on the indolence of Azeglio, and the dependence of the other ministers on his own administrative competence and mastery of parliament, to push through the *connubio*, but at first no one knew what Azeglio's reaction would be. That he had to accept a *fait accompli* was not at first apparent, but Cavour trusted that Azeglio would be reluctant to take any strong action. Azeglio, however, did not accept what Cavour had done without some, rather ineffectual, protest. When the *Indépendance Belge* published a statement to the effect that Azeglio had proposed and supported the election of Rattazzi, the prime minister sent a circular to the diplomatic agents in Turin, denying the fact, and saying that he had never agreed with the principles on which Rattazzi's ministry had been founded, and it would be impossible for him to associate his policy in any way with Rattazzi's.

Azeglio had plenty of reason to be angry with Cavour over what had happened. Only the day before Cavour's coup – on 13 March – the Centre Left had voted against the government on a measure approving extraordinary expenditure on the fortifications at Casale. The measure had been passed by only four votes, and would not have been passed at all without the support of the Right, whom Cavour was busy insulting. Azeglio wrote to his friend, Eugène Rendu, on 24 May 1851:

> Since the famous session of 5 February, the session of the *connubio*, I have been rather cold with Cavour. Just imagine – my dear colleague, without any warning, had arranged the whole under-hand affair with Rattazzi, and made his speech, which committed the ministry so heavily, without speaking to me of it.[3]

He went on to explain that he could not let the opposition in parliament see how isolated he had become in his own government, but that clearly the situation could not continue.

This letter was written before the formal election of Rattazzi as president. On the day when that step was taken, Azeglio was in bed and could not attend the debate. He immediately wrote to the king offering his resignation.

The king accepted the resignation of the whole government, but asked Azeglio to form a new one. In other words Vittorio Emanuele wanted to get rid of Cavour, rather than Azeglio, who now formed a new government omitting Cavour and Luigi Carlo Farini, who had worked closely with Cavour. In fact Azeglio was weary of politics, and eager to get out of it. Gioberti, however, at this moment, expressed the hope that Azeglio would remain, because he was believed, throughout Italy and abroad, to be much more 'Italian' than Cavour.

On 22 October 1852 Azeglio again tendered his resignation, and the king asked Cavour to form a government, with the stipulation that he should negotiate with the pope on the outstanding issues between Piedmont and Rome, and especially that of civil marriage. Cavour said that he could not give way in the dispute with the pope, and advised the king to ask Balbo to form a ministry. Balbo agreed to form a government, provided the right-wing leader, Revel, would join. Revel refused, partly because he knew public opinion would not welcome either him or a reconciliation with Rome. The king was obliged to return to Cavour, who agreed to form a government, while leaving open the question of relations with the pope.

By pushing through the *connubio*, Cavour had effectively driven Azeglio from office, and had himself secured the premiership. There was certainly a conspiratorial, if not a shabby, aspect to the operation. Some points can be made in Cavour's favour, however. While he had never had time for the extreme Left, who had continually made personal attacks on the government of a peculiarly unpleasant kind, the Centre Left had, since 1849, showed moderation in their language and Cavour felt that there was a sharp distinction between the two types of opposition. Often members of the Centre Left had voted with the government.

On the other hand the Centre Right, which was supposed to be the party of government under Azeglio, had become less reliable. It was divided within itself, and the individual members had idiosyncratic views which could never be anticipated. Cavour had come, then, to trust the leader of the Centre Left, Rattazzi, more than some of his own colleagues in Azeglio's government, not to mention Azeglio himself. The agreement which Cavour had reached with

Rattazzi included an assurance from the latter that he would give up any hint of republicanism and accept the *Statuto* completely. Beyond that they agreed, rather vaguely, to pursue a policy of 'civil and political progress', and maintain Piedmontese independence from foreign influence. For Cavour this almost certainly meant Austrian influence, though for Rattazzi it probably also meant French influence, and perhaps English influence, since the Left had always taunted Cavour with being too Anglophile, and had nicknamed him 'Milord Cavour'.

The charge that Cavour had acted behind Azeglio's back in arranging the *connubio* can hardly be refuted, but Azeglio had had warnings of what Cavour had in mind and these he had ignored, or preferred not to notice. Matteo Ricci, the husband of Azeglio's daughter, Rina, recorded that he was present when Cavour and Azeglio were lunching together, some time before any talk of a *connubio*. Alfonso Lamarmora, who was to be made minister of war by Cavour, was also present. There was at first a light-hearted conversation. Azeglio was always happier discussing the arts rather than politics, and was enthusing over a play by Dumas currently being performed in Turin. Cavour was bored by the subject, but, trying to keep the conversation light-hearted, made a joking remark about Azeglio's dislike of Rattazzi. Azeglio did not take it in a joking spirit, and the two men started to argue. Azeglio said he wanted to hear no more of Rattazzi, whereupon Cavour flung his plateful of lunch on the ground, and rushed out of the room. If the incident should have given Azeglio warning of what Cavour was plotting, it equally must have made it clear to Cavour that the idea of an alignment with Rattazzi would be anathema to Azeglio.

. . .

CAVOUR, PRIME MINISTER

In forming his government Cavour kept the ministry of finance for himself, but, perhaps surprisingly, gave the foreign ministry to a general, Giuseppe Dabormida, who was to play a somewhat negative role in the dramatic months ahead.

Cavour now had to grapple with the bitter struggle

between Church and State, in which Azeglio had shown himself to be something of a radical. The law abolishing the separate Church law courts met with the approval of most of the house, as it almost certainly did with public opinion, but twenty-six deputies of the Right voted against it. The general feeling was that these deputies wanted not only to retain the influence of the Church in Piedmontese politics and society, but to destroy the constitution, which they saw as incompatible with Catholicism. Still, the twenty-six deputies, having on this occasion voted against the ecclesiastical bill and the government, never voted against the government again, and Cavour decided that he would refrain from considering the Right in general as enemies.

Cavour was in a difficult position. He had promised the king that he would not make the passing of the law on civil marriage an issue of confidence in the government, though this, of course, was not the same thing as saying that he would drop the bill, or would fail to support it as an individual, from personal conviction. He could not simply keep silent upon a point on which he felt strongly, even if his position was opposed to the king's sentiments. Vittorio Emanuele was a simple man, who was concerned for his own soul. Although the pope irritated him, he believed that one day he would have to face his Maker, and he had a sneaking suspicion that the pope might know more about the whims of their Maker than he did.

Cavour was bothered by no such simple superstition. On the second day of the discussion of the bill – 16 December 1852 – two of Cavour's colleagues strongly defended the bill, and Cavour, interpreting his promise to the king literally, but perhaps not as the king had understood it, spoke with great warmth of civil marriage, both as a moral, as well as a political, cause. A vote was taken on 20 December in the senate. At first it seemed that the bill would pass, but after several disputed and contradictory votes, the government withdrew the bill, expressing its regret at the decision of the senate.

The Left was angry at the decision, and the matter was not improved when the Piedmontese bishops declared that anyone who might have obeyed the law would have been excommunicated. Angelo Brofferio, now the leader of the independent Left, attacked the government bitterly for giving way to a reactionary clerical faction. The Piedmontese public, he argued, expected Cavour's government to stand up to the reactionary forces. It was all very well for the ministers to speak in favour of civil marriage, but action, not words, was needed. 'We, deputies who are not in office, have only the pen and words, but you are in executive power, you have the obligation to take prompt and effective action. When you limit yourselves to speaking, you are falling short of your duties'. Brofferio's speech was greeted with loud applause from the gallery, and must have been painful to Cavour, who was walking a delicate tight-rope between the Left and the politically conscious people on one side and the Right, the king and the Church on the other. Since the bill had been rejected by the senate, Cavour had the choice of reintroducing it at a later date, and bitterly antagonizing the king, or of doing nothing. He decided to do nothing – to let sleeping dogs lie.

The prospect for Cavour on becoming prime minister was not a brilliant one. The little state of Piedmont had recently been defeated overwhelmingly in war. To anyone alive at the time it would have seemed very unlikely that a prime minister of Piedmont would secure a prominent place in European history. Cavour's only hope was for Piedmont to recover economically from her defeats, restore her reputation in Europe, and improve relations with the great Western Powers. He had already realized the importance for Italy of Louis Napoleon's *coup d'état* of December 1851, the stroke of policy by which Louis Napoleon became an authoritarian, rather than a democratic, president. A Bonaparte in dictatorial control of France was more likely to help Italy than the pacific July Monarchy, or the divided Second Republic had been.

In December 1852 Prince President Louis Napoleon proclaimed himself Emperor Napoleon III. Republicanism in France had been defeated, and would not be restored for eighteen years – long after Cavour's death. So far as Italy was concerned, however, Mazzini still had grandiose plans for revolution. He planned a rising against the Austrians in Milan for 6 February 1853. The Austrians suppressed the rising in its initial stages. A large number of Italians were arrested, and fifty men were executed.

As an attempted revolution of republicans, the movement in Milan represented a danger to the new emperor in France, but also to the Piedmontese monarchy. Cavour was saddled with an embarrassing problem. He could hardly ignore the fact that many Italians living in Piedmont – whether originally Piedmontese, or exiles from other parts of Italy, including Lombardy – were outspoken republicans, who might well have been involved in the Mazzinian movement, and should therefore be arrested. On the other hand, to do so would seem to be acting as an agent for the Austrians. He chose to divorce himself from the Italian nationalist cause, and had several Mazzinians arrested, including Francesco Crispi, Garibaldi's future political organizer in 1860 and prime minister of Italy in the 1880s and 1890s. The action brought him animosity from the Left, especially when the Austrian government thanked him for his actions.

The Habsburg government immediately put itself in the wrong, however. In February a decree was passed in Vienna taking over the property of Lombard refugees who had fled to Piedmont. Since these numbered some 20,000 households, an enormous amount of property was involved, including palaces of the aristocracy. It was an act of robbery on a massive scale. The ruling classes of Europe outside Austria did not like to see the property of the rich being sequestered by a government. Cavour was given a great opportunity, and believed that what became known as the 'sequestrations question' might one day contribute to a Second War of Italian Independence. He lodged a strong protest in Vienna.

.   .   .

THE CRIMEAN WAR

In 1853 a European crisis developed over the Eastern Question, a crisis which at first seemed not to concern Piedmont in any way. In its first phase it was a quarrel between Catholic and Orthodox Christian monks over rights in the holy places in Jerusalem. Napoleon III backed the Catholic monks and the czar, Nicholas I, backed the Orthodox monks. Given Piedmont's chilly relations with the papacy, it was unlikely that Cavour would get involved in the affair. In its second phase the Eastern crisis was a matter of the czar's ambitions to be the sole protector of the Christian population under Turkish sovereignty in the Balkans. The czar's claims antagonized the British government, who suspected that he had plans to re-establish a Christian empire – with himself as the emperor – in Constantinople, thus cutting the overland route to India. More immediately it was at least a question of whether Russian or British influence should predominate in the Turkish capital. Napoleon III's interests in the question were dictated partly by personal animosity towards an aggressive czar, partly by the need to secure an alliance with Britain so that he would not be isolated in Europe, and partly by the hope of securing the support of Catholic opinion in France. Napoleon's occasional desire to support Catholicism and the pepacy was to be a source of anxiety for Cavour for the remaining years of the Italian statesman's life.

Piedmont had no reason for going to war with Russia, yet in the course of 1854, after France and Britain were involved in a full military confrontation in the Crimea, Piedmont was drawn into the war as their ally. Historians used to credit Cavour with the initiative in taking Piedmont into the Crimean War, but studies of the primary sources in recent decades have led to the belief that he was pressurized into action by the British and French governments. The original interpretation, by which Cavour spontaneously decided that Piedmont could secure an alliance with France and Britain by going to war against Russia was first suggested by Cavour's own close friend, Giuseppe Massari, a Neapolitan who had settled in Piedmont and become a devoted follower of that country's government and of Cavour. According to Massari, Cavour had broached the matter to Vittorio Emanuele in January 1854 – even before Britain and France had gone to war with Russia, but when it seemed extremely likely that they would do so. He had suggested to the king that Piedmont might gain by entering the coming war as an ally of the Western Powers, and the king had immediately accepted the idea, saying that if he could not lead the army himself, he would send his brother. At that time it was assumed that the war would be fought in the Balkans. Massari recounted the exchange between Cavour and the king in direct speech, although he was not himself present, and his evidence really has no more validity than mere hearsay. In any case the proposition was not taken up at that time.

Massari's account became the basis of an attractive – but misleading – interpretation of the entire history of Italian unification. It was said that, by intervening in the Crimean War, Cavour had secured the good will of France and Britain, and this enabled him later to go to war with Austria, and start the process by which a United Kingdom emerged in 1861. This interpretation omitted to mention that in 1854 Austria signed a treaty with France and Britain, by which she gave them diplomatic support (with the unspoken threat of military support) against Russia, and it was the securing of this treaty which played the major role in British and French policy towards Piedmont in 1854. Franco Valsecchi was the first historian to put Cavour's policy in this more precise context.[4] According to Valsecchi Cavour's decision to intervene in the Crimea was a purely defensive one, made to avoid isolation in Europe, and determined upon only in the autumn of 1854. The Western Powers were negotiating with Austria. A Franco-Austrian alliance would be dangerous for Piedmont, threatening the independence of her policy in Northern Italy. Thus, when the British and French pressed him to provide troops against the Russians in the Crimea, he grabbed at this policy as an escape from isolation.

In spite of Massari's somewhat fanciful passage in his life of Vittorio Emanuele, there is reason to suppose that Cavour had not initially decided to intervene in the Crimean War. Denis Mack Smith has pointed out that there were two quite compelling reasons why Cavour should not adopt an aggressive policy towards Russia. One was that Vittorio Emanuele was attracted by the idea of fighting a war, and if possible leading his army into battle, and to this end might replace Cavour with ministers prepared to carry out his wishes. The other was that Piedmont depended to some extent on grain from Russia, grain which in normal times was easily shipped from Black Sea ports to the Mediterranean.

According to Mack Smith's interpretation, which contains much – though perhaps not all – of the truth, it was a move by the French which eventually drove Cavour to favour intervention. The French head of legation in Turin was the Duc de Guiche (later to become the Duc de Gramont, and, as French foreign minister in 1870, to bear a heavy load of responsibility for the outbreak of the Franco-Prussian War). De Guiche negotiated with Vittorio Emanuele, behind Cavour's back, to obtain Piedmontese intervention. The Austrians were afraid that if they became involved in the war in the East, the Piedmontese would stir up trouble for them in Italy, and the French had to take this fear into consideration in their attempts to secure some kind of alliance with Austria. The fear was ungrounded so far as Cavour was concerned: he had no intention of going to war with Austria so soon after the Piedmontese defeats of 1848 and 1849, and he certainly had no intention of stirring up revolution in Lombardy. But even ungrounded and foolish fears have to be taken into consideration by prudent governments, and Napoleon had evidently decided that Piedmontese involvement in the war was necessary to reassure Austria.

De Guiche therefore approached, not the Piedmontese prime minister, but the Piedmontese king, and Vittorio Emanuele was evidently pleased with a conspiracy by which he would ask Cavour to adopt a policy of intervention in the Crimea, or else ask for his resignation. The leader of the Centre Right in Piedmont, Ottavio de Revel, with whom Cavour had previously been on good terms, would then be asked to form a government, and the king evidently knew that Revel would carry through a policy of intervention.

If the king had calculated that Cavour would passively resign, rather than accept the ultimatum, he had not assessed his prime minister with any accuracy. Cavour already had his own reasons for adopting a policy of intervention, and so called the king's bluff. He remained in office, but now the policy of intervention had become his – Cavour's – policy, and he was to propagate it in parliament and the press with thoroughness and skill.

The British minister in Turin (head of legation, again, not strictly speaking, ambassador) was Sir James Hudson, who played a very much larger role in converting Cavour to a policy of intervention than De Guiche did. Hudson was a highly intelligent man and a close friend of Cavour. He had been appointed to the mission in Turin in 1852, when Cavour became prime minister. He had immense respect for Cavour and for Piedmont generally, and was inclined to disregard the wishes of his superiors in London if they showed any distrust of Cavour.

The British and French had two preoccupations so far as Piedmont was concerned. The first was the straightforward need for troops. This was greater in the case of the

British, since their forces in the Crimea were rapidly depleted by cholera, and the French army in the field considerably outnumbered them. The second preoccupation of the French and British was to get an understanding with Austria. Austria's interests were inevitably deeply involved in the war, even if only because of her trade route down the Danube to the Black Sea. The Austrian foreign minister, Count Buol, was enough of a conservative to hope that one day an alignment with Russia and Prussia could be re-established, but in the immediate situation he hoped to keep on good terms with France and Britain, and – perhaps more important – to end the war, which he had tried, but failed, to avert. The Austrians remained neutral, but not motionless. One of the reasons for the war had been the Russian occupation of the Danubian Principalities of Moldavia and Wallachia, referred to in diplomatic circles simply as 'the Principalities', and an autonomous part of the Ottoman Empire. The one positive action taken by the Austrian government was to persuade the Russians to evacuate the Principalities, so that an Austrian army could replace them. It was the Austrian presence in the Principalities which sealed off the Balkans from the war, and left the French and British with little alternative but to send their armies to the Crimea.

Napoleon hoped that Austria would go further than observing a benevolent neutrality, and he reminded the Austrian government that he could stir up revolution in Italy and elsewhere. The other side of the coin was that he could discourage revolution, or acts hostile to the Austrians from Piedmont, if the Austrians made it worth his while to do so. The Austrians were more worried by this argument than they need have been. After all, they had recently suppressed a Mazzinian rising in Milan with considerable ease, and, as we have seen, Cavour had no intention of giving them trouble.

Cavour's more immediate policy during the crisis must now be considered in detail. On 1 November 1853 the czar's government declared war on the Ottoman Empire. From then on a deepening crisis involved Britain and France, although they were not to join the war for some months. Cavour's representative in London was Emanuele d'Azeglio, the nephew of Massimo. He was on good terms with Cavour, evidently bearing him no grudge for Cavour's treatment of Massimo at the time of the *connubio*. Emanuele was a rather excitable, but able, man, who moved happily in the circles of the Whig ruling class, and was a friend of Palmerston. Cavour's official representative in Paris was Salvatore Pes di Villamarina, who never had the full confidence either of Cavour or of Napoleon. In the years to come diplomatic business of only the routine kind passed through Villamarina. For more confidential and more important matters links between Napoleon and Cavour were through unofficial agents, but perhaps for that very reason stronger than they might have been. Napoleon's foreign minister in 1853 was Drouyn de Lhuys, who was more sympathetic to Austria than to Italy. He did not make things any easier for Cavour, but Napoleon was already conducting his own foreign policy, without much reference to his ministry of foreign affairs.

There had been no war between the great powers in Europe since Waterloo. Russia and the Ottoman Empire had fought a minor war in the 1820s, but the first half of the nineteenth century – at least since the fall of the empire of Napoleon I in 1815 – had been exceptionally peaceful in the whole context of European history. The saying that it was in the nineteenth century that men had stopped carrying swords, and had started carrying umbrellas, reflected one aspect of the truth, even if it related only to Western Europe. Even in Western Europe, though, only the rich had been able to afford swords; and the history of the umbrella remains to be written. Nevertheless, the peaceful nature of the period from 1815 to 1854 is undeniable. The 1815 settlement had contributed to a *Pax Europea*, that had been disturbed, but not ended, by the revolutions of 1848–49. Metternich had said that he 'had ruled Europe sometimes, Austria never', and his European regime from 1815 to 1848 had at least been one of peace. It had, however, been a regime of repression, both of individual liberties and of nationalist aspirations. In the twentieth century there has been a remarkable analogy with that phase of international politics in one respect. Historical comparisons are often misleading, but this one has a certain validity. From 1945 to the fall of the U.S.S.R. individual liberties and nationalist aspirations were also repressed in Eastern, and much of Central, Europe, and this enabled peoples to live at peace, free from the outbreaks of the grosser barbarisms of inter-ethnic warfare. The breakdown of Communism in the U.S.S.R., Eastern and Central Europe, and the Balkans has been accompanied by the disappearance of peace, and an undoubted increase in human suffering, but it is to be hoped, that, in the long run, the price paid for freedom will have been worth it. The breakdown of the Metternich system led to fighting between ethnic groups in the Habsburg Monarchy in 1848–49, fighting which was subsequently to include Cavour's war of 1859, and, before that war, to the Crimean War, with its heavy toll of human life.

Cavour's brief, but dramatic, intervention in international affairs can thus be seen as part of the borderline between nearly half a century of comparative peace and the half century which saw limited wars between the great powers – the wars of 1866 and 1870 – and the incessant possibility of wars, in the absence of the kind of respect for treaties which Metternich's period, with all its negative features, had displayed. However, the price paid for the peace of the Metternich period was political stagnation and oppression, with a mindless censorship not only of the press, but of works of literary expression. Once the European peoples – and among them, pre-eminently the Italians – felt a desire to rule themselves, and to express that desire, the 1815 order was doomed, and political change, even if accompanied by violent revolution and warfare, was almost certain to follow.

In March, 1854, however, the Western Powers – France and Britain – still hoped that Austria could maintain her role as a stabilizing force in Europe, and might, going beyond that role, force the czar, Nicholas, to come to terms with them, before heavy fighting became necessary. After making himself emperor, in 1852, Napoleon III had tried to establish close relations with the czar, but had been rebuffed as an illegitimate parvenu. The sense of personal insult had fuelled Napoleon's hostility towards Russia and had made him eager for friendship with Britain, and – at least for the moment – with Austria. His strong desire that his cousin, Prince Jérome Napoleon, should marry into the ancient House of Savoy must be seen in this context of his search for legitimacy and respectability.

British governments, Whig, Tory or Peelite, still paid lip service to the 1815 settlement, and hesitated to abandon it completely. Palmerston professed to be pro-Austrian north of the Alps, but anti-Austrian south of the Alps. To be more precise, he would regard the emancipation of Lombardy and Venice from the Austrians as an act of natural justice, but, while he had sympathized with the Hungarians in their struggle against the Habsburgs in 1848–49, he was not going to take positive steps to endanger the integrity of the Habsburg Monarchy in any absolute sense. The securing of independence for Lombardy and Venice could be seen as a modification of the 1815 settlement, not a complete abandonment of it. It was a modification that the Austrians should allow for their own good – and Palmerston was always ready to tell foreign governments what they should do for their own good. He believed firmly that he knew better than they did, and it must be said that he was sometimes justified in this vain conviction. However, the immediate issue in March, 1854, was the securing of Austria in an alignment against Russia, and the preoccupation of the French and British governments was that nothing should be done in Italy to alarm or antagonize Austria.

Britain and France went to war with Russia on 28 March. In London the prime minister was Lord Aberdeen, a dour Scotsman, who had little sympathy for Italy. He had been the recipient in April 1851 of the famous letter from Gladstone, subsequently published, denouncing the Neapolitan regime as 'the negation of God erected into a system of government'. The letter had made a greater impression on the British public than on Aberdeen. The foreign secretary in Aberdeen's government was Lord John Russell until February 1854, when he was replaced by Lord Clarendon at the Foreign Office, though Russell himself remained in the cabinet. Russell was to be a good friend of Italy, though perhaps more an admirer of Garibaldi than of Cavour. While still at the Foreign Office, on 26 January, Russell had told Emanuele d'Azeglio that he hoped Piedmont 'would not forget the rules of prudence and reserve, and would not thrust itself on to a dangerous slope'. Azeglio replied, quite truthfully, that Piedmont desired peace, and that developments in the East were 'far from being a direct interest of Piedmont'.[5]

In the winter of 1853–54 the press in Turin discussed the possibility of Piedmont playing an active role in the Eastern crisis. However, once the Austrian government had declared its neutrality – in other words, that it had no intention of supporting Russia – the general assumption was that there was no reason for Piedmont to get involved. This was also the attitude of Cavour's colleagues to the cabinet; he was probably more prepared for an active policy than any of them. The foreign minister, Giuseppe Dabormida, who had taken office after a career in the army, was determined on neutrality. Another member of the government, also a general, Alfonso Lamarmora (sometimes written as 'La Marmora'), was very close to Cavour. He was not eager to use the army in action yet: he had carried through important military reforms since the defeats of 1848 and 1849, but felt that it was too soon to put them to the test.

Writing from Turin to Azeglio in London, Dabormida was expressing the general attitude of the Piedmontese government when he said that they were still 'nursing the hope of seeing Europe escape from the crisis which threatened her, without an appeal to the calamities of war'. Certain foreign newspapers credited Piedmont with having 'belligerent dispositions', but he could make 'the most sincere vow' that these charges were false. Even if there were to be a war, Piedmont would trust the 'two great maritime powers' to limit hostilities to the East. He went on:

> In this state of things it seems to us that our natural role, in the midst of a debate opened by a question in which we have no direct interest, is to maintain a prudent reserve, so that events – stronger than men – in lighting a general conflagration, will not lead us to take part in the struggle. In the eventuality of such a conflagration, which we like to think is a remote one, we would be happy to know how the Cabinet of Her Majesty the Queen of England, from a friendly point of view, sees our situation . . .[6]

It seems unlikely that Dabormida would have written in these terms without having first consulted Cavour, who certainly always wanted to have the good will of the British government, and at this stage of the crisis had no plans for involving Piedmont in the Eastern Question. Azeglio's reply was not particularly comforting. He commented: 'I can scarcely conceal from Your Excellency that Lord Clarendon is not in general very favourably disposed to defend Italian interests warmly'.

Clarendon was one of the English political leaders with whom Cavour was going to have to work. Cavour assumed in 1856 that Clarendon was very sympathetic to Italy, and historians have tended to accept his assumption. The evidence, however, suggests that the Whig minister, Clarendon, felt rather less warmly towards Italy than did the Tory minister, Lord Malmesbury, with whom Cavour was also to have close dealings.[7] But if the former Peelite, Aberdeen, was distinctly unsympathetic towards Italy, another former Peelite, Gladstone, was passionately supportive. It is a mistake to generalize along party lines when assessing the attitude of the British to the Italian Question, and Cavour himself was sometimes too ready to do so.

In February 1854, however, Emanuele d'Azeglio reported that Clarendon might have more sympathy for Piedmont than for Italians in general, but that at that moment the British foreign secretary was wholly absorbed by the Eastern Question, and took only 'a few rare hours of sleep' a night. 'Austria', Azeglio continued, was 'the key to the position', 'her attitude' was 'the decisive weight in the balance'. He believed, though, that she would make up her mind within a month, and whichever decision she made, Piedmont could profit. If she came down on the side of the Western Powers, Piedmont could ask them to mediate (his logic here was not too clear, and not entirely shared by Cavour). If Austria refused to work with France and Britain, Piedmont would obviously have an opportunity to score against Austria.[8]

The Austrian government would have liked the British government to declare its acceptance of, and in effect to guarantee, the existing boundaries of the Italian states. Clarendon would not go that far, but he was eager to reassure Austria regarding Piedmontese policy. The ground was being prepared for an intervention by Sir James Hudson and Cavour, working in close co-operation, though Cavour was not yet aware of it, or ready for it.

Clarendon wrote to Hudson on 23 March, saying that it seemed that Austria was ready to act 'cordially with us, against the disturber of the peace of Europe', by whom he meant, of course, Czar Nicholas. But Clarendon was still troubled by the fact that Austria could 'not get over fears and suspicions of Piedmont'.

> Under the circumstances we should very much regret that any insurrectionary movement took place in Italy to disturb the attention and divide the forces of Austria. We could give no encouragement whatever to it, and if Austria is faithful to us we are bound to be so to her, although at the close of the war we shall anxiously endeavour to secure better government and a different order of things in Italy.

Clarendon was suffering from the misconception shared by all British governments that Cavour and Piedmont were waiting for an opportunity to stir up 'insurrectionary movements'. If Clarendon had reflected for a moment, he would have remembered that only the year before Cavour had arrested Piedmontese revolutionaries after the abortive rising in Milan. Cavour, no less than Clarendon, would have regretted an 'insurrectionary movement'. It was, however, the implication in the final sentence of the passage just quoted that made Hudson and Cavour optimistic with regard to Clarendon's future policy – an optimism that was to prove largely unjustified.[9] Clarendon continued his despatch of 23 March by saying that Piedmont should be discouraged from taking 'advantage of the war for selfish purposes'. He had heard rumours that Vittorio Emanuele had been making some 'not very prudent' remarks, and he hoped the rumours were unfounded.

Ambassadors and heads of legation are, of course, supposed to work through foreign ministers, which was why Hudson at this stage was working through Dabormida rather than Cavour. However, Cavour was never one to stand on ceremony and although he had appointed Dabormida, it was not likely that he would leave the foreign minister in control if important decisions had to be taken. It can be concluded, then, that until mid-April 1854 he did not regard the Eastern Question with any great urgency, and it was to Dabormida that Hudson went, on 13 or 14 April (the exact day is not known) with two important documents.

The first of the two documents had alarmed Clarendon. It had been sent to the Foreign Office by the British minister in Tuscany, Sir Peter Scarlett, and referred to a rumour current in Austrian Italy to the effect that the Piedmontese were encouraging revolution in Italy, and that such an influence would prevent Austria from lending her aid to France and Britain against Russia. The Austrians, it was being said in Florence, wanted to occupy the garrison town of Alessandria, as a guarantee of good behaviour by Piedmont. The second document was from Clarendon to his minister in Florence, and showed that whatever the British foreign secretary thought of the truth of the rumour, he was determined to deny it. Clarendon went so far as to say that Britain would not let the Austrians occupy Alessandria, nor, indeed, any Piedmontese territory. Nevertheless, since Clarendon secretly felt that there might be something in the rumour, he had passed the two documents to Hudson for comment. Hudson knew Cavour's aims far better than Clarendon did, and could honestly say to Dabormida that he knew the rumour to be an absurd one. Dabormida, who was more eager than Cavour to keep Piedmont out of the Eastern crisis, could deny the rumours with great warmth. He was a cautious, rather unimaginative man, and Hudson knew that Dabormida's personal opinions did not carry much weight in London. Hudson therefore took the matter to Cavour, and the Piedmontese prime minister was at last involved in the whole affair.

Hudson read Scarlett's despatch, with its reference to the rumours that had alarmed Clarendon, to Cavour, and suggested that the time had come for Cavour to make an 'explicit declaration' which would reassure Clarendon 'and set all these Austrian fancies at rest'. Such a declaration on Cavour's part 'would enable Austria to march against Russia if she was honest and would deprive her of the excuse for not marching if she were false'.

> I said, 'Your Army is 45,000 strong – too many for Peace and too few for War in Italy – Austria suspects you ungenerously and unjustly, if you were asked to diminish your Army by One Third at this moment you would decline, under existing circumstances, and I quite agree with you. But supposing as a guarantee for your conduct in Italy, Austria having declared war against Russia you were invited to send one third of

your army to the Danube to fight by the side the Allied
Army would you do so?

Cavour replied, simply, directly and briefly in the affirmative,
and suggested that they should put the question and answer
in writing. Hudson concluded: '. . . here then is the Duke of
Genoa and 15,000 good bayonets at Your Lordship's orders
if you think proper to demand them'. The conclusion was
a little over-enthusiastic. Apart from the fact that the Duke
of Genoa, the king's brother, knew nothing about these
plans to send him off to the East with an army, Hudson's
question and Cavour's answer related only to the eventuality
of Austria going to war.

Hudson enclosed with his letter the written version of the
conversation that Cavour and he had had, and which went:

> Mr Hudson – 'What would the Sardinian Government
> do, if Austria having declared war on Russia, it were to
> be invited by England and France to take part in the
> Eastern war?
>   The Count of Cavour – My personal opinion is that in
> that case the Government of the King would accept the
> invitation and send 12 to 15,000 men to the East.[10]

Cavour was not a reticent man, and it seems a little out
of character that he should simply have said 'Yes' to
Hudson's question, even if he added the reservation 'my
personal opinion'. He was probably restrained, however,
from elaborating on his answer by the knowledge that his
cabinet was even less ready for intervention in the war than
he was. It is perhaps inevitable that Hudson's account of
this exchange should suggest that he made all the running,
and Cavour merely responded. Cavour must clearly have
speculated along such lines already, but the account which
is preserved for us in the Clarendon Papers in the Bodleian
is the earliest reliable documentation of such speculation.

It was apparently only after the exchange with Hudson
that Cavour brought the matter to the Piedmontese cabinet.
They were not happy about contemplating war, even in
an eventuality that had not yet arisen – and might never
arise. Dabormida felt that even if an Austrian army had
been despatched to the East, it would be unwise for the
Piedmontese to break up their army and send one third of

it to the East also. There was also some unease at the thought
of fighting as an ally of Austria. Lamarmora, still concerned
about the army he had so recently reformed, argued that a
military expedition would be a costly affair, and to let the
British finance the expedition would be virtually to have the
Piedmontese troops treated as mercenaries. Cavour seems
to have played a more subdued role at the cabinet meeting
than he usually did. Without the ebullient Hudson beside
him, he was evidently less enthusiastic for a positive policy.
After all, he knew all the drawbacks, and he could see the
force of the arguments of his colleagues. He agreed with
them that the question of how such an expedition should be
financed should be clarified, and he visited Hudson at ten
that evening to discuss the question. Hudson was obviously
unable to give any promises regarding financial support
from Britain, and in view of the attitude of the Piedmontese
cabinet, the two men felt it necessary for Hudson to send
a more cautious despatch to the Foreign Office, pointing
out that the other ministers were less ready than Cavour
to commit Piedmont. There was a paradoxical element in
what had happened. Clarendon had originally intended to
caution Cavour, but Hudson had so contrived it that Cavour
had been partly persuaded to adopt a belligerent policy – but
only, of course, in the event that Austria moved first. In one
respect only did Hudson represent the policy of the British
government. He, like them, was concerned to secure the
attachment of Piedmont to Britain rather than to France. He
hoped, in particular, that a Piedmontese contingent would
eventually serve under a British officer.

For several centuries the House of Savoy that was now
ruling Piedmont-Sardinia had retained its independence,
and had expanded into a not inconsiderable kingdom by
its diplomatic efforts. It had followed Machiavelli's advice
by employing the cunning of the fox, since it did not
possess the strength of the lion. Its major achievement in
recent decades had been the acquisition of the great port of
Genoa in 1815. The independent Republic of Genoa, that
had survived for centuries, had not been restored, although
the British government had promised to respect Genoese
independence. Instead, the British government had agreed
with the other victorious powers that Piedmont should be
rewarded for its opposition to Napoleon I, with this valuable

prize, which had made Piedmont a maritime power, and a power more firmly oriented towards the rest of Italy. The British preoccupation had been to make Piedmont as strong a state as possible to provide an initial bulwark against any future French attack. Anglo-French rivalry was still, in the 1850s, to be a major concern of Cavour. Although Britain and France were allies in the Crimean War, it was to be an uneasy alliance, and Napoleon – still hoping that ultimately he could have an alignment with Russia – was to prove more eager than the British to end the war. When Nicholas I died in 1855, during the war, Napoleon rightly assumed that an understanding with the new czar, Alexander II, would be possible.

The diplomatic situation of which Cavour had to take account was thus a complex one. He had to keep on good terms with both Britain and France, and to the extent that he could play them off against each other, he had to do so with some subtlety. He had to remember that both of the Western Powers, at that moment, needed an alignment with Austria, though, in the long run, Napoleon knew that he must break with Austria, if he was to scrap the 1815 settlement. One aspect of the 1815 settlement – the Treaty of Paris, to be precise – had recognized the Bourbons as the legitimate rulers of France, and had laid down that all members of the Bonaparte family were to be permanently banished from France: not one of them must ever cross the frontiers into France again. Since one of the family had not only crossed back into France, but was now the emperor of the French, it was fairly clear that that feature of the 1815 settlement was being politely overlooked. The British, on the other hand, still spoke of the sanctity of the 1815 settlement, and the extent to which this was a genuine point of policy, or a paying of lip service which was convenient for the argument of the moment, had to be determined. The assessment of this, and all the other imponderables, was a task for which Cavour's agile mind was well suited.

Austria remained neutral throughout the summer of 1854. Finally, on 29 November, Clarendon wrote a private letter to Hudson, asking him to secure a body of Piedmontese troops for the war which was now being fought in the Crimea. The figure Clarendon now suggested was 10,000, and Hudson was to check with Cavour how such a request would be received, if made officially.

While Cavour had been at the centre of these negotiations, his role had been a somewhat negative one up to this point. Nevertheless, he obviously believed that Piedmont should get something tangible out of intervention in the war, if intervention there was to be. At least there should be a promise from the French and British that the Italian Question would be discussed at the end of the war. The French disliked the idea, since they felt that any such promise would antagonize Austria too much. The British cabinet met on 19 December. The majority of its members agreed with the French that Cavour could be given no promises, but Palmerston, Gladstone and Russell (who was now a member of the cabinet without portfolio) pressed Clarendon to give Cavour some more substantial support. Russell believed that Hudson, working with Cavour, had gone a long way towards securing Piedmontese intervention. Russell wrote to Clarendon: We must at all events admire Hudson's despatch. Had he been at Vienna last summer Austria would have joined us in August with 300,000 men.[11] The figure which Hudson and Cavour had concocted in so casual a manner – 15,000 men – was the one which the treaty joining Piedmont with France and Britain in the war against Russia in December 1854 eventually cited, and it was in the event 15,000 men who were sent to the Crimea in the spring of 1855.

In the course of 1854 Cavour had come to the conclusion that Piedmont must satisfy the requests of Britain and France – but more particularly of Britain – to enter the war, even if he could obtain no promises from the Western Powers of any future advantages. The conclusion followed his whole line of thought. His commercial treaty with France had been economically unfavourable to Piedmont, but had seemed to him justifiable as providing a political link between the two countries. If it had been possible to obtain guarantees from France and Britain for future help in Italy, he would have obtained them, but when this proved impossible, he was prepared to trust in an uncertain future – to cast bread upon the waters.

When Cavour finally decided on intervention he knew that there was a strong likelihood that two of his colleagues –

Dabormida and Lamarmora – would not go along with the decision. Partly to appease them, he tried to get better terms from France and Britain, in discussions with De Guiche and Hudson, but, having failed in the attempt, he accepted the resignation of Dabormida, and took the foreign ministry himself, while, of course, remaining prime minister. In the end Lamarmora, with the rest of the cabinet, remained in office.

Piedmont's act of accession to the Anglo-French Treaty of 10 April 1854 was signed at 8 p.m. on 10 January 1855, with a military convention attached to it. It was Cavour's major act of foreign policy since coming to power. It was signed in Turin, so that Cavour's first despatch as foreign minister was to his legation in London, announcing that the treaty had been signed 'on the friendly invitation' of the ministers of England and France.[12] This was nearer the truth than the subsequent interpretation put across by some historians, according to whom the initiative had been entirely Cavour's, and had been a stroke of spontaneous genius on his part. It was rather that Cavour's policy had been a prudent and careful one, and would reap benefits eventually, though not for three or four years.

The details of the military convention were settled on 26 January 1855. Piedmont was to provide 15,000 men 'under the command of a Sardinian general', and the Western Powers were to 'guarantee the integrity' of Piedmont during the war. A supplementary convention, also signed on 26 January, arranged for a loan from Britain to Piedmont of one million pounds, half of it to be paid at once, and the other half six months later. Gladstone, as Chancellor of the Exchequer, had recommended that the interest to be paid on the loan should be 4 per cent, and this figure was included in the convention. By the standards of the time these were not excessively generous terms from Britain, but Cavour, who always had a realistic notion of Piedmont's financial needs, never haggled over such details. Britain was to pay for Piedmont's costs in transporting the army to the East.[13]

Lord Aberdeen's government fell from office in February 1855, after *The Times* had exposed the incompetence with which the war was being waged. Palmerston became prime minister, but Clarendon remained as foreign secretary. Cavour was evidently happy at the arrival of Palmerston, as well he might be, since Palmerston, although reluctant to take positive action on the Italian Question, was appreciably more sympathetic to Cavour than Aberdeen had been. Cavour wrote to Azeglio, saying that the new prime minister has 'too often given unmistakable proofs of the interest which he takes in our country, and in everything which could be advantageous to it, for us not to applaud' his appointment. Of Clarendon's remaining at the Foreign Office, Cavour wrote:

> The benevolence illustrated by the relations we have had with this Minister, the delicate sentiments which he has frequently expressed . . . make us attach a quite particular value in seeing him continue in high office.[14]

Cavour's praise of Clarendon was sincere, but undeserved. After the Congress of Paris he was understandably to develop doubts about the Englishman's good faith.

Only on 4 March 1855 did Cavour finally declare war on Russia, after the ratification of the Treaty of 10 January with the Western Powers. He sent a circular to all the Powers announcing the event. The Russian government was understandably outraged. They had taken no step of a hostile nature towards Piedmont, nor had the declaration of war even been preceded by an ultimatum. The Russian foreign minister, Count Nesselrode, had already written, in the name of the czar, to Turin on 17 February (5 February by the Russian calendar) a note, which Cavour said was 'in a language full of bitterness'. This was before Cavour had declared war, but after he had signed the treaty with Britain and France. Vittorio Emanuele, Cavour said, had read the Russian note 'with painful surprise', since he had not yet declared war. The surprise was somewhat hypocritical. Scratching around for some reason for feeling hostility towards Russia, Cavour hit on the fact that the Czar's government had broken off diplomatic relations with Piedmont at the time of the Piedmontese war against Austria 'without any motive', and that Nicholas I had further, in 1849, refused to receive a letter informing him of Vittorio Emanuele's accession to the throne.[15]

The Crimean War was unlike other wars in that negotiations continued while hostilities were taking place, because, since Austria remained neutral, it was possible for the belligerent powers to keep in touch with their enemy as well as their allies, through Vienna. Thus in the spring of 1855 a conference was in session in Vienna, with the Western Powers trying to use the good services of Austria to force Russia to come to terms, or, alternatively, to get Austria to enter the war. In the Vienna Conference Cavour deliberately played a small role, being represented only by a *chargé d'affaires*. Again he was throwing bread upon the waters, in the sense that he was trying to please the French and British by abstaining from embarrassing the Austrians, though he was getting no immediate returns for his restraint.[16]

Azeglio, in London, was always more impetuous than Cavour, and more inclined to speak his mind to the British ministers, with whom he was, after all, on very close terms. In a sense he did not represent Cavour's cautious policy too well, and on one occasion Cavour told him 'not to be a goose'. It was difficult to restrain Azeglio, and perhaps not altogether necessary. After the Vienna Conference he wrote to Lord Lansdowne, a cabinet minister without office, and to Lord John Russell, telling them that Vittorio Emanuele had been 'justly hurt at the less than secondary role' which Piedmont had been allowed at the conference.[17] Although Cavour kept a low profile during the conference, he had reminded the British government before the conference started that Piedmont had commercial interests in the Black Sea, and he had even gone so far as to say that the czar had always given 'encouragement and protection' to Piedmontese commerce.[18]

Piedmont's military contribution to the Crimean War has often been treated somewhat contemptuously by British historians. It has been pointed out that Piedmontese loss of life was only one twentieth that of Britain's.[19] The British losses were mostly due to the cholera, however, and when the Piedmontese contingent arrived. British troops in the field numbered less than 20,000. The war had thus become, in military terms, a Franco-Russian one, though every British schoolboy and schoolgirl ever since has thought of it as an Anglo-Russian one. The Piedmontese contingent alone was three-quarters the size of the British, while the French army numbered 90,000.[20]

Cavour was not too happy with the fulfilment by the British of their promise to provide transport for the Piedmontese expedition. He had been promised twenty-one British ships in the Gulf of La Spezia, but complained that these would be insufficient, as the expedition would consist not only of infantry, but of six squadrons of cavalry, six batteries of artillery, and, of course, the relevant number of horses and equipment.[21] Eventually, however, the fleet with the contingent started to leave La Spezia on 25 April 1855. The commander-in-chief was Alfonso Lamarmora, who resigned from the cabinet to take up this honourable task, and embarked on 28 April, reaching Constantinople on 5 May. His force fought effectively in one engagement against the Russians – the Chornaya Rechka. Their number was increased to 18,000 before the end of the war.[22]

In addition to the contingent from the regular Piedmontese army, the idea was floated that there might also be a volunteer force assembled in Piedmont from all over Italy. Cavour wrote to Azeglio on 3 June 1855 to say that the British (or more specifically Hudson) 'will insist on the formation of an Italian legion. Without giving the impression that we attach too much importance to this, you will also press this argument . . . The formation of an Italian legion on our territory cannot make our relations with Austria worse than they are already'.[23] The proposal came too late for anything to be made of it. Had such a force fought in the war, it would clearly have had a greater significance in the history of Italian nationalism than the presence of the Piedmontese regular force had, and would to some extent have anticipated the formation of Garibaldi's volunteer forces of 1859 and 1860. That Cavour was not opposed to the creation of such a force suggests that there was already an element of the Italian nationalist in his complex personality.

Cavour's immediate preoccupation was with the fortunes of the Piedmontese regular force. Even before they sailed he was complaining that the British command had changed its plan, and was not sending the Piedmontese to the front line, and that Napoleon had not been told of the decision. Cavour wrote to Azeglio:

> The proceedings of the English government in this instance cannot seem less than strange to us. We have no objection to our troops placing themselves

immediately in the war theatre. We are sending them to the East, not to indulge in a vain parade, but so that they should fight as well, and as soon, as possible.[24]

The victory of the Chornaya reassured Cavour that the prestige of Piedmont was growing with the war, but, like the British, and unlike Napoleon, he would have preferred the war to have lasted a little longer and provided Italian troops with a few more laurels.

. . .

THE CONGRESS OF PARIS

Cavour was in Paris in December 1855, and when he met the emperor on the 7th, Napoleon asked him what he could do for Italy. Cavour's reply took the form of a letter to Count Walewski, the French foreign minister. Walewski was an illegitimate son of Napoleon I and the Polish Countess Marie Walewska. Cavour was to have many dealings with Walewski, who was considerably less sympathetic towards Piedmont and Italy than was Napoleon III. The original of Cavour's letter was drafted by Costantino Nigra, then a young attaché in the Paris embassy, but signed by Cavour and was probably largely Cavour's work. It was written on 21 January 1856 and is in the foreign ministry archives in Paris. It is worth quoting from at length, since it shows precisely the aims that Cavour had at that moment – and the limitations of those aims:

Austria, having had so great a part in the recent events, must be considered by a diplomatic fiction, to have rendered a conspicuous service to Europe, we must start by assuming that we will not ask of her, for the moment at least, any territorial sacrifice in Italy . . .

In the first place, while renouncing any claims on Austria for a modification of the treaty of Vienna, claims which would be in keeping with the true interests of Europe, the strong influence which the Emperor has acquired over Austria suggests to us that he could ensure that she renders justice to Piedmont, and that she adopts a less oppressive and more tolerable régime over her Italian subjects.

After the pledges which Sardinia has given to the cause of order by sending her soldiers to fight in the Crimea, Austria has not even the shadow of a pretext for violating, on her part, the principles of equity and the formal engagements which received a new sanction in the treaty concluded between these two powers in 1851 (here Cavour is referring to the commercial treaty between Austria and Piedmont); or in maintaining the sequestrations of the property of those who had become Sardinian citizens after breaking the links which attached them to their old country.

Cavour, then, was not aiming high. He was still concerned with the old question of the sequestrations, and he added to it points which seemed even more marginal: Austrian refusal to co-ordinate railway building with Piedmont, and to improve police regulations regarding commercial and personal relations between Sardinians and Lombards.

The ending of the military régime, which has for eight years oppressed the populations of the Lombardo-Venetian kingdom, would be a real benefit for them, and would not for the moment at least, expose Austria to any true danger. Concessions made at the moment when this Power (Austria) signs a favourable peace, would not be interpreted as an act of weakness . . .

What the Emperor can obtain from Austria by friendly advice, he can impose on the King of Naples. He can, now that the preoccupations of the war no longer make vigorous diplomatic action dangerous, insist that this prince should cease from making odious the monarchical principle by a conduct which is as absurd as it is violent. In forcing him to open the prisons where for so long so many illustrious and innocent victims have suffered . . . France will render a true service, of which Austria herself would not complain . . .

The state of things in the provinces which Austria possesses in Italy, like that of the Kingdom of Naples, is conditioned by the stipulations of the treaty of Vienna which for the moment the Western Powers – England at least – do not want to touch. One is therefore forced to agree that the action of France in their regard is restrained within narrow and unbreakable limits.

This was not the case, Cavour continued,

> for an important portion of Italy . . . the States of the Pope, and especially of those provinces between the Apennines, the Adriatic and the Po.

While these provinces were 'in name' under papal sovereignty, they 'in fact' belonged to Austria, which was an infringement of the Treaty of Vienna.

> I therefore consider that it would be of supreme interest for France and for England, as a glorious task worthy of the sovereign to whom Europe owes the humiliation [*abaissement*] of Russia, to bring to an end Austria's occupation of the most beautiful provinces of central Italy.

However, he continued, he recognized that Austria could not withdraw her troops from the Papal States unless the government of those States were reformed. Modern peoples hated rule by priests even more than military oppression – a truth proved by the fate of Charles X's clerical regime in France. Even the Austrians must realize this. 'The only effective, durable remedy' for the state of affairs in the Legations would be 'to place them under the regime of a temporal prince'.

> And since one would not want to increase the fragmentation of Italy, it would be necessary to give them either to the Duke of Modena or to the Grand Duke of Tuscany. This combination, which is not in any sense anti-Austrian, would involve a territorial rearrangement, in which Piedmont could find a just compensation for the sacrifices she has made.

Although he felt little enthusiasm for the governments of Tuscany or Modena they were at least preferable to that of the Papal States.[25]

Cavour's letter was frank, but cautious. He knew that Austria could not be forced out of Lombardy and Venice at that moment. The 1815 settlement must be respected, but Cavour allowed himself the parenthetical comment that a modification of it 'would be in keeping with the true interests of Europe'. He wanted a tough line to secure reforms in Naples, but above all he wanted a withdrawal of Austrian troops from the Papal Legations. There was a strong military consideration in this latter aim. He was even prepared to see Bologna and Ravenna placed under the Duke of Modena, provided that the Austrian troops then withdrew.

In January 1856 the new czar, Alexander II accepted defeat, and agreed to send plenipotentiaries to a peace congress in Paris. That Paris was to be the venue of the congress indicated to the world that the France of Napoleon was restored to her old position of prestige. The Congress of Paris lasted from 25 February to 16 April. That the war was over owed much to Austria, and this fact ensured that no great ideological challenge was to be made on behalf of the nationalist movements – Polish, Rumanian, Hungarian – or Italian. Cavour was therefore not hopeful of making any substantial gains for Piedmont or for Italy. The French and British governments had promised him nothing, and he was at first inclined not to attend himself. He knew that Massimo d'Azeglio was immensely respected in London and Paris – perhaps more than he deserved – and Cavour was initially disposed to send Azeglio as chief plenipotentiary at the Congress. However, he probably decided that Azeglio's indolence was less likely than his own energy to extract whatever could be extracted from the peace, and somewhat reluctantly decided to go himself. His chief contact among the major plenipotentiaries in Paris was with Clarendon, who was, of course, the first British plenipotentiary, rather than with the first French plenipotentiary, Walewski, who was also president of the congress.

Inevitably the main purpose of the Congress was to draw up a peace settlement in the East. Piedmont was not uninterested in such a settlement, but it was obviously not Cavour's major concern. In the weeks before the Congress Cavour and Clarendon appeared to enjoy cordial relations. Count Buol, the first Austrian plenipotentiary, had put the whole weight of Austria against Cavour's attendance at the Congress, but he had been overruled. Walewski was not much more helpful, and did his best to insist that Cavour's role was a subordinate one. It was therefore understandable that Cavour should feel grateful for the apparent cordiality of Clarendon. On 27 March Cavour wrote to Clarendon, going over some of the points he had already made to Napoleon, via his note to Walewski of 21 January. He pointed out the illegality of the Austrian occupation of the Papal Legations, an occupation which meant that the pope was no longer sovereign in those lands. Cavour did not discuss the question as to whether the pope wanted the Austrian army there or not. He simply pointed out that the European Powers had not been consulted on this effective diminution of the pope's sovereignty. No international agreement had given permission for a large Austrian army to occupy the territory of a neighbouring sovereign state. In other words Cavour's argument was not based on the claims of Italian nationalism, but on the rights of the Concert of Europe. The Austrians still felt that the implicit – though never overt – recognition by the Congress of Vienna in 1815 that Italy was a legitimate sphere of Austrian influence was valid. Castlereagh, long ago, had agreed with Metternich on this point. But Cavour knew that the time had long passed when Austria could make such a claim, while Clarendon and a Whig government were not likely to accept it.

On the same day, 27 March 1856, Cavour sent another long note to Walewski, recording that he had proposed to the emperor an ending of the occupation of the Papal States by foreign troops. He argued that since Britain and France had shown such a lively interest in the fate of the Greek and Slav Christians in the Orient, they could hardly fail to show the same concern for peoples of the Latin race who were 'even more unfortunate because of the degree of civilization they had reached, which makes them feel more sharply the consequences of a bad government'. 'The system of repression and violent reaction' introduced after the revolutions of 1848 had become even more rigorous. 'Never have the prisons . . . been more full of people condemned for political reasons'.[26]

The Treaty of Paris, signed on 30 March, settled the Eastern Question in its main lines for some twenty years, and only after the treaty had been signed were other issues – including Italy – discussed. Buol tried to resist the discussion of Italy, arguing that 'the Italian Question' did not exist beyond the disturbed minds of revolutionaries, but again he was overruled.

On 8 April Clarendon addressed the Congress on the Italian Question in a speech which was to become famous in the mythology of the *risorgimento*. It was to be regarded by Cavour and many subsequent historians as a milestone on the path leading to the independence of Italy. In fact Clarendon dealt with only two specific points. They were, however, largely inspired by the letters Cavour had been writing to him. Clarendon repeated Cavour's argument that the Austrian occupation of the Papal Legations had not been approved by the other great powers, but he used the argument mainly to attack the papal administration. He also attacked the King of Naples, and demanded that Ferdinando should reform his absolutist and repressive regime. It was perhaps the tone and vigour of Clarendon's speech, rather than its content, that pleased Cavour, and impressed European diplomacy generally.

So far as the Italian Question was concerned, all the French and British governments did in practice immediately after the Congress of Paris was to break off diplomatic relations with the King of Naples, when it became apparent that he had no intention of reforming his government. It is possible that Ferdinando was relieved, rather than otherwise, to see French and British diplomats depart from Naples: all they had ever done was to give him unwelcome advice, advice which he considered impertinent. The British government had not had formal relations with the papacy since the Reformation, so there was no question of breaking them off now. Napoleon had made no demands on the papacy, and certainly had no intention of breaking diplomatic relations with the pope.

Far from receiving immediate help of any kind from the French or British governments, Cavour was disappointed a month after the Congress to learn of a secret treaty, signed by Britain, France and Austria, guaranteeing the independence of the Ottoman Empire. Cavour heard of the treaty only by reading the French newspapers on 8 May. He had good reasons for feeling offended. Piedmontese troops had fought and died in the Crimea to defend the Ottoman Empire, while Austria had remained neutral. Surely the

Piedmontese government had had the right at least to be informed that the treaty was being signed. On 9 May Cavour wrote to Emanuele d'Azeglio in London to complain of this shabby treatment from the Western Powers:

> while in the course of negotiations in Paris the most friendly understanding reigned – as was right – between us, while both sides were happy with the reciprocal confidence which was not lacking, even after the signature of the Treaty of 15 April, we might have received at least confidential information of this new treaty from Lord Clarendon who has honoured me with so many signs of friendship and confidence which I dare to believe I have deserved.

Cavour was beginning to realize just how hypocritical the British government could be. Azeglio was told to ask Clarendon for an explanation of Piedmont's exclusion from any knowledge of the treaty, but no explanation was forthcoming.

Cavour feared another slight three weeks later. The Treaty of Vienna in 1815 had declared that rivers which flowed through more than one country could, by agreement between the Powers, be declared 'international rivers', on which trade would be free and international control enforced. In 1815 only the Rhine was designated an 'international river'. In 1856 the Treaty of Paris declared the Danube to be also an 'international river', and two commissions were to be set up to control navigation on the Danube. One, a 'riverain commission' was to be formed from representatives of the countries through which the Danube flowed – in effect, Austria and the Ottoman Empire or an independent Rumania, if and when such a state should come into existence. The second commission was to be an 'international' one, representing the Powers. Cavour was concerned that Piedmont should be represented on the international commission, both out of respect for her part in the war, and, more relevantly perhaps, because she depended on much trade on the Danube and the Black Sea. When rumours reached Cavour that Piedmont was again to be excluded, he informed Azeglio that if even Prussia, but not Piedmont, were to have a seat on the international commission, he would have to make a formal protest, because our exclusion would be interpreted as a consequence of the treaty of 15 April and as a proof that this treaty had modified, to the advantage of Austria, the friendly relations which existed during the war between England and Sardinia.[27]

This time Clarendon listened to Cavour's request – or insistence – and supported Piedmont's claim, which led to acceptance by the other Powers, Austria included. At least Cavour's diplomacy could be said to have had a positive achievement. For once Piedmont was being treated as a major power – even before she had expanded to become the Kingdom of Italy.

A more important issue regarding the Danube, however, was the so-called 'Principalities Question'. The principalities of Moldavia and Wallachia were still under nominal Turkish sovereignty, but a strong Rumanian nationalist movement demanded that the two principalities should be united under a single prince, as a first step towards the autonomy – and then, independence – of a Rumanian state. The Austrians were bitterly opposed to such a progression. The impoverished province of Transylvania was a Rumanian-speaking area within the Habsburg Monarchy, and if a Rumanian state were to exist the people of Transylvania would probably become rebellious against the Habsburgs. Napoleon III, with his professed belief in 'the principle of nationality' sympathized with Rumanian nationalism, and the new czar, Alexander II, shared his sympathies, if only because he hoped that an independent Rumania could become a satellite of Russia: Russian troops had occupied the principalities, posing as liberators, on more than one occasion in the past. The British attitude towards the Principalities Question had not been consistent. While in Paris at the Congress Clarendon had given the impression that he agreed with Napoleon, and sympathized with the Rumanians, but on his return to London he came under the influence, more directly, of Palmerston, and the traditional pro-Turkish policy of the British reasserted itself. While the Congress lasted, then, Cavour had little difficulty in supporting the case for the unification of the principalities, since it was apparently supported by France and Britain. When the British stance changed, it was impossible for

Cavour to change course without offending Napoleon. Cavour had no particular sympathy for Rumanian nationalism, but Piedmontese interests seemed to dictate an alignment with France and Russia, rather than with Britain, Austria and Turkey.

This chapter has been concerned to a great extent with Cavour's relations with Britain. In the next two chapters his relationship with France becomes very much more important. His patient policy from 1852 to 1856 was to bear fruit in the increasing drama of the years 1858 to 1861.

. . .

NOTES AND REFERENCES

1. *Epistolario*, VI, p. 33.
2. Chiala, I, p. 521.
3. *ibid*, p. 259.
4. F. Valsecchi, *Il Risorgimento e l'Europa. L'Alleanza di Crimea* (Mondadori, Milan and Verona, 1948; new edition, 1968).
5. Turin, 124 (1854 and 1855), *Confidentielle*, XXVIII, Azeglio to Dabormida.
6. Rome 285/21, No. 620, 3 February 1854.
7. On Clarendon, see Harry Hearder, 'Clarendon e l'Italia', in *Il Risorgimento e l'Europa. Studi in onore di Alberto M. Ghisalberti*, edited by Vittorio Frosini, (Bonanno, Catania, 1969).
8. Turin, No. XXX, *Confidentielle réservée*, Azeglio to Dabormida, 14 February 1854.
9. Clarendon, (1854), deposit C 128, Clarendon to Hudson, 23 March.
10. *ibid*, (1854), deposit C 21. Hudson's casual grammar and punctuation have been preserved. He usually wrote to Clarendon, of course, in English, but this brief record between the two men is in French. The translation is mine.
11. Clarendon (1854), deposit C 15.
12. Rome, vol. 21, No. 707.
13. Valsecchi, *op. cit.*, pp. 418–81; Di Nolfo, pp. 10–13.
14. Rome, vol. 21, No. 725, 21 February 1854.
15. *ibid*, vol. 21, No. 730.
16. Di Nolfo, p. 43.

17. Turin, 124 (1855), No. 62, *Confidentielle*, Azeglio to Cibrario, 13 June 1855.
18. Rome, vol. 21, *Confidentielle*, Cavour to Azeglio, 22 March 1855.
19. Denis Mack Smith, 'Cavour and Clarendon', *Atti del XXXV congresso di storia del risorgimento italiano* (Instituto per la storia del risorgimento italiano, Rome, 1959), p. 238.
20. Cristoforo Manfredi, *La spedizione sarda in Crimea nel 1855–56* (Stato Maggiore Esercito – Ufficio Storico, Rome, 1956).
21. Rome, vol. 21, No. 734, Cavour to Azeglio, 14 March 1855.
22. Di Nolfo, p. 47.
23. *Epistolario*, vol. XII, p. 339.
24. *ibid*, p. 201.
25. Carlo Pischedda and Giuseppe Talamo, editors, *Tutti gli scritti di Cavour*, 4 vols., (Centro Studi Piemontesi, Turin, 4 vols., 1976–78), vol. IV, pp. 1876–1878. This document has been printed in several publications, but this is the only accurate version.
26. *Archives du Ministère des Affaires Etrangères*, Paris: Italie, 1856, vol. 36, 'Note sur l'état des Legations'.
27. Frosini, editor, *Il Risorgimento e l'Europa, op. cit.*, p. 184.

Chapter 5

THE ALLIANCE WITH FRANCE, 1856–59

. . .

RELATIONS WITH NAPOLEON III IN 1856 AND 1857

In forging the alliance with France in 1858 Cavour's starting point was far stronger than it would have been before the Crimean War. Napoleon had written to Vittorio Emanuele on 5 February 1856, saying:

> I will do everything I can to ensure that in the peace negotiations Italian interests are not forgotten: but I cannot hide from myself all the difficulties which I shall have to surmount.

As we have seen, the difficulties indeed prevented Napoleon from doing anything positive for Italy at that stage, but his sincerity was genuine enough. After the Congress, on 12 April 1856, he again wrote, in an apologetic tone to the Piedmontese king, saying., however:

> I must say that Count Buol promised me that he would do whatever was humanly possible for Italy, since I did not hide from him that there [in Italy] alone was there delicate ground between us.[1]

A point that has escaped historians up to now is that Napoleon was already speculating on the formation of an Italian confederation of states as early as March of 1856. The fact is apparent from a document in the French foreign ministry archives, a note sent by the emperor to Walewski. After commenting on the dangerous state of Italian affairs, Napoleon wrote:

> I believe that today there is something which would satisfy almost everyone. It would be the creation of an

Italian confederation under the nominal domination of the Pope, after the pattern of the German Confederation, that is to say, that without changing the borders of countries nor the rights of sovereigns, we could create in Rome a diet nominated by the different states, and which would concern itself with the general interests of the country.

Thus Austria, through its possession of its Lombard states, would find itself vis-à-vis the Italian confederation as Holland finds itself vis-à-vis the German Confederation. This diet would not only concern itself with the great general interests of Italy, such as customs, the army, the navy, finance, etc., but to a degree it would administer, and its decisions would be sovereign on everything relating to the general interests. Each state would have one representative for every million inhabitants. Thus Piedmont would have 9 voices, of which one would be Sardinia [evidently the Island]; Lombardy 4 voices; Tuscany 1 voice; Parma and Modena 1 voice; the Pope 3 voices; Naples 4 voices, of which one would be for Sicily = Total 18 voices.[2]

Napoleon's addition was faulty and he overlooked Venetia in the blueprint for an Italian confederation, but what was more important was the radical nature of the proposal in some respects. Indeed, the wide-ranging concerns of the central diet suggest that the term 'federation', rather than 'confederation' would have been more accurate. On the other hand the participation of Austria, and the suggestion of an analogy with the German Confederation, give the proposal a conservative character. Certainly in 1856 Cavour was unaware that any such proposal was being considered in Paris.

In another conversation with Count Buol, on about 16 April, Napoleon evidently took a stronger line. He told Cavour that he had said to Buol that he 'was sorry to find himself in direct contradiction with the Emperor of Austria on the Italian Question'. If Napoleon had really spoken like this to the Austrian foreign minister he was clearly anticipating what he was to say to the Austrian ambassador in January 1859. On the later occasion, when the remark was to be made more publicly, it was to cause a storm in European diplomatic circles. In 1856 Buol had, according to Napoleon, gone to Walewski and spoken very humbly, saying that Austria was eager to please Napoleon 'in everything', since France was Austria's only ally and it was therefore 'necessary to conform to her policy and her desires'.[3]

Cavour was understandably incredulous at this piece of information, and seized the opportunity to say that he had prepared a protest against Austria, which he would submit to Walewski the following day. The emperor hesitated at that point, and suggested that the next stage would be to reach agreement with Palmerston. He knew, of course, that Palmerston was not likely to embark on an active policy, and that discussion with the British would be merely a delaying tactic. That Napoleon had really spoken to Buol along the lines he claimed seemed confirmed to Cavour, when Buol made a point of going to Cavour to assure him of Austria's good intentions towards Piedmont, of her desire to live in peace, and not to interfere with Piedmont's institutions. Cavour refused to accept Buol's attempt to be friendly, and replied that Buol had given no proofs of such a desire while he was in Paris. The exchange between Cavour and Buol became animated, and several home-truths were exchanged, if in a polite manner. Cavour avoided any reconciliation with the Austrians of a kind that could be misinterpreted either by European diplomacy or by public opinion in Italy.

On returning to Piedmont after the Congress of Paris Cavour received praise from most quarters. On 29 April the king awarded him the 'Annunziata', a high honour, still valued in the last years of the Fascist era – perhaps the equivalent of the Garter in Britain.

Already in the summer of 1856 Cavour was speculating on encouraging a revolution in Central Italy. Such a revolution could give him an excuse, perhaps not for war immediately – since he did not yet have an alliance with France – but for increasing the tension against Austria. The marble mountains of Massa and Carrara, which seem geographically to belong to the Tuscan coastal region, were incongruously under the rule of the Duke of Modena. In July 1856 the Piedmontese authorities in Liguria allowed revolutionaries to cross the border into Massa. Whether Cavour really imagined that anything would come of an attempted rising in Massa-Carrara at that time is not clear, but when no rising developed he quickly washed his hands of the affair, and even had ten ringleaders arrested on their return to Piedmont. If a revolutionary movement had developed he might well have utilized it in some way. As it was, he appeared a friend of the reactionary and Austrophile Duke of Modena.

For a year Franco-Piedmontese relations did not appreciably improve. In the summer of 1857, Cavour's friend, Count Roger de Salmour, wrote from Paris to say that Napoleon's popularity was fading, but that this might not be a bad thing for Italy, since it might encourage the emperor to wage a popular war on Italy's behalf: 'certainly he will profit from the means which we offer him to strengthen his throne by chasing out the Austrians'.[4] However, Napoleon would not fight a war for Italy, Salmour assured Cavour, unless he were certain that it would not unleash revolutionary passions. He therefore wanted to be reassured that Piedmont was strong and reliable, and Cavour was the man who could give this reassurance. After dinner Salmour heard the emperor say to one of his guests that he would be happy to have two ministers like Cavour.

In subsequent exchanges with Napoleon, Salmour was captivated by him, and deeply flattered by the attention which the emperor was giving him. Salmour assured Cavour, modestly if not ingratiatingly, that these attentions were, of course, aimed at Cavour, Salmour being only the intermediary. In July Salmour was at Plombières, and again had polite exchanges with Napoleon, and an invitation to return to Plombières the following year. In the event a rather more important meeting was to take place at Plombières in July of 1858. A few days after Salmour wrote to Cavour from Plombières in 1857, the official Piedmontese minister in Paris, Villamarina, was writing to tell Cavour how friendly Walewski was to Piedmont. Cavour replied, in his droll manner, that he was glad to know that Walewski was, 'basically, our friend, more than appearances would suggest'.

.   .   .

THE LAST MAZZINIAN ATTEMPT AND THE *CAGLIARI* CRISIS

The year 1857 was a comparatively dormant one in the history of the Italian Question so far as Cavour was concerned. It was more important for the Mazzinians, who made a desperate attempt to regain the initiative. A Neapolitan socialist, Carlo Pisacane, believing that the Italian peasants should play a central role in the Italian movement, and that it might be possible to start a spontaneous rising in the impoverished region of Calabria, organized an expedition from Genoa to Sapri, a point well to the south of Naples. He was in touch with Mazzini, who returned to Genoa on 11 May 1857 to organize a rising in Piedmont to coincide with the one in the South.

Cavour knew, better than Mazzini, that a republican revolution in Piedmont was unlikely to succeed, but Pisacane's action involved the Piedmontese government in another sense. Pisacane's movement began with the hijacking of a small Piedmontese civilian ship, the *Cagliari*, owned by the Genoese firm of Rubattino and Company. With some thirty followers, Pisacane took possession of the ship, and forced its captain to sail first to the Neapolitan island of Ponza, where over three hundred prisoners were released to join the revolutionary force. The greatly enlarged, but still hopelessly inadequate, revolutionary band then landed at Sapri, where they were defeated by the royal Neapolitan army. Rather than face capture and imprisonment by the Neapolitan regime, Pisacane killed himself. Hearing of the disaster of Pisacane's expedition in June, Mazzini tried to call off the revolution in Genoa. Some of his followers were arrested by the Genoese authorities, and Mazzini himself was obliged to return once more as an exile to Britain.

Pisacane's tragic venture need not have involved Cavour directly had it not been for the role played in the outcome by the Piedmontese ship, the *Cagliari*. The captain of the ship was, of course, a Piedmontese civilian: the *Cagliari*'s normal function was to take mail to and from Genoa, Cagliari in the island of Sardinia, and Tunis, where there was a considerable Italian colony. When Pisacane landed at Sapri, the Piedmontese captain, Stizia, was allowed to regain control of his ship. According to his account, he then sailed northwards towards Naples to report the revolutionary attempt, but on the way was intercepted by Neapolitan warships, and, with his crew, put into custody in Naples. Cavour was to be involved because the Neapolitan government had, according to his account, not only illegally taken possession of a Piedmontese ship, but had thrown a wholly innocent Piedmontese merchant and his crew into one of those Neapolitan prisons about which Gladstone had written so eloquently.

The role of the Rubattino company in the history of the Risorgimento could bear further enquiry. It seems something of a coincidence that two ships belonging to the same company were seized by Garibaldi's expedition in 1860. However, Cavour, who had corresponded with Rubattino on non-political matters, could certainly claim that there was no evidence whatsoever that Captain Stizia of the *Cagliari* had collaborated with the revolutionaries, or that Rubattino was anything but an innocent commercial firm, normally performing a civilized and important task.

Cavour probably felt that one favourable aspect of the case was that the British government – much against its will – was involved by the fact that the engineers of the *Cagliari*, Henry Watt and Charles Park, were British subjects – Scotsmen to be precise – and that they, like Stizia and the rest of his crew, were incarcerated by the Neapolitans. The trial of these unfortunate sailors did not start until February 1858, by which time a more important episode in the history of Italy had intervened – Orsini's attempt on the life of Napoleon III. The Orsini Attempt will be considered in a moment, but the story of Cavour's role in the *Cagliari* affair must first be concluded.

The Piedmontese and British sailors, and the Piedmontese ship, had thus been in Neapolitan hands for some seven months before the trial had even started. The Neapolitan government seemed genuinely to hold the absurd belief that the Pisacane expedition had been planned by Cavour, in spite of the fact that Mazzini had tried to start a rising in Genoa to coincide with the one in the Kingdom of Naples. Since Ferdinando's government was acting in such an impossible manner against subjects of both Piedmont and Britain, Cavour assumed that the two governments could make common cause against Naples. He claimed that the capture of the *Cagliari* on the high seas by Neapolitan frigates was an infrigement of international law, and as such must surely be of concern to a mercantile nation like Britain, quite apart from Britain's own case against Naples. The Neapolitan government declared that the *Cagliari* was 'war booty', and had no intention of returning it to Genoa.

The British, however, made no attempt to help Cavour. A legal dispute developed in Britain, with Emanuele d'Azeglio securing a verdict from Dr Phillimore, a famous liberal lawyer, against the legality of the Neapolitan capture of the *Cagliari*, while the British Law Lords argued that the Neapolitans had been justified in capturing the ship, but not in keeping it as 'war booty'. The last point might have seemed obvious to anyone, since Piedmont was not at war with Naples. However, given the ruling of the British Law Lords, the Palmerston/Clarendon government refused to link their demands with those of Cavour. When the Tory government came into office they were no more obliging than the Whigs. Lord Malmesbury, the Tory foreign secretary, concentrated exclusively on the British case, following legal advice on the lines that the argument should not be blurred by mixing it up with the quite separate Piedmontese case.

Walewski had also disagreed with Cavour over the question of the *Cagliari*, since the French government was always appreciably more lenient towards Naples than the British government was. Malmesbury actually seems to have believed that Cavour was contemplating war with Naples, a war in which Britain clearly did not want to be involved. In the event, Cavour never allowed things to run to extremes. Eventually he expressed the fear that discussions with Britain on the *Cagliari* might be getting tedious, and, in Hudson's words, Cavour 'would rather be considered anything save a Bore'.

The crisis was ended suddenly by a capitulation on the part of the Neapolitan government, who agreed to release Watt and Park, the Scottish engineers, and to pay them an indemnity for wrongful imprisonment, and the handing over of the *Cagliari* and the rest of her crew, not to Piedmont, but to the British government. It was a considerable slight to Cavour. The Neapolitan government still claimed that its legal arguments were valid, and that it was surrendering only to the superior might of Britain. The British government, of course, handed the *Cagliari* back to Rubattino and Company in Genoa. The whole episode suggested that Cavour had secured the moral support of neither Whig nor Tory governments in London. Consequently he needed all the more urgently to gain the support of the French, and perhaps of allies elsewhere in Italy.[5]

In November 1857 there were general elections in Piedmont, and the results were surprising. They showed a sharp turn to the right. Cavour was re-elected, but he was alone among ministers in having an overall majority. The right-wing leader, Solaro della Margarita, on the other hand, was returned by a large majority. There seems little doubt that devout Catholics, in what was after all traditionally a devout country, disapproved of the government's anticlerical policy. A number of priests were elected, but their elections were found to be invalid on slightly dubious grounds. Cavour went to some lengths to exclude other elected members on grounds of irregularity in the elections. There is little doubt that his approach to this election result was a very partisan one, and is an example of the ruthlessness of the man. Opposing Cavour was not an agreeable or easy task.

Don Margotti, the editor of a Catholic newspaper, organized a Catholic boycott of future parliamentary elections and in so doing anticipated the action of Pius IX, who, by the *Non expedit*, was to forbid Catholics to take part in the parliamentary life of the united Italy after 1870. Cavour was probably relieved at the consequences of Don Margotti's boycott. But the results of the 1857 elections necessitated a change of domestic policy for Cavour. He had to recognize that, in a sense, the *connubio* – the move to the left - had not been a success. He dropped Rattazzi from the government, which, apart from anything else, pleased Napoleon, who believed that Rattazzi was too close to revolutionary politics in Piedmont.

Napoleon was seeking action against the Piedmontese Left on another issue. Mazzini's Genoese newspaper, *Italia e Popolo*, and *La Ragione*, which was even further to the left, were tried for publishing articles attacking the French emperor. The juries found the editors not guilty, and in so doing enraged Napoleon, who asked that the Piedmontese press laws should be modified to prevent such verdicts in the future. A further article in the *Italia e Popolo* that Napoleon found particularly offensive appeared in December 1857. When the French minister in Turin protested at the article, Cavour said that it would be difficult to take legal action, and tried to laugh the matter off, in a characteristic fashion, by saying that 'he hoped people had now realized that newspapers in Piedmont had no influence at all and were not worth all this trouble', but he then said firmly that 'present political circumstances made any new press law impossible'. Simply to warn the newspapers or to impose a stamp tax would be counterproductive. A tax would simply diminish the number of papers, and those that remained would gain in importance. It was the true liberal speaking: if newspapers annoy you, you do not ban them or censor them or tax them; you simply encourage more to appear, in the knowledge that if there are enough of them, their diatribes will cancel each other out. Cavour, however, was careful not to be drawn into an argument with the French, while at the same time making no promises about policy with regard to the press.

. . .

CAVOUR AND THE NATIONAL SOCIETY

In August of 1857 a group of Italian nationalists assumed the name 'the National Society'. They were never to have more than 4,000 followers, and thus in numerical terms never compared with Mazzini's republican movement, but long before they assumed the title of 'National Society' they had been influential in Piedmont, not least on Cavour. It was the tragic failure of Pisacane's expedition – yet another Mazzinian attempt – that convinced these men that they had to work with the Piedmontese monarchy for the liberation of Italy.

The origins of the National Society can be traced back to 1855, and to the ideas of the Marchese Giorgio Pallavicino and Daniele Manin. Pallavicino was a Lombard republican revolutionary, who had been arrested and imprisoned by the Austrians in the notorious Spielberg prison. Manin was a Venetian lawyer of Jewish extraction, who had led the revolution of 1848 in Venice, and had for a while been the president of the revolutionary Republic of St Mark. Before the end of 1855, with a Piedmontese army fighting in the Crimea, both men had decided, a little reluctantly, that the difficulties in founding a united Italian republic were too great, and that unity under the Savoy monarchy was a more feasible proposition. Manin had letters published in

The Times and the *Siècle*, letters of which the key statement read:

> Convinced that above all Italy must be made, that this is the first and most important question, we say to the Monarchy of Savoy: 'Make Italy and we are with you. – If not, not'.
>
> And to the constitutionalists we say: 'Think about making Italy and not of enlarging Piedmont; be Italians and not municipalists, and we are with you. – If not, not'.[6]

In 1856 Pallavicino and Manin are joined by Giuseppe La Farina, who was to become an active agent of Cavour two or three years later. At that time La Farina, a Sicilian, was preoccupied with the possibility that Cavour might support the claims of Napoleon Murat to the throne of Naples. Napoleon III often toyed with the idea of re-establishing the Murats in Naples. Joachim Murat, the son of an innkeeper, had been a brilliant cavalry general under Napoleon I, whose sister he had married, and who was briefly King of Naples in the Napoleonic period. His surviving son, christened 'Napoleon Lucien Charles', was thus a relative of Napoleon III. He had always retained a party of supporters in Naples.

La Farina explained to Cavour that, while he could understand the attitude to Murat taken up by the Piedmontese government, he could not possibly support Murat himself. To re-establish the Murat family on the throne of Naples would imply an abandonment of Italian unity. La Farina asked whether Cavour could assure him privately, without necessarily making a public statement, that his government would not support Murat for the throne of Naples. If he could not get this assurance, La Farina would ask for his passports, and settle in Paris. Cavour, in a personal meeting with La Farina, evidently reassured him, since La Farina remained in Turin. Cavour's attitude to Murat was to be important in his future dealings with Napoleon III.

Manin, who was living in Paris, met Cavour there in February 1856, and again in April. Although Manin was still a republican at heart, he was convinced that Cavour genuinely wanted to unite Italy, should such an aim prove feasible. Cavour was probably careful not to let Manin realize the gulf which lay between their ideas as to what was practically possible. At that moment Cavour regarded the unification of Italy as a dream rather than a political aim, but he believed that the idealists of the National Society could be useful for him.

Someone of far greater importance than the Pallavicinos and the La Farinas was put in touch with Cavour through the National Society: Giuseppe Garibaldi. A myth of considerable potency had already grown up around the name of Garibaldi. Even before 1848 he was well known as a hero in the fight for freedom of the peoples of South America, and more specifically of Uruguay. His brilliant campaign against the Austrians in 1848 had allowed Italians to believe that they could fight successfully against the powerful army of a great power – a belief that was confirmed by Garibaldi's yet more brilliant defence of the Roman Republic in 1849. If the pope had been restored in Rome after 1849, and if little remained of the achievements of the revolutionary years, it was certainly not due to any failing on Garibaldi's part.

Garibaldi joined forces in July 1856 with the men who were to form the National Society, and they were henceforth to become an important, if intermittent, link between Garibaldi and Cavour. Garibaldi met Pallavicino in Genoa on 6 August, and complained to him that the Piedmontese government was doing nothing to further the Italian cause. On 13 August Garibaldi was in Turin, and met Cavour. Pallavicino was also present, and recorded the meeting:

> Cavour welcomed him with courtesy and friendliness and hinted that he could rely on considerable official help. Cavour even authorized Garibaldi to pass on these hints to others. It seemed that he was seriously thinking about the great political redemption of our peninsula ... It was all an act! What Cavour wants, and *I am sure of it*, is just for Piedmont to be enlarged by a few square miles of Italian soil ...

La Farina saw Cavour in September, and of that meeting he recorded, several years later, that Cavour was hoping for the unification of Italy some day, though clearly did not then regard it as part of a working programme. Still, Cavour hoped that he could use La Farina and his friends to agitate at the right moments, but could not offer them any open support from the Piedmontese government. Manin's assessment of Cavour's position with regard to the unification of Italy was more perceptive than either Pallavicino's or La Farina's, which is not surprising, since Manin was the most intelligent of the three men. He wrote, on 27 September:

Cavour is extremely able and is well known abroad. It would be a grave loss not to have him our ally, as it would be a grave danger to have him our enemy. I think we must not overturn him but urge him on. We must work incessantly to form public opinion, because as soon as opinion is clear and forceful, Cavour I am sure will follow it . . . Only if public opinion is strong for Italy and if Cavour refuses, then we can think again. But I think Cavour to be too intelligent and too ambitious to refuse the Italian enterprise if public opinion demands it strongly enough.

'Too intelligent and too ambitious' – Manin understood the basic characteristics of Cavour. Here was a man not content to be prime minister of the Piedmont of 1856. An enlarged Piedmont, dominating the peninsula as Austria had dominated it, would have been an improvement, and perhaps the Cavour of 1856 would have been well content with that result to his life's work. However, as Manin realized, if Cavour were offered grander vistas by events, he would not close his eyes to them.

Pallavicino had a different impression. He believed that all Piedmontese politicians limited their hopes to the creation of a North Italian kingdom with the two centres of Turin and Milan. 'Cavour', he wrote, on 1 October, 'is one of the most *Piedmontese* of them all; we shall harness him to our chariot only when we have a knife at his throat'.[7]

In 1857 one difficulty for Cavour came from an unexpected source – the decision of the Austrian government to relax its rule in Lombardy. Since 1849 the administration of Lombardy had been essentially a military one, under the ancient Marshal Radetzky, who was popular with his troops, but hated by the Italian civilian population. The government in Vienna, in replacing Radetzky on his retirement, sent to

110

Milan the Archduke Maximilian, a liberal and intelligent man who, a few years later, was to be made emperor of Mexico by a French army, and whose execution by a Mexican republican firing squad was to inspire one of the earliest Impressionist paintings – the large masterpiece by Edouard Manet. Maximilian's arrival in Milan was greeted with relief by many Italians, and some of the exiles from 1853 returned from Piedmont. Cavour was not happy with the thaw in Austrian rule in Lombardy, and it was probably a factor in his decision to prepare a policy of war against the Habsburgs, before the Lombards could show any gratitude to the Austrian authorities. Austrian policy was never consistently generous to Italy, however. Having partly appeased the people of Milan, by removing the military nature of their occupation, the Austrian government now broke off diplomatic relations with Turin for no obvious reason.

If Maximilian's policy in Lombardy was a source of concern to Cavour, its influence was far outweighed by that of his own economic policy, which had made Piedmont economically the most successful part of Italy. For some reason British historians have sometimes suggested that Austrian Italy was more advanced economically than Piedmont, and while this may have been true of 1850, it was certainly not true of 1856. Cavour's decade was one of dynamic development. In particular the growth of the railways shows the striking achievement of those years. In 1848 Piedmont had only eight kilometres of railway line, while the other Italian states already had 357 kilometres. At the beginning of 1859 Piedmont had 850 kilometres, and the other Italian states 986; Austrian Italy – Lombardy and the Veneto – had only 524 kilometres. The Piedmontese network comprised 47 per cent of the lines in the entire peninsula, and more than 40 per cent of those in process of construction.

Cavour's commercial policy had also contributed to a striking development. From 1850 to 1858 Piedmontese imports grew by about 130,000,000 lire to 321,000,000 lire, and exports from 73,000,000 to 236,000,000. Figures for the commerce of the other Italian states did not compare with these. Piedmont had only 20 per cent of the population of Italy, but in these years was responsible for 39 per cent of the imports, and 27 per cent of the exports. In 1858 Piedmontese commerce was worth 114 lire per head of population. Austrian Lombardo-Venetia was worth only 72 lire per head of population. Modena and Tuscany were about the same as Lombardo-Venetia, while the Papal States and Naples had, of course, very much less commerce. Piedmont, in fact, was enjoying a more dynamic life than the majority of West European countries. The picture, however, must be modified in some respects. The comparatively low figure for the commercial life of Austrian Italy was mainly due to the more sluggish economy of the Veneto. If Lombardy is considered alone, the figure is very comparable to that of Piedmont. Nor, of course, can Cavour take all the credit for the striking economic growth of Piedmont in the 1850s. The acquisition of the important port of Genoa by Piedmont in 1815, and the position of Piedmont on the routes from the Mediterranean to France would eventually have borne fruit in the railway age. The fact remains that Cavour's policy of comparatively free trade, and his conviction of the significance of the railways, at that precise moment, were immensely important.

It should also be added that the improvement of the Piedmontese economy, while bringing substantial benefits to the middle class – illustrated by a considerable increase in the consumption of food, clothes, and luxury articles – did little to help the poor. It is a sad but basic fact of social and economic history that the expected trickling down of wealth rarely, if ever, occurs. A working day of eleven to thirteen hours remained the norm for the wage earners; working conditions were as unhealthy as ever and 65 per cent of the population remained illiterate in 1858, though this figure was to fall appreciably soon afterwards.[8]

. . .

THE ORSINI ATTEMPT AND ITS AFTERMATH

Cavour kept several links with Napoleon III from 1856 to 1858. One was Napoleon's doctor, Conneau, who had also been the doctor of Napoleon's mother, Hortense de Beauharnais, the daughter of the Empress Josephine by her first husband. Conneau had promised Hortense when she was dying that he would always be at hand if Louis-Napoleon needed medical attention. He had kept his word; he was with Louis-Napoleon at the time of the attempted coup against Louis-Philippe in 1840, as the result of which Conneau had shared imprisonment with Louis-Napoleon in the fortress of Ham. Even when Conneau had served his term of imprisonment in 1846, he preferred to remain voluntarily in prison rather than to leave Napoleon. When the two men were back in England, Napoleon bought a medical practice for Conneau in London.

Another link was Napoleon's cousin, Prince Jérome Napoleon (nicknamed 'Plon-plon' because of his speaking manner) an ardent friend of Italy, and a not unimportant influence on Napoleon. Before the birth of Napoleon III's son in March 1856 Plon-plon was the heir to the imperial title. Both Conneau and Prince Napoleon became close friends of Cavour. A more consistent link with Napoleon was supplied by Cavour himself in the shape of his private secretary, Costantino Nigra, who was in Paris at significant moments. Nigra was to have a distinguished career in the diplomatic service, but in Cavour's time was a wholly unofficial contact, to a degree supplanting the formal diplomatic links through Villamarina and Walewski. An even less official contact had been the Countess Virginia Castiglione, a Tuscan cousin of Cavour. In 1856 Cavour had suggested to this very beautiful girl of nineteen that she should go to Paris with the express purpose of sleeping with the emperor. Lady Holland, the great Whig hostess, remembered the young Countess 'as being absolutely faultless, alike in figure and feature, from the crown of her head to the sole of her foot'. Of no other woman that she had ever met, Lady Holland commented, could this be said.[9] Countess Castiglione evidently regarded the assignment Cavour had given her as an interesting one. She carried it out without difficulty. Whether her nights with the emperor had any influence on his policy is one of those imponderable questions which are not decided by historical documentation.

In January 1858 a former follower of Mazzini, Felice Orsini, organized an attempt on the life of Napoleon III. Orsini was living in England, where he had three large bombs (known at the time as 'infernal machines') made, and with three fellow-conspirators – one of them a hired assassin, but the other two ardent Mazzinians – he transported the bombs to Paris, via Brussels. On 14 January the bombs were thrown at Napoleon and the Empress Eugénie as their coach arrived at the Opera. Seven people were killed outright; one died later; about 150 were hurt. Napoleon escaped unharmed, and Eugénie had only a glass splinter in the corner of her eye, which was easily removed. Orsini had hoped that by killing the emperor he could stimulate revolution in France, and that a French republican government would go to the help of Italy. Since the Second Republic of 1848 had been singularly unwilling to help Italy, Orsini's proposed scenario had been absurdly optimistic.

Orsini's extraordinary *volte face* at the trial opened possibilities for Italy which were more significant than any which might have resulted from Napoleon's death. Saying, in a letter read to the court, that he knew that he was about to die, he declared that he had been mistaken in trying to kill Napoleon, and that on the contrary Italy's salvation could come from a living emperor. A patriot on the steps of the scaffold, Orsini appealed to Napoleon to help Italy secure her independence, and 'the blessings of 25 million citizens would follow him to posterity'.

Orsini was guillotined, but Napoleon was to react as though he had been persuaded by his would-be assassin. The whole extraordinary episode of the trial may have been engineered by Napoleon, whose police chief had visited Orsini in prison. It surprised Cavour as much as it surprised most people. Cavour had naturally been appalled at learning that an Italian had tried to assassinate the emperor, and was relieved, if mystified, at the path taken by the trial.

Immediately after the attempt, and before the trial, Napoleon understandably experienced a sense of outrage, which extended to those countries which he felt to have been in some way involved in Orsini's plans. He made sweeping accusations against the press of four friendly countries: Belgium, Britain, Switzerland, and, of course, Piedmont. The license the press in these countries was permitted, according to the French government, was a danger to the life of the emperor, and a tighter control should be imposed.

The Orsini attempt made it much more difficult for Cavour to resist Napoleon's demands that something should be done to increase censorship and control of the Piedmontese press. He decided to move against the *Italia e Popolo*, instructing his Intendant at Genoa to take action, saying that he was 'ready to use all available means'. One means which he favoured was to impose 'frequent, even daily, confiscations', even though he recognized that such a policy might not be 'altogether legal'.

> Should there be refugees from other Italian states among its [the *Italia e Popolo*'s] contributors, they must be expelled from the country forthwith, whatever the articles they write. Even the theatre critic should be driven out. The mere fact of contributing to such a criminal paper makes any *émigré* unworthy of our hospitality. We must wage war to the death against that assassin's gazette. It is a disgrace and a danger to society, and its destruction would be an eminently patriotic act.[10]

The episode is one of the less attractive ones in the life of Cavour. A passage in one of his letters to another agent, Angelo Conte, was suppressed by Luigi Chiala in the standard edition of Cavour's letters, but published by Alessandro Luzio in the *Rivista Storica Italiana* in 1930. The following is Denis Mack Smith's translation:

> It is impossible to achieve our purpose by legal means, because of the pretence of moderation which Mazzini's paper puts up. So other means must be found. The first and most obvious would be the refusal of the printer to go on printing, perhaps in return for a suitable bribe. Or we could terrify him into giving up his help for such a wicked and hostile journal. Love of lucre and fear are potent motives in many minds. See to it that you set one or other or both of them in motion so as to achieve the aim I have indicated; and you will have done the country an inestimable service.[11]

Fifty issues of the *Italia e Poppolo* were confiscated over a period of a few months, and it inevitably went bankrupt.

Immediately after the Orsini Attempt a sharp Anglo-French crisis developed. In Napoleon's eyes the British were more responsible than any other nation for the atrocity. Orsini had been living in England for some years, and had been giving revolutionary addresses to large, admiring audiences. He was a dramatic figure, with his black beard and his account of his escape from a papal prison, and, unlike Mazzini, he was a fine orator. The three bombs that had been thrown at Napoleon (as it happened, none of them by Orsini personally, but by his three accomplices) had been made in Birmingham. Soon after the attempt, Walewski protested to Clarendon, and asked that something should be done to curb the excesses of the revolutionary exiles in England. Palmerston's government, uncharacteristically, bowed to French pressure, and introduced a bill to parliament making 'conspiracy to murder' a 'felony', instead of merely a 'misdemeanour'. The bill passed its first reading, but was then defeated by a combination of Tory and Radical votes. It was because of this defeat that the Palmerston/Clarendon government resigned, and was replaced by Lord Derby with Lord Malmesbury at the Foreign Office. The bill was quietly dropped and Walewski and Malmesbury patched up the affair, in spite of the fact that at the height of his rage Napoleon had threatened to break off diplomatic relations with Britain if the bill were not passed.[12]

If Napoleon could be so tough with Britain – even if only momentarily – it was not surprising that he was equally tough with Piedmont, and that Cavour found it necessary to destroy the *Italia e Popolo*. Napoleon continued to express his displeasure with Cavour's government in a meeting with a Piedmontese general, Enrico della Rocca. On 5 February 1858 Della Rocca wrote to Vittorio Emanuele to report on the meeting with the emperor. It was after an official dinner which had been postponed because the news of the acquittal of the Piedmontese journal, *La Ragione*, had had 'a very bad effect here' – and the postponement of the dinner dated from even before the Orsini Attempt. Della Rocca reproduced Napoleon's words as well as he could:

> . . . your Press is much too free. There is no respect for morality, religion, order, persons. You do not have sufficient laws to repress it. You must have the force and energy necessary to propose and make the laws which are lacking, and to modify the existing ones. I am not saying that you must send away all the emigrants,

but it is absolutely necessary to send away the bad ones, and to keep the rest under observation. What I say to Piedmont, I say to Belgium, to Switzerland, to England which is a great Nation. I would have to have no blood running in my veins to tolerate murderers on my frontier. . . . I say then to Piedmont, I love your country, I love your King, I have a great sympathy for your flag, for the cause that it represents in Italy, but if you do nothing, if you do not find a way of repressing the press . . . my friendship will fade and I shall be forced to form a closer link with Austria . . .[13]

What would Piedmont then do?, Napoleon asked. She would be mistaken to depend on England, who would give her money perhaps, but not a single man.

Villamarina also had an interview with Napoleon, and wrote to Cavour on 6 February. To Villamarina, Napoleon repeated the same theme: 'I can assure you, my dear Marquis, that I speak to Piedmont just as I speak to any other Power, England included'. And he added: 'I can tell you frankly that, if England should refuse to accept my rightful demands, our relations with her will gradually weaken until we are on the brink of hostilities'.

What, Napoleon then asked, would Piedmont do in the event of a serious break between Britain and France? Speaking bluntly, he said: 'There are two possibilities: to be with me or against me'. He pointed out, with some justification, that 'England has no army, and furthermore for a long time to come she is going to be embroiled in India and China'.[14] It was true that the Indian Mutiny had been quelled only the year before, but in China France was an ally – and a belligerent ally – of Britain against the Chinese Empire, so that it was a little dishonest of Napoleon to pretend that Britain alone was 'embroiled in China'. It would have been more exact to admit that he was himself 'embroiled in Indo-China'. In the event, French policy in Indo-China was laying the foundations for generations of suffering for the unfortunate people of Vietnam: though that, of course, Napoleon could not know.

Concluding his tough interview with Villamarina, Napoleon added that if Piedmont sided with Britain against him, he would be obliged to 'seek Austria's support', even though the

Austrian 'government has always aroused and still arouses my deepest disgust'. Villamarina's account of the interview could have left Cavour in little doubt of the emperor's feelings. Cavour was facing one of the gravest crises in his stormy career.

On 9 February, when Della Rocca's letter of 5 February had been received in Turin, Cavour drafted a letter for Vittorio Emanuel to send to Della Rocca, and for Della Rocca to read to Napoleon. It strongly refuted the emperor's arguments, and was a masterpiece of calculated daring. It constituted a brilliantly successful gamble on Cavour's part.

The emperor's words, Vittorio Emanuele's ghost writer said, included

> reproaches or threats (things to which I am very little accustomed) especially when the Emperor speaks of uniting with Austria against us if we *do not act immediately to obey his wishes*. This seems a little violent, since neither I nor my country deserve anything of this kind. The Emperor says that he speaks to us in the same sense as he speaks to England, Belgium and Switzerland; I hope that he does not intend to compare us in every respect with these Gentlemen when he enjoys the loyal and frank affection and sympathy which I and my country have always shown him on every occasion.

Cavour's draft then passed to details, listed as 'press, Police, Emigrés, England'. So far as the press went, 'the Emperor knows that our press is free, but there is a repressive law . . . which has always served us well in the past, when newspapers offended religion or foreign sovereigns. It was unfortunate that the jury had absolved *La Ragione*, but a law was being planned to prevent a repetition of that unfortunate event.'

With regard to the police, the letter argued that Mazzini had eluded the police far longer in Paris than in Piedmont, and Orsini had been in Paris for several days before 'the frightful event'.

On the subject of the émigrés: 'we constantly expel a great quantity of émigrés; when we know that they are dangerous we turn them into cargo for America', but, adding a sarcastic twist, 'the greatest portion of them, at least a great number, come from Marseilles'.

Where England was concerned: there was no Piedmontese alliance with England. 'The Emperor must know how little I love England, her policy and her Lord Palmerston'.

The letter ended with a dramatic peroration, which may have been composed by the king himself, since, while the rest of the manuscript is in Cavour's hand, the last passage is in Nigra's hand. Della Rocca was to tell the emperor.

that he was dealing with a faithful ally; that I have never accepted violence; that I follow the path of honour – always spotless honour, and for this honour I answer only to God and my people; that for 850 years we have held our head high, and no one will make us bow it; and that, with all this, I desire only to be his friend.[15]

Cavour instructed Della Rocca to read the letter to Napoleon, but not to leave him a copy because of the passage about 'England and her Lord Palmerston', which would cause embarrassment if it were quoted. Della Rocca read the famous despatch to Napoleon at 1.30 p.m. on 13 February, and wrote to the king at 4 p.m. He could report that the emperor had assured him that he did not want the Piedmontese government to do anything which could lead to a change of ministers, and that Napoleon was in an altogether happier and more conciliatory mood than he had been at the previous interview. Cavour's tough line had paid off.

In defending his action Cavour made one of his more brilliant parliamentary speeches on 16 April 1858. After the defeat of Novara, he argued, Piedmont had to choose between two paths. She could close in on herself, ignoring everything that was happening beyond her borders and thinking only of domestic matters. Or she could adjust to the hard facts of the situation, but at the same time remember the courageous policy of Carlo Alberto, and continue that policy – but in the field of diplomacy rather than warfare. The first path would have had certain advantages: the Piedmontese government would simply have concentrated on retrenchment, and economic revival; but it would have involved a renunciation of any hopes for the future, and an abandonment of the glorious traditions of the House of Savoy. It would mean a renunciation of the sad but splendid inheritance from Carlo Alberto. The references to

Carlo Alberto, not wholly deserved by that monarch, were nevertheless greeted with cheers in the chamber. Vittorio Emanuele, Cavour continued, therefore could not fail to choose the second of the two paths, and to make clear his choice he had appointed Massimo d'Azeglio prime minister, which implied a liberal and 'Italian' programme. Azeglio followed the second path, which meant demonstrating to Europe that the Italian people [and Cavour said 'Italian', not 'Piedmontese'] were capable of governing themselves in a spirit of freedom, and of reconciling a system of freedom with civil order, in contrast with the social disturbances threatened in other parts of Europe. To reconcile freedom and order involved an active diplomacy in the interest of the other parts of Italy.

Azeglio's successors – by which Cavour meant himself – retained the aim of reconciling freedom and order, and so of keeping the respect of European governments. By their intervention in the Crimean War they made it clear that they were on the side of justice and civilization. Cavour did not, of course, weigh up the relative claims to justice and civilization of the Russian and Turkish Empires, though he would probably have argued – with some reason – that Russia was strong and aggressive, while Turkey was weak and crumbling, and that therefore the danger to justice and civilization in 1854 had come from St Petersburg.

In the Congress of Paris, Cavour claimed, for the first time an Italian power had been able to defend the Italian cause before the chief powers of Europe. He would perhaps have preferred to make a bigger claim than this, but so far as it went, it was a valid one. Solaro della Margarita had argued that it had been a mistake to ask the great powers of Western Europe to interest themselves in Italy. The mistaken policy was now rewarded by an attempt by the French emperor to interfere in Piedmontese affairs. Cavour replied that, far from asking for foreign intervention in Italy, he had protested against the Austrian presence in Italy. His reply, of course, was a half-truth: he was already counting on French intervention to remove the Austrian presence.

Solaro della Margarita had also complained that Britain and France were intervening in Italian affairs by their verbal attacks on the Kingdom of Naples, verbal attacks which were followed by the breaking of diplomatic relations. To this complaint Cavour protested his innocence: if the two great Western powers felt that the conditions of the Kingdom of the Two Sicilies were such that they could no longer maintain diplomatic relations with that kingdom, that was entirely their affair. And, in any case, the removal of diplomatic relations from Naples could hardly be considered intervention. Cavour was exercising considerable polemical skill, tempered with a judicious economy of the truth. He then answered the charge made by both della Margarita and Revel that Piedmont's involvement in the Crimea had been a waste of men and money since not a single province, not a single commune, had been gained. Though territorial gains had not been made, Cavour insisted that there had been moral gains. Europe had been warned that she would not enjoy real peace until the Italian Question had been settled, and the warning had not been contradicted. The European press, apart from the ultra-reactionary and Austrian papers, had become not only far more interested in Piedmont, but far more sympathetic towards her. There was sympathy too from America: the people of Boston, 'the Athens of the North', had presented Piedmont with 'a magnificent cannon'.

It was essential for Piedmont to have alliances with the great powers. Angelo Brofferio was still pursuing the argument that Carlo Alberto had expressed with the words 'Italia farà da se' ('Italy will go it alone'). It was a mistake. If international questions were decided like questions of civil law, argument and eloquence would be enough. Unfortunately, international questions were not settled in this way. When diplomatic notes, protocols, memoranda, legal arguments failed, the nations took to arms, and then, as in the days of Frederick the Great, 'fortune was the friend of the big battalions'. Cavour preferred to quote Frederick the Great, rather than Napoleon, who had put it more graphically by saying 'God is on the side of the big battalions'. Cavour left God out of it.

Brofferio, Cavour generously believed, would modify this argument by saying that if there must be alliances, they should be with peoples who had the same institutions as Piedmont – in other words, with liberal nations. But in history free peoples had often found it necessary to ally themselves with 'governments founded on quite different principles', and Cavour had many examples to give of such paradoxes, examples which displayed quite an impressive and accurate knowledge of modern history. Some of his critics, however, Cavour said – critics not in parliament, but in the press – made Brofferio sound like a moderate. The remark was greeted with hilarity, but Cavour went on to explain that he referred to writers who believed that Piedmont should be allied neither to autocracies, constitutional monarchies, nor republics, but to the revolution. Such writers, Cavour said, loved 'the revolution more than Italy'. His government, on the other hand, sought friendship with all governments except the Austrian. With Russia they had better relations than they had ever had, and good relations with Prussia had been established after the Congress of Paris.

Cavour then turned to a consideration of Mazzini and the republican movement, which he depicted as having been a generous one before 1848, but having been turned into a bitter and murderous one by the failures of 1848 and 1849, and by the sad experiences of exile. Far from home and loved ones, the radical exiles had taken to the planning of assassinations and evil acts. It was partly their fault, but it was also partly the fault of the corrupt and despotic states from which they came – and he was thinking particularly of the Papal States. It was important, however, that the one free state in Italy – Piedmont – should make it clear to Europe that she was opposed to assassinations, especially as there were now reliable reports that attempts on the life of Vittorio Emanuele were planned.[16]

The purpose of the speech, then, was simply to justify the government in tightening the censorship of the press, and the rules for trial by jury, but Cavour made it a vote of confidence in his government, and in effect a verdict on his whole policy to date. The speech was immediately printed, and thousands of copies were circulated, not only in Piedmont, but throughout Italy, and it made quite an impact abroad.

. . .

PLOMBIÈRES

In April 1858 Cavour seemed to be trying again to stir up a crisis over the affairs of Massa and Carrara. In the foreign ministry archives in Rome there is a strange document which seems to have been overlooked by historians. It is a despatch from Cavour to Emanuele d'Azeglio, in which he says that a grave state of affairs existed in Massa and Carrara, where there was risk of a revolution. The facts which he had to relate, Cavour wrote, seemed scarcely credible, but were asserted by completely reliable informers. Massa and Carrara had been in a state of siege for six months. An Austrian captain had been placed in command of the troops there, and another Austrian officer had been named '*auditeur de Guerre*'. All laws and justice had been replaced by the arbitrary rule of these two men. No one was allowed to leave their home after nightfall. All trials were secret. Refugees crossed the border into Piedmont every day. Cavour was seeking advice from London and Paris.[17] If he hoped to stir up a crisis with this report, he failed to do so. Neither London nor Paris reacted. The accounts he was reporting were almost certainly exaggerated, and he himself was not likely to have understated them. Nevertheless, the idea of Piedmontese intervention in the event of revolution in Massa and Carrara was to be revived at Plombières in July.

In May there were indications from Paris that Napoleon was thinking seriously of a war with Austria, and was preparing to discuss an alliance with Cavour. The first hints were conveyed by Prince Jérome Napoleon, the emperor's cousin, and already included Napoleon's wish that the Princess Clotilde, daughter of Vittorio Emanuele and a girl of fifteen, should be married to the Prince. Beyond this they included Napoleon's intention to make war on Austria, and subsequently to create a Kingdom of Upper Italy. To visit Paris himself seemed to Cavour likely to 'make everyone suspicious', so he suggested, on 6 May, that Dr Conneau should bring more specific proposals from Napoleon to Turin. The suggestion was delivered to Conneau by Costantino Nigra in Paris. Conneau, perhaps timid of accepting so heavy a responsibility, declared ignorance of the proposal Prince Napoleon had made, but consulted the emperor himself. Nigra telegraphed the result of the meeting to Cavour, in cypher, on 9 May. It confirmed the three sensational points. Napoleon, however, was already expressing concern that a plausible motive for the war should be found.

Cavour was eventually summoned by Napoleon to visit him in Plombières in July of 1858. Plombières was a charming French spa town near the Swiss border. It was used as a resort by many of the Bonapartes and is still full of memories of the family. The agreement that was to be reached between the two men was perhaps Cavour's first major achievement, and one of his three most significant acts of policy, the other two being his manoeuvring Austria into war in the following spring, and his regaining of the initiative in the Italian Question from Garibaldi, in the autumn of 1860. However, it was at Plombières that he drew up a plan with Napoleon for the waging of an offensive war against Austria by a Franco–Piedmontese alliance, and it was that alliance and that war which broke the mould in nineteenth-century Italian history, and started the rapid and dramatic process by which Italy secured independence and unity.

Cavour took with him to Plombières several sheets of notes, some of them in his handwriting, some of them in Nigra's. They anticipated the course the conversation was to follow to some extent. One sheet reads as follows:

Questions which it will be necessary to address with the Emperor or which could be raised by him.

1st   What will be the aim of the war?
2nd   What will be the causes or the pretexts? . . .
3rd   The manner of France's co-operation: importance of the land and sea forces employed in the Italian war.
4th   What will be the base of operations of the French army? . . .
5th   In what proportions will France and Piedmont support the needs of the war?
6th   How will the administration of the provinces delivered from the Austrian yoke be organized?
7th   What will the conduct of the allies at the beginning of the war be towards:
    The Duchess of Parma
    The Duke of Modena
    Tuscany
    The Pope
    The King of Naples?
8th   Will it be necessary to sign a treaty and a military convention?

9th   The marriage of the Princess Clotilde with Prince
Napoleon. How to reply if the Emperor makes this a
sine qua non of the alliance? . . .[18]

Our knowledge of what happened at Plombières comes from
a solitary source – Cavour himself. He sent a brief telegram
from Plombières, but then went to Baden-Baden where he
wrote his king what he called 'an endless epistle', written 'on
the corner of a table at an inn, without any time to copy it,
nor even to reread it'.

On his arrival Cavour was shown into the emperor's study.
Napoleon at once said that he had decided to support
Sardinia with all his power in a war against Austria. There
was, of course, no need to justify this decision to Cavour.
Both men accepted the unstated assumption that Austria
had no natural right to the possession of Lombardy and
Venetia, since those regions were so obviously Italian in
every sense. A war to place them under an Italian sovereign
– in effect, Vittorio Emanuele – must, then, be a just war.
It was undeniable that in social and ethnic terms Lombardy
and Venice were wholly Italian, the only German-speaking
people there were the military and a few administrators, and
even many of the administrators were Italian.

Both Napoleon and Cavour knew, however, that these
unspoken assumptions must remain unspoken. Napoleon
therefore immediately stressed that the war could be
undertaken only for a non-revolutionary cause, which could
be justified in the eyes of the diplomatic circles, and, still
more, of the public opinion of France and of Europe. The
discussion thus centred, at this point, on the false 'cause'
for which the war was to be fought. Cavour first suggested
'Austria's bad faith in not carrying out her commercial
treaty with us'. Napoleon understandably rejected this as
'a commercial question of mediocre importance' (*'d'une
importance médiocre'*, rather loosely translated by one American
historian as 'of piddling importance') which 'could not be
made the occasion for a great war which would change the
map of Europe'.

Cavour then suggested taking up the arguments raised at
the Congress of Paris: the treaty of 1847 between Austria
and the rulers of Parma and Modena; the occupation of
the Romagna and the Legations; and the new fortifications

the Austrians were building around Piacenza. Napoleon also rejected this idea on the grounds that it had not led to French or British intervention in 1856, and could hardly justify a war now. Napoleon also added – much more to the point – that since he had troops in Rome he could hardly go to war with Austria for having troops in Ancona and Bologna. Cavour gave up this line of argument reluctantly, and admitted that he had no other clear proposals to make. 'The Emperor came to my aid, and together we set ourselves to traversing all the States of Italy, seeking grounds for war; they were hard to find'. Cavour's frank statement expresses the total dishonesty of this part of the negotiation.

They finally settled on Massa and Carrara, and so returned to an idea that Cavour had considered on previous occasions – or, at least, a new version of the idea. The plan now proposed was for the people of Massa and Carrara to send a petition to Vittorio Emanuele, asking for protection from their oppressive sovereign, and perhaps even for annexation by Piedmont. Vittorio Emanuele would decline the latter, but would send a provocative 'and menacing' note to the Duke of Modena, who would reply 'in an impertinent manner', giving Piedmont justification for war. Austria would come to the help of Modena. Cavour added the point that the Duke of Modena had not recognized any French sovereign since 1830, though whether he pointed this out to Napoleon is not clear from his letter. It seems highly probable that he did so.

Napoleon then issued a word of warning: there were two grave difficulties in the Italian Question: 'the Pope and the King of Naples', both of whom had to be treated with caution, the first because of French public opinion, and the second because of the feeling of the czar. Cavour replied to this word of warning that the pope could feel safe so long as French troops were in Rome, even if he were deprived of those parts of his principality occupied by the Austrians, while the King of Naples had failed to carry out the reforms recommended by France and England in 1856, and 'his subjects should be left free to disencumber themselves of his paternal domination if they seized the chance'.

Rather surprisingly, Napoleon was 'satisfied' with this argument. They then passed to the main purpose of the war.

The Emperor agreed readily that it was necessary to drive the Austrians out of Italy once and for all, and to leave them without an inch of territory south of the Alps or west of the Isonzo'.

They next discussed the organization of Italy after the war. 'We generally agreed to the following principles, recognizing that they were subject to modification by the course the war took.' This last reservation showed that the two men – perhaps at Cavour's suggestion – remained aware that the war would stir things up to such an extent that nothing too precise could be laid down at that stage. But what was agreed was clear enough:

> The valley of the Po, the Romagna, and the Legations would be constituted the Kingdom of Upper Italy, under the rule of the House of Savoy. Rome and its immediate surroundings would be left to the Pope. The rest of the Papal States, together with Tuscany, would form the Kingdom of Central Italy. The borders of the Kingdom of Naples would be left unchanged, and the four Italian states would form a confederation on the pattern of the German Confederation, the presidency of which would be given to the Pope to console him for the loss of the major part of his estates.

The assumption that the pope would be grateful for being made president of an Italian confederation was to be proved a mistaken one, and might have seemed a little unrealistic even at the time. The idea that the confederation should follow the pattern of the German Confederation must have been more attractive to Napoleon than to Cavour. The German Confederation, established in 1815, when any sympathy for nationalist movements was at a low ebb, had ensured the disunity rather than the unity of Germany, the independence of the German princes rather than an effective centralizing body. Napoleon is revealed by this phrase to be nervous of a strong united Italy. He wanted, after all, only a Piedmontese ally, rather stronger than the existing Piedmont, but nothing that could act independently of French wishes. Cavour's interpretation of the proposed confederation was revealed by the next paragraph: 'This arrangement seemed to me quite acceptable. For Your

Majesty, sovereign in law over the richest and most powerful part of Italy, would be sovereign in fact over the whole peninsula'.

'Sovereign in fact over the whole peninsula' – the phrase shows that Cavour's ambitions were not small ones, even if they could still be described as 'the Piedmontization of Italy'.

Napoleon and Cavour then considered who should be made sovereigns of the Kingdoms of Central Italy and Naples. Leaving 'the borders of the Kingdom of Naples unchanged' obviously did not imply leaving the Bourbons as sovereigns. Napoleon suggested, though apparently not forcefully, that Murat might be made king of Naples. Cavour evidently raised no objection to the idea, and suggested that the Duchess of Parma – a Bourbon – might be made sovereign in Florence, presumably as 'Queen of Central Italy', since the term 'Kingdom', rather than 'Grand Duchy', was being used.

Napoleon's reward for the territorial settlement of Italy was to be his acquisition of Savoy and Nice. It made sense for Savoy to be part of France in strategic terms, since it was on the French side of the highest mountain range of Europe, and the population was French-speaking. So, although Savoy was the home of the ruling Piedmontese family, its people looked towards France. Nice was another matter. Its population in 1858 was predominantly Italian-speaking, and even in the late twentieth century there is a considerable Italian colony there. Strategically, however, it could again be said to be more valuable to France, since it is to the west of an impressive and very beautiful coastal mountain pass. Cavour refused to commit himself on Nice, pointing out the distinction from Savoy. Napoleon, according to Cavour, 'stroked his moustaches several times', and said that Nice and Savoy 'were for him quite secondary questions which there would be time for later on' – not, perhaps, the most sincere of comments.

Napoleon then emphasized the need to isolate Austria – 'the grounds for war' must 'be such as would not alarm the other continental powers, and would be popular in England'. He considered that the grounds they had chosen satisfied this condition and believed England would be neutral, but advised Cavour to influence English public opinion so far as he could, because the British government was 'a slave to public opinion' It was an unintended compliment to the British political system. Thus Britain would be neutral, and so too would be Prussia, because of 'the antipathy of the Prince of Prussia toward the Austrians'. So far as Russia went, Alexander II had made a 'formal and repeated promise . . . not to oppose his Italian projects', and Cavour was inclined to believe that the war would indeed be limited to France, Piedmont and Austria.

Napoleon stressed that to defeat Austria, even if she had no allies, would present 'immense difficulties'. For some fifteen years Austria had resisted Napoleon I, and it was Austria, 'in the terrible battle of Leipzig', that 'contributed most to the defeat of the French army'. Just defeating Austria in 'two or three victorious battles in the valley of the Po or the Tagliamento would not be enough'; it would be necessary to march on Vienna.

It was with this assumption that Napoleon estimated that 300,000 troops would be needed – a large army by nineteenth-century standards: the French had defeated the Russians in 1855 with only 90,000 men. But 100,000, Napoleon said, would be needed to 'block the fortified places of the Mincio and the Adige and close the Tyrolean passes'. This was surely an absurd overestimate, especially since it left only 200,000 to march on Vienna. Of the whole 300,000 'France would provide 200,000 men, Sardinia and the other Italian provinces 100,000'. That Sardinia, with volunteers from other parts of Italy, should be required to provide half as many troops as France may seem in retrospect a heavy imposition, but to Cavour at the time it seemed necessary to explain the 'weakness' of this figure to Vittorio Emanuele. To maintain 100,000 in the line, Cavour pointed out, would require '150,000 under arms'. There would be, Cavour explained to his king, 'two grand armies, one commanded by Your Majesty and the other by the Emperor personally'.

They then turned to the question of financing the war. Cavour recorded that Napoleon offered 'to provide us with whatever war materials we need' – a rather sweeping offer – 'and to help us negotiate a loan in Paris', and recommended that 'cautious use' should be made of 'contributions of the Italian provinces in money and material'. The recommendation reflected a fear of Mazzini, and of Mazzini's ability to raise money: money from such a source brought with it danger.

The discussion in Napoleon's study had lasted from 11 a.m. to 3 p.m. Rarely in European history have four hours of talk made such sweeping decisions. Napoleon asked Cavour to return at 4 p.m. Three p.m. was a normal time for lunch with the upper classes of nineteenth-century Europe, but evidently the two men did not lunch together. Nor was there much time for a siesta on this summer afternoon. When Cavour returned at 4 p.m. it was not to continue the discussion in the Emperor's study, but to go for a ride in 'an elegant phaeton drawn by two American horses' which Napoleon drove himself, 'through the valleys and forests which make the Vosges one of the most picturesque parts of France'. Cavour was a civilized man – deciding the fate of hundreds of thousands of human beings did not prevent him from enjoying the scenery.

An archaic, dynastic character was now given to the Pact of Plombières at the wish of Napoleon, who began the conversation during the afternoon drive by opening the question of marriage of his cousin, Plon-Plon, to Vittorio Emanuele's young daughter. As we have seen, the Piedmontese king had already heard rumours to the effect that Napoleon was thinking of proposing the marriage, but did not know what importance the emperor attached to it. The situation was embarrassing because Napoleon had evidently discussed the possibility of the marriage with Dr Conneau, who had refused to elaborate on the fact when pressed by the king and Cavour.

Cavour said that his king wanted to do 'what he could to be agreeable', but 'was very reluctant to give his daughter in marriage because of her youth and could not impose an unwelcome choice upon her'. The Princess Clotilde was, in fact, not yet sixteen. Cavour added that if, however, 'the Emperor strongly desired it', the king 'would not have irremovable objections to the marriage, but wished to leave his daughter entirely free to choose'. Napoleon immediately made it clear that he was 'very eager for the marriage'. 'An alliance with the House of Savoy was what he wanted more than anything else'. Conneau had not been instructed to discuss the matter with the king, because Napoleon could not risk a refusal to an open proposal.

Both men knew that society in general did not have a favourable impression of the character of Prince Jérome. Napoleon laughingly commented on his cousin, saying that 'he had often been angry with him; but that at bottom he loved him tenderly, because he had some excellent qualities'. Cavour confirmed Napoleon's good opinion of Plon-Plon, citing the 'loyalty he has shown to his friends and mistresses'. Loyalty to past mistresses was regarded as a virtue in the Paris of the Second Empire; it may have seemed less of a virtue to a young future wife in the more inhibited atmosphere of Turin. Cavour elaborated on the point of Prince Napoleon's loyalties: Rachel, a woman who had been the prince's mistress for many years, who had borne him a son, but from whom he had been separated for four years, had been dying in Cannes, and Prince Jérome had not hesitated to abandon the pleasures of the carnival in Paris to hasten to her deathbed. Queen Victoria's reaction to Plon-Plon had been more typical. She had noted in her Journal in 1855: 'his manner is rude and disagreeable in the highest degree. *Il me fait peur*, and has a diabolical expression . . . He seems to take a pleasure in saying something disagreeable and biting, particularly to the Emperor, and with a smile which is quite satanic'.[19]

Cavour was careful not to commit the Piedmontese king to this unhappy idea of a marriage of his young daughter to a middle-aged man with a complicated past private life. In parting, Napoleon said: 'I understand the King's repugnance at marrying his daughter so young; nor do I insist that the marriage be immediate; I am quite willing to wait a year or more if necessary'. According to Cavour, Napoleon's last words on parting were: 'Have the confidence in me that I have in you'.

Cavour stressed that the emperor had not made the marriage a *sine qua non* of the alliance, but without it, Cavour believed, Napoleon would bring to the alliance 'quite a different spirit from the one which he would have brought, if, in exchange for the crown of Italy which he offers Your Majesty, Your Majesty had granted him his daughter's hand for his nearest relative'. Apart from the fact that the Empress Eugénie, or their son, might be considered nearer relatives to Napoleon than was Plon-Plon, Cavour was exaggerating somewhat in saying that Napoleon was 'offering the Crown of Italy' to Vittorio Emanuele. However, Cavour was not in the habit of understating points in his argument. He tried to frighten Vittorio Emanuele by stressing the danger of offending Napoleon III, or Prince Napoleon, who was 'still more Corsican than his cousin', and would 'vow deadly hatred against us', if the offer of marriage were rejected. At this point Cavour was surely going over the top. Apart from the fact that there was nothing 'Corsican' in Napoleon III's psychology, if by 'Corsican' was meant 'revengeful', the offer of marriage was a very secret one, and, while its rejection would have disappointed the emperor, it is unlikely that he would have regarded it quite so bitterly as Cavour was suggesting. Cavour continued his argument with a prophecy which was soon proved false:

> If the consequent war is successful, the Napoleonic dynasty will be consolidated for one or two generations; if it fails, Your Majesty and his family run the same grave dangers as their powerful neighbours.

The partial success of the war of 1859 was not, in the event, to save the Napoleonic dynasty in the long run, though it allowed the Savoy dynasty a brilliant immediate future, and survival for nearly a century. Cavour went on to discuss the advantages of the marriage in surprising detail: Prince Napoleon 'is separated from the throne only by a two-year-old child', but it was true that 'the main objections which can be made to this marriage lie perhaps in the personal character of the Prince and on the reputation that has been placed upon him'. Cavour then wrote, not about the personal character of the prince, but about his political instability: he had been exposed to revolutionary ideas at an early stage, but was now a moderate; he had never disavowed defeated friends, even when his loyalty involved confrontations with the emperor. To marry Clotilde to a member of an ancient regal family might be more disastrous, and Cavour then gave examples (which were not hard to find) of relatives of Vittorio Emanuele who had married royalty but had been miserably unhappy, like the third daughter of Vittorio Emanuele I, who had married the Emperor Ferdinand of Austria, who was unfortunately 'impotent and an imbecile'. In truth there were few eligible princes whom the Princess Clotilde could marry with any prospects of happiness. In the event the marriage of Clotilde to Prince Napoleon was the first part of the Pact of Plombières to be implemented. As might have been expected, the marriage was an unhappy one, partly because Clotilde saw herself as a martyr, but partly because she really was a martyr.

Cavour had to conclude his 'endless epistle' by asking the King to preserve it, since there was no other copy in existence.[20]

The Pact of Plombières was a dark secret from the European diplomatic world, although everyone knew that the meeting had taken place. Count Hübner, the Austrian ambassador in Paris, wrote in his diary:

> The interview at Plombières follows me day and night.
> What sort of a deal have those two conspirators made?
> Nobody knows, not even Walewski . . .
> I gave Count Walewski to understand that if Cavour was making a new effort to kindle the flames of discord between the powers, which certainly would be the case if the name 'Italy' was spoken aloud in the conference [a conference being held on the Principalities Question], then I should have to hold to my instructions, which read very explicitly. These would forbid even my passive presence at a debate over Italian questions.

Walewski assured Hübner that 'there would be no more talk of Italy in the conference', though he based this belief on the somewhat less reassuring statement that 'Cavour's purposes go beyond that. It is not words he needs, it is deeds . . . To save himself he needs some event that he can exploit in the sense of the Italian cause. The Cagliari affair was good business for him . . . Now obviously he is trying to make up another Cagliari case . . .'

Hübner did not realize that the affair had gone far beyond the *Cagliari* case, but he could report that Napoleon had written to him 'in his very own hand that he, in order to please *my* Emperor, had refused to make common cause with Cavour'. And Hübner concluded: 'I need not add that I am keeping my eyes open and shall endeavour to get to the bottom of this new secret of Cavour's'.[21]

The Piedmontese prime minister was still at the mercy of Napoleon's changes of mood and of policy. By September

1858 the emperor was suggesting that war should be delayed until the spring of 1860, or at the very earliest July or August of 1859. Cavour countered this by saying that Maximilian was trying to win over the Milanese middle class with 'semi-liberal jargon' and free festivities. However, Napoleon was not likely to be too interested in pro-Austrian, or anti-Austrian, sentiment in Lombardy. Cavour would have to do a great deal more persuading, arguing, and, finally, gambling, before he could ensure that the Pact of Plombières bore fruit, or before he could goad Austria into war.

. . .

NOTES AND REFERENCES

1. *Cavour-Nigra*, I, pp. 40–41.
2. *Archives du Quai d'Orsay*, Italie, vol. 36, 'Note de l'Empéreur sur l'Italie', 22 March 1856.
3. Chiala, I, p. 225.
4. *Cavour-Nigra*, I, p. 42.
5. A more detailed account of the *Cagliari* crisis can be found in Harry Hearder, 'La cattura del *Cagliari*', in the *Rassegna Storica del Risorgimento*, XLVII, April–June 1960, pp. 226–235.
6. Mack Smith, p. 215.
7. *ibid*, pp. 216–218.
8. All these figures are from Giorgio Candeloro, *Storia dell'italia Moderna*, IV, (Feltrinelli, Milan, 1964), pp. 210–211.
9. David Duff, *Eugénie and Napoleon III* (Collins, London, 1978), p. 131.
10. Mack Smith, p. 231.
11. *ibid*, p. 232.
12. H. Hearder, 'Napoleon III's threat to break off diplomatic relations with England during the crisis over the Orsini Attempt in 1858', in the *English Historical Review*, July 1957.
13. *Cavour-Nigra*, I, p. 59.
14. *ibid*, pp. 61–63.
15. *ibid*, p. 65.
16. Camilio Benso di Cavour, *Discorsi parliamentari*, edited by Delio Cantimori, (Einaudi, Turin, 1962), pp. 123–182.
17. Rome, Inghilterra, Cartella 85, Confidential, Cavour

to Azeglio, Turin, April 1858. No day given. Received 19 April.

18. *Cavour-Nigra*, I, p. 100.
19. Queen Victoria, *Leaves from a Journal* (1855), quoted in Duff, *op, cit.*, p. 122.
20. This important document is printed in its original French in *Cavour-Nigra*, I, pp. 103–114. An English translation can be found in Mack Walker, *Plombières. Secret Diplomacy and the Rebirth of Italy* (Oxford University Press, 1968), pp. 27–34.
21. Mack Walker, *op. cit.*, p. 38.

Chapter 6

THE WAR OF 1859: ITS PREPARATIONS AND CONSEQUENCES

· · ·

THE TREATY WITH FRANCE

At the close of 1858 Cavour was thinking of the creation of an Italy dominated by an enlarged Piedmont, but not of a single united Italy. He warned Villamarina on 25 November 1858:

> If anyone talks to you either seriously or jokingly about the reconstitution of Italy, you must be bold and maintain that this can be solidly established only if Piedmont rests her head on the Alps and her feet on Ancona.[1]

This was not the only occasion in 1858 and 1859 when Cavour spoke of Ancona as marking the limits of his ambitions for Piedmont, though, of course, he was working for Piedmont to dominate, rather than to rule, the whole peninsula.

Confirmation of Plombières, giving a distinctly different twist to that agreement, and in a much shortened form, was incorporated in a treaty arranged by Cavour with France in January 1859. It was backdated to December 12, 1858, to conceal the fact that the marriage of Clotilde and Plon-Plon had been part of the deal. The treaty was as secret as the original pact.

In writing to his agents Cavour had been citing slightly different terms for the coming treaty from those which were eventually recorded. Thus he had referred to a population of the Kingdom of Upper Italy of 'about ten million', and of the cession of Savoy to France, but of the fate of Nice as something to be discussed at the peace settlement after the war. Questioned secretly by a parliamentary commission about the treaty, Cavour denied that there was any question of ceding Nice or Savoy. The cession of the two provinces – or even only of Savoy – was clearly the most delicate part of his arrangements with Napoleon. Other clauses in the treaty that the Piedmontese public would not have liked were his agreement that their armies would be under French overall command, and that Piedmont was to pay the total expenses of the war. They were inescapable conditions, however; Cavour realized that in military terms there had to be a united command, while he was prepared to secure finances, by one means or another, for waging the war. Floating public lotteries, or securing loans from the European bankers, were not operations which unduly worried him, though in the last resort, he knew that the French would be unable to exact full payment.

At this important moment for Cavour's policy, his relations with the king were not good. Vittorio Emanuele had not been happy at the sacrifice of his young daughter to political interests, and had been torn between his desire to become king of Northern Italy through a marriage alliance with Napoleon, and his natural paternal feelings for his daughter's happiness, feelings which were certainly sincere. An even sharper cause of dispute between Cavour and his king was Vittorio Emanuele's decision to marry his mistress, Rosina Vercellana, now that the queen was dead. By the perverse morality of the time, a king was supposed to marry a member of another ruling house, or at least a noblewoman, not a former commoner who happened to be his mistress. But Cavour's hostility to the marriage was not, of course, conditioned by puritanical considerations. He merely feared that Rosina would become an uncontrollable influence on the king, and that in the eyes of monarchical Europe she would lower the tone of the House of Savoy. Although he cited the second of these two reasons, it was probably the former which was the operative one. Rosina had in fact been the king's mistress for twelve years, and had borne him children: it was a little late in the day to suggest that she brought disrepute to the Piedmontese monarchy, though even a morganatic marriage was, of course, a rather different matter from a long-lasting affair. Cavour had been antagonizing the king by opposing his liaison with Rosina since 1856, and in retrospect it seems surprising that he had made so big an issue out of a matter that the king regarded as a personal, rather than a political, one. In the event, however, the marriage was postponed for some years.

Cavour's relations with his king did not endanger the treaty of January 1859. Article 1 of the treaty stated the basic agreement:

> In the event that, following an aggressive act by Austria, war should break out between H. M. the King of Sardinia and H. M. the Emperor of Austria an Offensive and Defensive Alliance will be concluded between H. M. the Emperor of the French and H. M. the King of Sardinia.

[It is important to note the phrase 'will be concluded' (*sera conclue*). Before Bismarck introduced the system of defensive close alliances from 1879 onwards an 'alliance' was, strictly speaking, something which existed only in wartime. The alliance which Napoleon and Cavour was planning was something which would exist only if war came about. Bismarck's alliances post-1879 continued to exist whether there was war or peace. The distinction was to be of considerable importance for Cavour during the first months of 1859, since Napoleon did not regard himself as being bound to an alliance with Piedmont unless certain circumstances led to war between Piedmont and Austria.]

Article 2

The end of the Alliance will be the freeing of Italy from Austrian occupation, to satisfy the wishes of the population, and to prevent a return to the complications which led to war, and which put the repose of Europe ceaselessly in danger, by constituting, if the issue of the war permits, a Kingdom of Upper Italy of about eleven million inhabitants.

[This complicated sentence reflected a somewhat subtle idea: the war was to be fought to end a situation which could lead to war. It was, in a sense, an early example of the idea of a 'war to end wars', which became so popular during the First World War. Since then the world has become less optimistic about the results of any particular war, but it must be said that Lombardy was to enjoy greater stability as part of Italy, after the war of 1859, than she had enjoyed, since 1815, under the Austrians, or, in earlier days, under the Spanish.]

Article 3

In the name of the same principle the Duchy of Savoy and the Province of Nice will be reunited with France.

[This clearly marked a retreat by Cavour. Nice was now definitely to go to France, if the rest of the treaty was to be observed.]

Article 4

Whatever events follow from the war, it is expressly stipulated, in the interest of the Catholic Religion, that the Sovereignty of the Pope will be maintained.

[The Pope, then, would remain sovereign of a state, but he was not necessarily promised the retention of all his territory.]

Article 5

The expenses of the war will be borne by the Kingdom of Upper Italy.

Article 6

The contracting parties agree to receive no overture, nor proposition, tending to the ending of hostilities without previously conferring together.

[This clause was to be blatantly broken by Napoleon.]

Military Convention

Article 1

The forces of the Allies in Italy will be built up to about 300,000 men, namely:
>200,000 French
>100,000 Sardinians.

Six other articles dealt with military and naval details, including an article allowing the Piedmontese to use 'volunteers', provided they were 'trained and well disciplined'. Clearly if Garibaldi's volunteers were to be considered: 'well disciplined', they had to be fighting for Vittorio Emanuele, not for some wild Italian republic.[2]

.   .   .

THE BUILD-UP TO WAR

The year 1859 had started with an event calculated to give Cavour hopes that a Franco-Austrian war was not far off. At the annual New Year's Eve reception given by Napoleon in the Tuileries, the emperor seemed to go out of his way to indicate polite hostility to Austria. Saying to the Austrian ambassador that his personal affection for Francis-Joseph remained unchanged, he added that he regretted Franco-Austrian relations were not good. The remark was evidently intended to be overheard by the other diplomats present, and created a stir in the European chancelleries, and a sharp fall on the stock exchanges.

Villamarina reported to Cavour on 4 January that there was much discussion of the incident among the diplomats in Paris:

> Everyone noticed that the countenance of Baron Hübner, usually so firm and assured, was this time profoundly shaken ... The Austrian Nuncio who shares the sentiments and opinions of the Austrian representative at Paris, immediately changed colour, and became *hic et nunc* pale as death. And it was not surprising, since I saw with my very own eyes that the Emperor, while addressing the relevant words to Baron Hübner, kept his eyes permanently fixed on the representative of the Holy See.[3]

According to Hübner himself the famous statement was made 'in a genial tone' and was interpreted in several different ways by the people who heard it. Yet the very next day Hübner noted in his diary: 'Everyone is talking of war between France and Austria'. It is at least possible that Napoleon had no intention of stirring up war fever at that moment, and was surprised at the effects of his words. For Cavour, however, the interpretation placed upon the incident was a godsend. It was important for him to keep up the temperature, until Austria reached breaking point.

To this end, and to ensure a deterioration in Austro-Piedmontese relations, Cavour decided that the king should make an emotional appeal to Italian nationalism on the occasion of his speech at the opening of parliament in January, 1859. Cavour's draft of the speech ended with a rather bland reference to 'the Great Mission entrusted by Divine Providence' to Vittorio Emanuele. Cavour was now sufficiently dependent on Napoleon III to send him a copy of the draft for his approval. Napoleon found the reference to 'Divine Providence' 'too strong', and suggested instead as a concluding sentence: 'We cannot remain insensible to the cries of pain which come to us from so many parts of Italy'. Cavour was pleased with this, rightly believing that it was 'a hundred times stronger'. The king himself made a few changes before making the speech, his changes being improvements in a rhetorical sense. Thus he changed 'cries of pain' to the singular – 'cry of pain' (*grido di dolore*). The phrase had a greater appeal than anything Cavour or Napoleon had written. The idea of a single cry from a suffering nation, reaching the ears of a warrior king, had a touch of genius about it, and suggests that Vittorio Emanuele was less limited than is often suggested.

When Cavour was told that the British public and the British business world were alarmed by the speech, he told Azeglio in London that he was not surprised, but that it should not be taken out of context. After all, it stated only what everyone already knew. A danger much graver than any Piedmontese intentions was threatened by the massing of Austrian troops in Lombardy and on the frontier. Cavour claimed to have information that the Austrians intended to invade. Their railways had suspended normal transport of merchandise, to concentrate exclusively on war material. There were, Cavour said, about 17,000 men around Milan, and 15,000 on the frontier. It cannot be said that this statement was an extravagant one: while these figures may have seemed large for peacetime, they were hardly enough for Austria to employ in an aggressive war against Piedmont.[4]

A few days later Cavour backed up his argument by writing that the *grido di dolore* speech, far from stirring up trouble in Italy, had produced the opposite effect. It had given some hope to Italy, in place of despair, and despair was the more dangerous emotion, likely to lead to revolution. After all, Italy had remained peaceful during the Crimean War, and afterwards, when it seemed, at the Congress of Paris, that the British and French were sympathetic to the Italian cause. Three years later, however, the Italian situation had not improved; the Papal States were still occupied by two foreign armies. The breaking of diplomatic relations with Naples by the British and French governments had had no effect; the Neapolitan government was now sending political prisoners to America, and most of them were so weakened by Neapolitan prisons that they did not survive the journey.[5]

In February Cavour was still extremely optimistic. He saw that the war that he had planned would be a revolutionary one so far as Austria was concerned, and consequently he forged links with Hungarian revolutionaries. He wrote to Prince Napoleon on 5 February: 'I consider the Hungarian insurrection as an essential element of the complete and prompt success of our plans'. His Hungarian contact was General Giörgy Klapka, who was a refugee in Paris. In the event, though, the great Hungarian rising of 1848–49 was not to be repeated in 1859.

On 2 February Cavour was writing confidently to Napoleon III about the coming war:

> If we still have many preparations to make I believe that Piedmont and Italy are in a good mood to handle the coming events. Partisanship has disappeared. Everyone is for the French alliance. Even the ultra-aristocratic and clerical party, who tried initially to oppose it, has had to recognize its powerlessness and to join with the immense majority of the nation.[6]

If, in February, Cavour was optimistic that war was coming, it was because he had not fully assessed the forces in Europe which would work for peace. In particular the British government was opposed to war, partly for sincerely humanitarian reasons, but partly because war on the European mainland was always bad for British trade. In March and the first half of April Cavour had to face a strong peace offensive, orchestrated by the British foreign secretary, the Third Earl of Malmesbury, and not opposed by Napoleon sufficiently firmly for Cavour's taste. Other members of the Tory cabinet – Lord Derby, the prime minister, and Disraeli, the chancellor of the exchequer, among them – were more sympathetic towards Austria. Malmesbury, on the other hand, had no affection for the Austrians, but knew Italy well. He had known Louis-Napoleon in Italy when the two were very young, and had mixed in revolutionary circles, which had included Byron's mistress, the Countess Guiccioli. His feelings towards Napoleon were mixed. He had been made foreign secretary in 1852, and again now in 1858, because of his earlier friendship for Napoleon, and he could not fail to look on Italy with nostalgia. But he no longer trusted Napoleon, and he felt distaste for Piedmont and Cavour. Malmesbury was not a party man, and Disraeli, who believed that he himself should be foreign secretary, felt that Malmesbury conducted a foreign policy of his own, without enough reference to the cabinet. Above all, Malmesbury wanted to preserve peace in Italy and Europe, and he was only too aware that Cavour was working for war.

A proposal for a congress on the Italian Question came at first from St Petersburg, but Malmesbury rapidly turned it into his own mission. Napoleon alarmed Cavour by supporting the idea of a congress. Even if such a congress were to bring changes advantageous to Piedmont, they would be far less so than those likely to be introduced by a victorious war against Austria. Worse still, the Austrian government argued that the congress should be a meeting of the great powers, with Piedmont unrepresented. The French and British governments rejected this argument, whereupon the Austrians argued that if Piedmont were to be represented, Naples, the pope and the rulers of the Central Duchies must be also. The plans for holding a congress went a long way. The venue was discussed, and the governments were considering who their plenipotentiaries should be. Malmesbury decided to send Sir James Hudson – a decision which suggests that he was prepared to give some support to Cavour, provided war could be avoided.

Although Cavour wanted to avoid a congress if possible, he prepared a fall-back position, should one become inevitable. He prepared a closely argued document for the attention of Napoleon. Cavour was briefly in Paris between 26 and 30 March (Nigra had been there since 27 February), and it was during these days that he prepared his memorandum.

Disarmament, he argued, would have a 'disastrous effect in Italy'. As for the proposal of a congress, it had

> shaken confidence and diminished the moral authority of Sardinia; Italy falls back into moral anarchy. It would consequently be highly desirable that this measure [a congress] should be avoided.
>
> All the same, if, so as not to irritate England any further, the Emperor judges it indispensable to give a hearing to the propositions, the undersigned declares that the response of Sardinia must be subordinated to a preliminary question: will Sardinia be admitted or not to the Congress on the footing of a perfect equality, with or without the other States of Italy?

If the answer were to be in the affirmative, it would be possible to think of some way of satisfying 'in part at least the desires of England and Prussia'. If the answer were to be negative, Sardinia would find it 'absolutely impossible' to disarm 'a single man of its army'. Cavour pointed out that, anyhow, the request from England and Prussia that Sardinia should disarm had a 'threatening and shocking' character, and he could not believe that France would join it. England had asked Sardinia not to attack Austria and had declared herself satisfied with the reply she had obtained. Why then did England now want France to associate in a request for Sardinian disarmament?

Piedmont, Cavour argued, had remained for a long time disarmed, while Austria made preparations for war: indeed, while she mobilized 30,000 men and sent four army corps into Italy. Austria should therefore take the initiative in disarming. If Austria would go back to the situation regarding armaments as it had been on 1 January, then Piedmont would do the same.

So far as the congress went, Piedmont should be admitted on an equal basis to the great powers. Her only role would be to represent the interests of Italy. Austria on the other hand, would have a double function – as a great power, and as an Italian power, and her two roles would contradict each other. If Piedmont were present, she would balance Austria's role. The other Italian states were dependent on Austria, and could be represented by her, but to avoid creating difficulties, Cavour would raise no objection to their presence on an equal standing to that of Sardinia. Cavour's argument was valid in real terms, but when spelt out so explicitly it sounded disingenuous.

If there were to be a congress. Cavour decided that he would demand:

(1) The Austrian evacuation of the Papal Romagna.

(2) The destruction of those Austrian fortifications at Piacenza and Ferrara constructed since 1849.

(3) The cancellation of Austrian treaties with the other Italian states.

(4) So far as the Papal States went, the pope could continue to govern Rome and the country immediately surrounding it, but 'serious municipal institutions' should be introduced for Rome, and these reduced Papal States should be placed under a guarantee of the Catholic Powers. The rest of the Papal States would remain under the sovereignty of the pope, but would 'enjoy an independent administration'. The population would be consulted on what administration they required.

(5) Austria would have to accept the principle of 'non-intervention' [quoted in English] on the right bank of the Po, and the 'secondary states of Italy would be invited to introduce into their interior organization representative institutions'.

(6)There would be an Italian confederation of all Italian states which had introduced representative institutions. There would be a customs union, a common currency and 'uniformity of military institutions' between these states.[7]

The striking point about these proposals was their moderation. If there were to be a congress – which Cavour fervently hoped to avoid – he would be content with these conclusions. There would evidently be no suggestion of a Piedmontese annexation of Lombardy, but it is interesting that the proposal that the pope should be president of the Italian confederation had been quietly dropped from Cavour's schemes. However, the fact that, as late as the end of March, he was prepared to step back from his real aims to this attempt at securing compensations if he had to accept a congress, suggests a sense of diplomacy and realism that he did not always command.

These were anxious days for Cavour, but tension was continually being increased, and to that extent war was coming nearer. Malmesbury's immediate task was now to get what the Foreign Office always called 'disarmament', but what today would be called 'demobilization'. The Austrian government was prepared to disarm, provided the Piedmontese government would disarm also. The Austrians simply could not afford to keep their large army in Italy on a war footing indefinitely, and therefore had to face war unless the Piedmontese could be persuaded to disarm.

On 19 April the Austrian foreign minister, Count Buol, drafted an ultimatum to be sent to Turin, demanding a promise to demobilize within three days. The twenty-eight-year-old Emperor Francis Joseph approved the ultimatum, which Cavour had no difficulty in rejecting, correctly and promptly. He had snatched war out of what had looked dangerously like becoming a peaceful handling of the Italian Question. Austria's ultimatum placed her entirely in the wrong in the eyes of European diplomacy. Even the Tory government in London sent a strongly worded protest to Vienna. Once before the Austrian government had made a similar blunder – but with far less serious results – when they had ordered the sequestration of the property of Italian aristocrats after the attempted Mazzinian rising of 1853 in Milan. They were to make another, not dissimilar, blunder – but with even graver consequences – when they sent an ultimatum to Serbia in 1914.

At the outbreak of war Cavour took the offices of minister of the interior, of foreign affairs, and of war, as well – of course – as remaining prime minister. Even for wartime this gave him a rather dictatorial position, but there was certainly no great opposition to his assuming all these roles.

. . .

THE WAR AND THE ARMISTICE OF VILLAFRANCA, APRIL–JULY

At the start of the war, Piedmont, with an army of only 60,000, had to face Austria alone. It took several days, in the first place, before the French Empire could declare war on Austria, and rather longer for a French army of 110,000 to be moved, partly over the Alps, and partly by sea to Genoa, to come to the assistance of Piedmont. The Austrian general,

Gyulai, lacked the brilliance and dynamism of his aged precursor, Radetzky, who had been so successful against Carlo Alberto in 1848 and 1849. Gyulai moved too slowly to be able to take Turin before the arrival of the French, his excuse being that he was hampered by heavy rain. The first minor battle was a victory for the Piedmontese, fighting alone against the Austrians.

The Second War of Italian Independence though limited in time and place was nevertheless a war of great horror and human anguish. The casualty rate was enormous – more terrible than that of the Crimean War. As commanding officer of the French army, Napoleon was appalled at the mountains of dead and wounded left on the battlefield. Without losing control of operations, he was in a state of nervous exhaustion, chain-smoking his way through the horror. For the first time in the history of warfare, the railway was used for moving these considerable armies. The steam locomotive, which Cavour regarded as an engine of advanced civilization, was indeed, on the whole, a vehicle of peace, but from 1859 to 1918 it moved vast armies of men to their death, the internal combustion engine taking over this invidious task only in the twentieth century.

There were two huge battles in 1859 in which the Austrians were defeated, but not overwhelmingly. In the battle of Magenta the French fought alone, since the Piedmontese did not arrive in time. Blood soaking through the blue uniforms of the French soldiers gave the world a new word for a new colour – magenta. In the battle of Solferino Vittorio Emanuele and the Piedmontese were also present and fought effectively. After both battles, although the Austrians had been defeated, an Austrian army remained in existence, and the Franco-Piedmontese forces had not broken through the formidable fortresses of the Quadrilateral. Not only had there been no glorious march on Vienna, but Venice remained in Austrian hands.

In addition to Napoleon's sense of horror at the human tragedies of the battle, he had three other considerations which persuaded him to end the war. One was the simple military fact that there was considerable doubt as to whether a total victory – with the acquisition of Venice – could be achieved. Another was the realization that developments in Central Italy, which will be considered in a moment, were beyond his control. His third preoccupation – perhaps the most important – was the mobilization of a large German army on the French frontier. Cavour had hoped that Prussia would remain neutral because of Austro-Prussian rivalry in Germany, and more specifically because Prince William, the future Emperor of Germany, had a strong sense of hostility towards Austria. Up to a point Cavour's hopes were realized. Prussia remained neutral, but her army and that of the German Confederation, were mobilized. The King of Prussia, Frederick William IV, had suffered a stroke in the summer of 1857, and his letters at this period show a lack of any sense of reality. His brother, Prince William, had become the effective sovereign, and in October of 1858 had been formally recognized as regent. But although the Prussian government was far from being a close friend of the Austrians, and was to go to war with Austria some eight years later, it would be unlikely to stand by if a French army marched on Vienna – that is, into the lands of the German Confederation.

On 11 July 1859 Napoleon and Francis Joseph met at Villafranca, eleven miles from Verona. At least Napoleon had got inside Venetian territory, but he had not liberated any of it. The truce he was to sign was to bring no joy to the Venetians. Mazzini had forecast that peace would be made somewhere on the plains of the Po with Cavour far away. For once Mazzini had been right. Even though Vittorio Emanuele was not far away, and seems to have wanted peace, believing it to be unavoidable, the pact of Villafranca was undoubtedly a Franco-Austrian agreement, in which Cavour had no part. The Plombières agreement may have been the basis of Villafranca, but it was radically modified, since Napoleon had not been able – or willing – to force the war to a full conclusion.

The most unrealistic element of Plombières – the Italian Confederation under the presidency of the pope – was preserved. The most important element was the cession of Lombardy to Piedmont. Before Plombières such a development had seemed a remote possibility to many people, though not to Cavour. Now it was accepted as an inevitable outcome of the Austrian defeat. Venice, on the other hand, remained part of the Habsburg empire. The Austrian governor remained; Austrian officers would still sit in the cafés in the Piazza San Marco for another seven years – until five years after Cavour's death. The most reactionary element of Villafranca was the decision that 'the Grand Duke of Tuscany and the Duke of Modena will return to their states'. Leopold II, the Grand Duke of Tuscany, had been liked by his Italian subjects before 1848, and had been much praised for granting a constitution in March of that year. However, since his restoration in 1849, and the scrapping of the constitution, he had been regarded with distaste even by the Tuscan nobility, who had once been his friends. The Duke of Modena was more thoroughly hated. To restore them would certainly require force from the Austrian – or perhaps the French – army. The Tuscan moderates would prefer annexation by Piedmont, rather than the restoration of these satellite princes of Austria.

In a strange way the armistice of Villafranca, by its unpopularity in Italy, united everyone who was working for some form of Italian nationalism. Baron Bettino Ricasoli, authoritarian landowner and strong conservative in Tuscany, where he did an important job in restoring his Chianti vineyards, was now as eager to end Tuscan independence, and to secure a united Italy, as was the most radical Mazzinian. Mazzini himself, of course, regarded Villafranca as a hideous betrayal of the Italian cause by Napoleon III, whom he had hated since 1849. For Cavour the betrayal was a more personal, and so a more hurtful, one. The man with whom he had plotted, and whose confidence he had spent so much energy to secure, had come to terms with the enemy – and the Austrians were as much Cavour's enemies as they were Mazzini's.

When Cavour realized that Vittorio Emanuele had accepted the peace of Villafranca without consulting him, he had what can only be described as a mental breakdown. He cursed and swore at the king and threatened to join revolutionary resistance to the peace. After a violent scene he had little option but to resign, still in an unbalanced state of mind.

Cavour's resignation placed Italy – perhaps more than Piedmont – in a position of great danger. For the moment it seemed that Italy's fate would be settled by France and Austria working in agreement. However, developments in Central Italy, and the activities of two men – Ricasoli and

Farini – did something to fill the vacuum left by Cavour's temporary departure from the scene.

. . .

CENTRAL ITALY AND CAVOUR OUT OF OFFICE, JULY–SEPTEMBER

From the moment the war had started, dramatic events had taken place in Central Italy. A working-class demonstration in Florence had alarmed the Grand Duke, and, rather than shed blood, he had hastened to Vienna and exile. An aristocratic group, led by the formidable Ricasoli, had seized control, and asked the Piedmontese government to annex Tuscany. There was revolution also in the Papal Legations, where Piedmontese annexation was also invited. The situation in Tuscany was a complex one, and Cavour had been reluctant to take immediate action. However, he sent initially Massimo d'Azeglio, and later the dynamic and somewhat ruthless Luigi Carlo Farini to the Papal Legations to act as a temporary dictator. Napoleon III was unhappy at this treatment of the pope's territory before any permanent settlement of Italy could be made, but Farini had already taken power in Modena on June 19 and the Austrians had evacuated Bologna on the night of 11–12 June, after the battle of Magenta.

Another force played a role in filling the vacuum left by Cavour's absence from July 1859 to May 1860: the British government. The Palmerston/Russell administration was favourable to the total exclusion of Austria from Italy and although it was the French and Piedmontese who had driven the Austrians out of Lombardy, Palmerston, in his usual arrogant manner, now blamed Napoleon for having failed to finish the task by driving them from Venetia. In particular the restoration of the old rulers of the Central Duchies was condemned by the British government. Palmerston went so far as to suggest to the cabinet that Britain should go to war with Austria if the Austrians attempted to restore the Grand Duke of Tuscany by force. He talked loosely of shelling Venice, but the cabinet as a whole would not sanction such extravagance. Nevertheless Palmerston's attitude had some influence on Napoleon, and the Grand Duke was never to be restored.

After Cavour's resignation Vittorio Emanuele asked General Alfonso Lamarmora to take on the premiership, which he succeeded in doing. Cavour had trusted Lamarmora as commander of the forces in the Crimea, and as minister of war. But Lamarmora had none of Cavour's skill or vision, and was reluctant to annex the Central Duchies so long as Napoleon's attitude remained in doubt. In Florence Ricasoli held the fort, taking over virtually dictatorial powers. He organized elections for a parliament in such a way that no one wishing the return of the Grand Duke on the one hand, or with republican or socialist leanings on the other, would be elected. Once elected, the parliament stated its wishes very clearly by passing a complex motion asking for annexation by Piedmont, with the approval of Napoleon III, and a mediating role by Britain, Prussia and Russia. The Tuscans thus hedged around their request in such a way that no great power was offended, apart from Austria. Ricasoli retained power.

Elections in Modena produced a more radical assembly on 16 August. It, too, voted, on 21 August, for annexation by Piedmont. Farini in Modena, like Ricasoli in Florence, remained 'dictator', a term intended to imply temporary power during a time of crisis. He had already, on 18 August, assumed dictatorial powers in Parma, where the same process was followed, with an assembly voting on 12 September for union with Piedmont.

The revolution in the Papal Legations presented the Piedmontese government with a situation where the skill and courage of a Cavour would have been useful. Before his resignation he had taken the decisive step of sending Massimo d'Azeglio to Bologna. Before leaving Bologna on 16 July Azeglio had made the astute move of handing over power for the moment to a personal friend of Napoleon, Colonel Leonetto Cipriani, who followed Ricasoli's example by arranging for elections in such a way that a conservative parliament would be elected. On 6 and 7 September the parliament in Bologna voted the temporal power of the pope at an end, and asked for annexation by Piedmont.

The brief meeting of Napoleon and Francis Joseph at Villafranca had simply arranged the terms of an armistice, but they were terms which firmly anticipated those of a definitive peace. A conference to finalize peace terms met at Zurich on 8 August, and at this conference, of course, Piedmont was represented. The final Treaty of Zurich was not signed until 10 November. It confirmed that Austria would cede Lombardy to the French government, who would then pass the province to Piedmont. A European congress was to be called to discuss the other clauses of Villafranca – the creation of an Italian confederation under the pope, and the restoration of the old rulers of the Central Duchies.

With the signing of the Treaty of Zurich it seemed that Napoleon was still forgetting the spirit and much of the letter of the agreement of Plombières, and was working in collusion with Austria to secure the restoration of the old regimes in Central Italy, With Cavour out of office it seemed that he had forgotten his promises to Piedmont. But the unpredictable French emperor suddenly changed his tack once more. A pamphlet, published anonymously, entitled *Le Pape et le Congrès*, appeared in Paris in December 1859. It was leaked that the author was a Viscount Louis de La Guéronnière, who was close to the emperor and evidently writing under the emperor's instructions. The pamphlet made very specific recommendations to the pope, recommendations which were unlikely to be observed, and likely to be offensive to him. It was suggested that, in the first place, the pope should resign himself to a smaller state – a geographical limitation of his temporal power; in the second place, he should abandon the attempt to provide for his own defence, but should depend on an army of the Italian Confederation, of which he was to be president, and of which the diminished Papal States would be a member; and finally that the Catholic powers should provide him with an income.

Le Pape et le Congrès antagonized not only the pope, but also the Austrian government, who now declared that they could not take part in a congress which would recognize the doctrines pronounced in the pamphlet. Probably Napoleon had sincerely wanted a congress. He always retained memories of the splendid Congress of Paris of 1856, when the Second Empire had been at the peak of its power, and Eugénie had provided him with an heir. However, the idea of a congress to confirm the terms of the Treaty of Zurich, taking into account *Le Pape et le Congrès*, had to be abandoned. The British government had opposed the congress for a reason quite different from that for which the Austrians opposed it. Palmerston and Russell were still furious with the terms of the Treaty of Zurich, and to agree to a congress on Italy would have seemed an acceptance of those terms. Not to attend such a congress, though, would have been a surrender of the British right to have a voice in the future of Italy. With the congress abandoned, Russell could now make his own proposal, which was an eminently sensible one: that the Powers should adopt a policy of non-intervention in Italian affairs, and allow the Italians to determine their own future. Russell made his proposal in January 1860. The other powers accepted it, Austria very reluctantly. It set the stage for Cavour's return to power – and also for his final struggle with Garibaldi.

. . .

NOTES AND REFERENCES

1. Mack Smith, p. 255.
2. *Cavour-Nigra*, I, pp. 312–313.
3. Turin, Lettere Ministri, Francia, 1857–9, vol. 285, Confidential.
4. Rome, Gran Bretagna, 1859, Cartella 88, Confidential, 16 January.
5. *ibid.* 21 January.
6. *Cavour-Nigra*, II, p. 1.
7. Carlo Pischedda and Giuseppe Talamo editors, *Tutti gli scritti di Cavour*, (Centro Studi Piemontesi, Turin, 1976), the volume for the years 1850–1861, pp. 2,026–8.

Chapter 7

CAVOUR AND GARIBALDI IN THE FINAL STRUGGLE TO UNITE ITALY, 1860–61

· · ·

CAVOUR RETURNS TO POWER

Although Cavour had been out of office for six months, he had remained in touch with the ministers, many of whom were his former colleagues, and with the complex developments in Central Italy. He decided that the time was ripe for his return to power when Napoleon had *Le Pape et le Congrès* published. In spite of Napoleon's liking for congresses, the publication of this pamphlet suggested that he no longer wished to act with Austria. His alignment with Austria, which had in a sense existed since Villafranca, was ended, and there was to be a return to the spirit of Plombières. To enable his return to power Cavour now conducted a forceful campaign in the press, demanding elections and the recall of parliament. He saw parliament, where he could always command support, as a counterweight to the king, whose influence would keep him from office if possible. In Turin four leading newspapers supported Cavour, as did two in Milan, and one in Genoa. The British government, through Hudson, made it clear that it favoured a recall of parliament. In the middle of January Cavour met the king, and, in an emotional exchange, 'promised that he would not talk any more about Rosina'.[1] The king reluctantly asked him to form a government.

Cavour took for himself not only the premiership, but also the foreign ministry and the ministry of the interior. His power in this culminating period of his career was to be firmly based. Manfredo Fanti, who was to play an important role in the confrontation with Garibaldi, and in the early years of the Kingdom of Italy, was made minister of war. Fanti was also in command of the army of central Italy:

154

his role suggested that Cavour was prepared for a forward movement of more annexations. People whom he wished to conciliate without giving them posts in central government Cavour made local governors. Men of the Left handled in this way were Lorenzo Valerio, who was made governor of Como, and Depretis, the future prime minister of Italy, who was made governor of Brescia. Massimo d'Azeglio was made governor of Milan, a city he knew well from his younger days. The formation of this government illustrated Cavour's skilful control of power, although he was charged by his opponents with being unduly influenced by foreigners – specifically by Hudson and Lord John Russell. He had the moral support of the British in returning to power, but could certainly have managed without it at this juncture. The journal *Opinione* commented:

> The previous Cavour administration meant the war of independence; the new one means annexation. The whole of Italy sees this idea personified in the famous statesman ... Count Cavour has the enviable good fortune of re-taking the reins of government sustained by public opinion and supported by the faith of the whole nation.[2]

There was some exaggeration in the comment, but there was an element of truth in it. Cavour became prime minister again on 21 January 1860. In the intrigues which led to this result Sir James Hudson had played a far from negligible role.

. . .

THE ANNEXATION OF THE CENTRAL DUCHIES AND THE QUESTION OF SAVOY AND NICE

The two questions – that of the Piedmontese annexation of what had once been the Grand Duchy of Tuscany, the Duchies of Parma and Modena, and the Papal territory of the Romagna, on the one hand, and that of the French annexation of Savoy and Nice, on the other hand – were not linked by any formal understanding, yet they were inextricably linked in the minds of Napoleon and Cavour. The Piedmontese statesman was faced, as always, with the unpredictable and unreliable attitude of the French emperor. Perhaps one of Cavour's greatest skills was that of grappling with the tergiversations of French policy. He had the good sense to realize that in dealing with Napoleon it was not so much what the emperor said, as what he felt, that mattered. In the case of Savoy and Nice, Cavour calculated that Napoleon needed the acquisition of the provinces in order to convince the French public that the sacrifices of the 1859 war had brought some tangible advantages to France. It could also be argued that Savoy and Nice fell within the 'natural frontiers' of France, if the term was taken in its geographical and strategic sense, rather than a nationalistic or ethnic one. Even ethnically Savoy was 'naturally' French, though Nice, as Cavour had pointed out at Plombières, was quite another matter.

Cavour was under no legal, nor even moral, obligation to surrender Savoy and Nice, nor could Napoleon claim that Cavour was bound by his promise, since Venice remained Austrian, and the terms of the Pact of Plombières had thus been only partly fulfilled. However, in the delicate processes of having Central Italy annexed to the emerging Kingdom of Italy, and Savoy and Nice annexed to France, it had to be made clear that both annexations were in accordance with the wishes of the populations. Before annexing central Italy, Cavour took the rather imaginative step of asking Ricasoli and Farini to arrange for the election of deputies in Tuscany and Emilia to sit, not in the parliaments of those regions, but in the parliament in Turin. An undramatic measure, it nevertheless anticipated annexation in an unprovocative, but persuasive, manner.

Cavour took another step, which Napoleon might well have considered more provocative. Before annexing Tuscany and Emilia, he circulated to the great powers a remarkable, unsigned, document, claiming that the annexations were necessary in order to free Italy from French influence. The circular was perhaps intended primarily to please the British government, but the French may have been less concerned about Central Italy than Cavour feared. The French foreign minister, Edouard Thouvenel, was announcing early in February that the French government was ready to open negotiations concerning the 'formation of an Italian kingdom of eleven million souls'. Cavour, of course, was delighted with this new attitude of Napoleon, but commented that things were going 'too well', and suspected that Napoleon had some undeclared motives that went beyond the acquisition of Savoy and Nice.

There were three ways by which the wishes of the peoples of central Italy could be determined. One way had already been tried, and had been decided in a pro-Piedmontese sense. This was by vote of the revolutionary assemblies, which had not been elected democratically, but which – it could be argued – represented the responsible section of the community. The second way would have been by the election of a constituent assembly, by universal suffrage – an assembly which would then debate and vote democratically on future steps for the unification of Italy. This second method was the one recommended by Mazzini, but considered impractical and dangerous by Cavour. A third process was that adopted by the Napoleons – decision by plebiscite. It involved the use of universal male suffrage, but on a one-off occasion only. The poor and the illiterate would have one vote in their lives, but the Piedmontese constitutional Charter would ensure that they were never to vote again. The male population was to be asked a question that appeared, on the surface, to be a simple one: Do you want annexation by Piedmont, or not? It was not, of course, in reality a simple question, since the consequences of voting 'No' were by no means clear. For Cavour, however, it served the useful purpose of conforming to Napoleon's practices, and its democratic character was rather apparent than real. The last thing Cavour wanted was real democracy in the Mazzinian sense, but he would probably not have favoured unification by plebiscite, if it had not been made fashionable by the two Napoleons.

Decrees were published on 1 March 1860 in Tuscany by Ricasoli, and in Emilia by Farini, announcing that in ten days' time the choice could be made between 'Annexation to the constitutional monarchy of King Vittorio Emanuele II', or 'A separate Kingdom'. What exactly 'A separate Kingdom' meant was not defined, but all men over the age of twenty-one could vote. The use of the word 'Kingdom', as opposed to 'Grand Duchy' or 'Duchy', almost certainly implied that the restoration of the old rulers was no longer a possibility. The results of the plebiscites seemed overwhelmingly to confirm a wish for annexation. An apparent eagerness for Vittorio Emanuele to become their king was displayed by the men of Tuscany by 386,445 votes against 14,925, and by the men of Emilia by 427,512 against 756. Cavour had decrees published in Turin declaring Tuscany and Emilia merged with Piedmont. The acquisition of Tuscany by Piedmont could be interpreted as the central event of the *risorgimento*. A modification of the Tuscan dialect had been accepted as the correct form of the Italian language, and the rich cultural history of Florence made her in many respects the civilized heart of Italy.

Piedmontese annexation of Tuscany and Emilia – even with the loss of Savoy and Nice – meant that Cavour's policy had increased the country's population by 11,137,000. On 1 April 1860 Piedmont – or the Kingdom of Upper Italy, as it should perhaps now be called – was the seventh largest country in Europe in terms of population.

While the plebiscites were being held, and while the decrees announcing the annexation of Central Italy by Turin were being drafted and published, the cession of Nice and Savoy to France was being formalized. Cavour's policy on the surrender of Savoy and Nice was a tortuous one. Up to the last moment he denied that the annexations were going to happen. A new governor of Savoy on 10 January 1860 was assured that 'in Turin there had never been a question of surrendering Savoy to France', and nineteen days later the governor himself said that 'the Government . . . has never entertained the design of surrendering Savoy'. Cavour repeated the assurances to Hudson, who reported them to London on 3 February, yet on 2 March Cavour was assuring the French that the wishes of the people of Savoy would be respected, the clear indication being that the people wished for union with France.

On 12 March a treaty was signed by Vittorio Emanuele in Turin, and two days later by Napoleon in Paris, passing Savoy and Nice under French sovereignty. It was to be confirmed by plebiscites 'as soon as possible'. In the event the plebiscites were not held until the middle of April, but, as usual, they confirmed the action already taken by the governments. A vast vote of 130,583 in Savoy favoured annexation by France, against only 235 who still wanted to remain subjects of Vittorio Emanuele, whose first and most ancient title as Duke of Savoy thus lost its validity while he was not to be King of Italy for another year. The population of the town of Nice was, of course, much smaller, and there the figures were 24,448 in favour of annexation, and only 160 against. That French agents and the presence of the French army in Nice contributed to the result can hardly be doubted.

. . .

GARIBALDI TAKES OVER: CAVOUR'S POLICY IN ECLIPSE

Paradoxically it was Cavour's cession of Nice that led to the next, immensely important, phase in the unification of Italy. Nice was not only Garibaldi's birthplace, but also his parliamentary constituency. He was so enraged at its cession to a foreign power that he began to assemble a volunteer force at Quarto, on the coast near Genoa, to attack the French in Nice. But a revolution had broken out in Sicily, and Francesco Crispi and others persuaded Garibaldi that an expedition to Sicily, though a desperate proposition, would not be quite so desperate as an expedition to Nice.

Garibaldi sailed from Quarto with his Thousand – or just over a thousand – young men on 6 May 1860. They were to fight under the slogan 'Italy and Vittorio Emanuele', but the 'Italy' Garibaldi envisaged was a democratic monarchy, with universal suffrage and a vast citizen army, with which Venice and Rome could be liberated. In other words, although 'Vittorio Emanuele' figured in Garibaldi's slogan, the radical idea for which he was fighting bore little resemblance to any institution in Cavour's immediate – or perhaps ultimate – plans.

That Garibaldi's force was poorly armed – mainly with rusty, unrifled and unreliable muskets – is beyond doubt. More debatable is Cavour's responsibility for this state of affairs. Modern rifles had been bought by voluntary donations for Garibaldi, but that the Piedmontese authorities prevented him for securing them seems to have been due to a personal decision of Azeglio, rather than any instruction of Cavour's. That Cavour had no sympathy for Garibaldi's aims is, however, quite certain. An often-quoted letter to Nigra in Paris probably expressed his genuine reaction, although it was written to give Nigra material for explaining the situation to Napoleon and his foreign minister, Thouvenel:

> I regret Garibaldi's expedition as much as he [Thouvenel] does, and I am doing and will do everything that is possible to see that it does not lead to new complications. I did not hinder Garibaldi from carrying out his plan, because it would have been necessary to employ force to do so. Just now the ministry is not in a state to brave the immense unpopularity which would have burst upon it if it had tried to stop Garibaldi. With the elections imminent, and counting on every type of moderate liberal to counter the intrigues of the opposition, and to get the treaty [regarding Nice and Savoy] adopted, I could not take vigorous measures to stop help being sent to Sicily. But I omitted nothing in my attempts to persuade Garibaldi to give up his mad scheme.[3]

Cavour clearly did not expect Garibaldi to succeed. After Garibaldi had taken Palermo, and seemed likely to take the whole of Sicily, Cavour had to revise his expectations. He then decided to allow arms to be sent. Waves of volunteers joined Garibaldi's original Thousand, and Cavour now hoped to be able to secure some control of Garibaldi, and if possible – when the time was ripe – annex Sicily to Piedmont. He sent La Farina, of the National Society, to represent him in relations with Garibaldi in Sicily. The choice was an unwise and unfortunate one. La Farina had not been on good terms with Garibaldi before the sailing of the Thousand. The most that could be said of him was that he was a Sicilian. When he arrived in Sicily he antagonized Garibaldi, and even more Crispi, by pressing for the immediate annexation of the island to Piedmont. At first Garibaldi was too occupied with the waging of his sometimes desperate, but ultimately brilliant and successful, campaign against the Bourbons, to concern himself with La Farina. But by 7 July relations between Crispi and La Farina had become impossible, and Garibaldi reacted by having La Farina arrested and expelled. His decision marked the lowest ebb of Cavour's influence in the whole process of Italian unification. However, a total break between Cavour's government and Garibaldi was avoided when the two decided on a replacement for La Farina. Agostino Depretis, who was one day to become prime minister of Italy, and one of the most skilful operators in Italian nineteenth-century history (second only, perhaps, to Cavour) had a personality very different from that of La Farina. He would not cause trouble between Garibaldi and Turin, but, equally, he was unlikely to give Cavour a firm grasp of the situation in the South.

Cavour's loss of the initiative lasted while Garibaldi conquered the island of Sicily, crossed to the mainland, and entered Naples on 7 September. The Piedmontese statesman's attitude to Garibaldi's crossing of the Straits has been the theme of some academic argument, but it seems fair to conclude that Cavour would have preferred the event never to have taken place. Napoleon III, too, might well have blocked Garibaldi's passage over the narrow straits of Messina, had it not been for the presence of the British Mediterranean fleet. Like Lord John Russell, British admirals were captivated by Garibaldi's achievements, and their support for the man Queen Victoria called a 'filibuster', ensured that French or Piedmontese warships would give him no trouble.

While Garibaldi had been conquering Sicily, Cavour's influence had clearly been in eclipse. He had been painfully aware of the danger. On 1 August he had written to Nigra:

> If Garibaldi passes to the Continent and establishes himself and his capital in the Kingdom of Naples as he has done in Sicily, he becomes absolute master of the situation. King Vittorio Emanuele loses almost all his prestige; in the eyes of the great majority of Italians he will become only the friend of Garibaldi. He will probably keep the crown, but this crown will shine only as a reflection of what a heroic adventurer judges good to shine on it. Garibaldi will not proclaim the republic at Naples; but he will not carry out annexation and he will keep the dictatorship. He will dispose of the resources of a kingdom of 9,000,000 inhabitants, and will be surrounded by an irresistible prestige. We will not be able to struggle against him.[4]

Cavour even believed at this point that a war against Austria for the acquisition of Verona and Venice might be necessary to take away some of the glamour of the Sicilian campaign, though he considered that such an extreme measure would not be necessary if a pro-Piedmontese revolution in Naples could be achieved. Once the King of Naples had been thrown out by revolution – before the arrival of Garibaldi – there would be a justification for a Piedmontese invasion to restore order. However, Cavour's attempt to regain the initiative by organizing a pro-Piedmontese revolution in Naples was to be a total failure.

Cavour knew very little of Naples, and his choice of agents to send there was no more inspired that his contacts among Neapolitans. The Bourbon King of Naples, Francesco II, had made a few desperately liberal attempts to counteract Garibaldi's arrival. He had restored the constitution of 1848 on 1 July, and had appointed Liborio Romano minister of the interior. Romano had links with the criminal *camorra*, but could pose as an instant liberal. Cavour, too, thought Romano was worth cultivating. Romano was prepared to betray the Bourbons and welcome the Piedmontese, just as he was later to welcome Garibaldi. He was not the kind of man to organize a genuine revolution.

Cavour started plans for his own revolution in Naples in the middle of July. He employed bribes on a big scale in an attempt to secure the support of anyone in the Bourbon army, or even in the royal circle. Villamarina, who had been the official Piedmontese minister in Paris, but had been demoted to the legation at Naples, was co-ordinating Cavour's efforts, and some twelve agents were sent from Turin. When Villamarina had been in Paris Cavour had never trusted him with his confidential dealings with Napoleon, which had been handled unofficially by Nigra, who had now replaced Villamarina at the Paris legation. The fact that no one in whom Cavour had greater faith than he had in Villamarina had been sent to Naples might suggest that Cavour was not serious in his attempt at revolution, but other evidence suggests that he was in deadly earnest. Villamarina himself was certainly optimistic. Before Garibaldi had crossed the Straits, Villamarina believed that a pro-Piedmontese rising in Naples would make annexation of mainland Naples comparatively easy. It was also the case that Ricasoli and Farini had plotted with Cavour for a rising in Naples to anticipate Garibaldi's arrival. A certain Nicola Nisco, a moderate liberal, was an intermediary between Cavour on the one hand, and Romano and a

Neapolitan general, Nunziante, on the other. Nunziante gave Nisco a letter from Vittorio Emanuele, offering support for the rising. However, the attitude of Napoleon III to this conspiracy had not been tested. Prince Napoleon agreed to speak to the emperor, and when he did so it became clear that Napoleon did not approve. He even told Plon-Plon to say in Turin that the plans had not been mentioned to him.

In spite of all his plotting, Cavour could yet stand back from the immediate scene and express his admiration for a brilliant revolutionary. He wrote to Nigra on 9 August:

> Garibaldi has rendered Italy the greatest services that a man could give her: he has given Italians confidence in themselves: he has proved to Europe that Italians know how to fight and die on the battlefield to reconquer a fatherland.[5]

He added: 'All the same it is eminently desirable that a revolution should take place in Naples without him', but Cavour was to lose the race to Naples, if, indeed, he had ever been a starter in that race. Garibaldi advanced from Calabria to Naples virtually unopposed, and entered the city on 7 September, King Francesco having withdrawn his army to Gaeta, on the farthest northerly point of the west coast of the Kingdom. Romano, true to form, handed over power to the most recent successful contender for it – Garibaldi. For once, Cavour's assessment of the reality of power had failed him.

. . .

CAVOUR AGAIN ON THE OFFENSIVE: THE CREATION OF THE KINGDOM OF ITALY

Garibaldi's supply of volunteers and arms had depended to a great extent on Dr Agostino Bertani, a former Mazzinian, who had operated from Genoa. Bertani prepared a force of 9,000 armed men for a direct invasion of the Papal States from the north, but Cavour took steps to prevent it from moving. He wanted, at all costs, to prevent a Garibaldian invasion of the Papal States either from the north or from the south. Such an invasion, he believed, would antagonize the great powers and probably lead to French intervention against the Italian movement. However, while it was possible to prevent any Garibaldi-inspired movement from Piedmont to the Papal States from the north, to prevent Garibaldi himself from marching on Rome from the south was a tougher proposition.

Cavour's decision to send an army through the Papal States to intercept Garibaldi can be seen as a natural sequence to his failed attempt to intercept Garibaldi at Naples by staging a pro-Piedmontese revolution. In a deeper sense it was much more than this, though. To go to war with the pope was going to be Cavour's greatest, and ultimately most successful, gamble. To justify the war he had to pretend that revolution was about to break out in the Papal States, and that Piedmont had to intervene to restore order. To ensure that there would be no intervention from the great powers the line to Paris had to be kept open. It had to be an informal and secret line, since Napoleon could not afford to say openly that he approved of a Piedmontese invasion of Papal territory. It was true that the Papal Romagna had already been annexed, but to move a considerable army right across the remainder of the Papal States, in the teeth of Papal resistance, was not likely to be applauded by French Catholics.

Nigra, however, was already reporting Napoleon's tacit and very cautious approval on 26 August:

> If there has to be a forward motion, between the two, between Garibaldi and Turin, the latter is to be preferred. His Majesty would not be astonished, nor perhaps annoyed, at efforts by us to retrieve the flag that Garibaldi has stolen from us.[6]

The cabinet accepted Cavour's proposal of an invasion of the Papal States on 26 August, and Farini and Cialdini were at once despatched to Chambéry, officially to carry Vittorio Emanuele's congratulations to the emperor on his acquisition of Savoy, which he was visiting for the first time, but unofficially to seek his approval of the plan of Piedmontese intervention in the Papal Marche and Umbria. The choice of the occasion was a subtle – or perhaps over-subtle – one. The emperor would clearly be feeling grateful to the Piedmontese for his beautiful new province, with its mountains snowcapped even in August.

Farini and Cialdini met Napoleon on 28 August. It is not, strictly speaking, known what the emperor said at this meeting, but it is believed that, although he did not give his formal approval to Cavour's plan, he made it clear that he would take no action. He would impose only three conditions: the action must be a swift one, so that European diplomacy would have no time to react; there must be no suggestion of collusion with France; and there should be a revolutionary movement of some kind in the Papal States to justify Piedmontese intervention. In short, Napoleon said: 'Do it, but do it quickly', or in Macbeth's words:

> If it were done when 'tis done, then 'twere well
> It were done quickly.

Cavour quoted Farini as saying that the emperor had reacted perfectly. He had said that it was too late to stop Garibaldi reaching Naples, where he would be proclaimed dictator, and that he must therefore be stopped in Umbria and the Marche. Diplomacy, said the emperor, would make loud noises, but would do nothing. The probability is that Napoleon was relieved at Cavour's decision: if Garibaldi had invaded the Papal States, the emperor would have been faced with the difficult choice between withdrawing his troops from Rome or fighting Garibaldi.

Of Napoleon's three conditions, the first – that the operation should be a rapid one – was faithfully carried out by Cavour's government. In an attempt to fulfil the third – that there should be a revolutionary movement in the Papal States – Cavour sent agents with bombs and cash into the Papal States. The National Society lent their support, on 3 September ordering their members to start a revolt and request Piedmontese help. Cavour then sent a somewhat outrageous ultimatum to Pio Nono, demanding that he should disband his army, since it was a threat to peace. It was embarrassing that the ultimatum was unaccountably delayed: it reached Rome on 10 September, and the invasion started on the 11th. Cardinal Antonelli's rejection of the ultimatum reached Cavour only on the 13th. The National Society's attempt to start a revolution in the Papal States was also an unconvincing one.

So, on 11 September, with Garibaldi in Naples, and the Bourbon army ready to make a last stand on the Volturno, south of Gaeta, a Piedmontese army, under Manfredo Fanti, invaded the Papal States. Numbering some 33,000 men, it was to meet stiff resistance. Pio Nono had carried out reforms of his army, and appointed a French commander, Louis de Lamoricière, who had served under the July Monarchy, and was no friend of Napoleon III. Even so, Napoleon had to take the token step of breaking off diplomatic relations with Piedmont, and reinforcing his garrison in Rome as a firm warning that the Piedmontese army must give the capital a wide berth. France was not alone in breaking off diplomatic relations with Turin. The Russian government did so also, as did – less surprisingly – the Catholic states of Spain, Portugal and mad Ludwig's Bavaria.

The campaign lasted for eighteen days, Lamoricière's force was perhaps a third as large as Fanti's. Not all the pope's forces could be used, since the whole territory had to be garrisoned for fear of risings. The campaign was effectively decided in one battle, at a little hill town near the Adriatic, called Castelfidardo. Although Lamoricière himself and a small force continued to resist in the port of Ancona for a few days, the bulk of the papal force surrendered.

When the Piedmontese army moved from the Papal States into what was still in theory the Kingdom of Naples, Garibaldi's army was facing a Neapolitan army that still numbered 50,000, in the broad valley of the Volturno. When Garibaldi tried to cross the river he was thrown back with heavy losses. For a moment it seemed that a successful counterattack of the Neopolitans might take them back to Naples, but Garibaldi's magic was not yet dimmed, and the Bourbon army was again defeated.

Garibaldi hoped that local assemblies in Sicily and Naples would now be elected by universal manhood suffrage, while he was still in command of the situation. That Cavour feared, and perhaps expected, a violent confrontation with Garibaldi is indicated by the fact that he gave orders to the Piedmontese navy, if possible, to seize the Neapolitan fleet. In the event, Garibaldi had already handed all naval forts and ships under his control over to Vittorio Emanuele. The period of Garibaldi's supremacy was approaching its end.

Rather than have assemblies elected for Sicily and mainland Naples, Cavour arranged for two more plebiscites to be held – one for Sicily and one for Naples. Since much had happened since the plebiscites for Central Italy had been held, the questions asked were now rather different. There was no longer a reference to 'annexation to Piedmont'. The question now was: *Italia Una Vittorio Emanuele* – 'Yes' or 'No'. Separate 'Yes' and 'No' slips were issued to be dropped in separate urns. The ballot for the city of Naples was held in the University. Anyone who is curious and can gain admission to the Royal Archives at Windsor Castle can see a 'Yes' slip, which was sent to Prince Albert. The question posed, then, was a simple nationalist one: 'Italy one'. Vittorio Emanuele had no numeral attached to his name, so that he appeared to be no longer merely a Piedmontese king. The results of the plebiscites seemed to suggest that the whole South had been converted to Italian nationalism, though subsequent events were to show that this was not the case. In Continental Naples 1,302,064 men voted 'Yes', and only 10,302 'No'. According to this vote, then, less than 1 per cent rejected Vittorio Emanuele. In Sicily the figures were 432,053 'Yes' votes, to 667 'No' votes; so that in the island a considerably smaller percentage voted 'No'.

So far as the invading Piedmontese forces went, Cavour played his cards with some skill. He did not persuade the king to lead the army initially, even though the presence of the king might have made the invasion more respectable. Rather, he preferred to wait and observe the outcome of the campaign. Then, on 3 October, Vittorio Emanuele joined the army in Ancona. His presence when the Piedmontese force met the Garibaldian force was of immense importance. By then Cavour could feel fairly sure – although he still had some agonizing doubts – that Garibaldi would not enter into conflict with an army led by his king.

In the event Garibaldi and the king met, with their armies, at a point north of the Volturno on 26 October. There was no armed confrontation, nor even apparent friction. To some extent Garibaldi was honest enough to feel grateful for military help in finally defeating the Bourbon forces, though he could probably have done so without help. On 7 November – two months after Garibaldi's original entry – he and the king rode into Naples together, amid cheering crowds. The cheers may have been more for Garibaldi than for Vittorio Emanuele, but they may also have been simply an expression of hope for a better future. Garibaldi was not yet ready to leave the scene entirely to the Piedmontese, and asked to be made Dictator of Southern Italy for one year. Perhaps inevitably, the request was turned down, and on 9 November he set off from Naples for his island home of Caprera, having refused all honours and rewards. Cavour was free of one enemy, but not for long.

Meanwhile plebiscites were held in those parts of the Papal States which had been annexed – or liberated – by the Piedmontese army. The figures repeated the apparent desire of Italians to belong to a single homeland. In the Marche, on the east coast, 133,765 voted for union, and 1,212 against, while in Umbria, the beautiful hilly region nearer Rome, 97,040 were for union, and only 360 against.

As has been seen, the emergence of a united Italy was greeted with sullen hostility by most of the great powers. Britain was an honourable exception. The British Foreign Office produced a despatch drafted by Russell to Hudson, and published in a blue book, explicitly stating that Britain would not follow the current trend to break off diplomatic relations with Vittorio Emanuele's government (not yet 'Italy'), but regarded 'the prospect of a people building up the edifice of their liberties, and consolidating the work of their independence' as a 'gratifying' one.

Cavour's life did not have long to run. But on 27 January 1861 he could arrange for the election of a parliament for the Kingdom of Italy, an event that had been his boyhood's dream, but which ten years before he would have believed inconceivable in his lifetime. The parliament met on 18 February in Turin, deputies from all over Italy having to travel to this rather remote little city, which had always been Cavour's home, however much he may have enjoyed stays in Geneva, Paris and London. Recently he had left it only briefly – once on a trip to Florence. He had avoided visits to Naples.

On 17 March parliament recognized Vittorio Emanuele 'King of Italy', this time with the numeral 'II' attached, although there had never been a 'Vittorio Emanuele I' of Italy. The parliamentary act was in keeping with the political philosophy of Cavour. No priest blessed the king, but equally no huge, popularly elected assembly bestowed powers upon him. Instead a small gathering of deputies, elected on a very restricted franchise, incorporated him as part of a parliamentary monarchy. It was the kind of event which

168

the British landed nobility, for whom Cavour had always felt admiration, could smile upon. It was not democracy; but it was not tyranny. In an imperfect world it may have seemed the best option. It was Cavour's *juste-milieu* in power.

Cavour still had Garibaldi to reckon with, however. Garibaldi's immediate preoccupation was with the fate of the officers of his army, whose dedication and courage had made Cavour's Kingdom of Italy possible. General Fanti, as minister of war in the first Italian government, tried to exclude as many as possible of Garibaldi's officers from commissions in the new Italian army. Fanti even preferred to enrol the officers of the old Bourbon army, even though they were not likely to feel great loyalty to the Kingdom of Italy. Outraged at Fanti's decisions, Garibaldi returned from Caprera in April 1861, to intervene in a parliamentary session, which ended in turmoil as Garibaldi condemned Cavour as a reactionary influence on Vittorio Emanuele. It was a sad conclusion to the history of the stormy relations between Cavour and Garibaldi.

In the elections for the first Italian parliament a large majority of Cavour's supporters – now to be known as the Party of the Right (*La Destra*) – had been returned. Only eighty members of the Party of Action – former Mazzinians – had been elected. If Cavour's career is seen as that of a parliamentarian, it can be considered to have concluded with a great electoral victory. His power had always been based on parliament, and it was fitting that this comparatively small assembly, which represented only a minority of the population, but which contained intelligent and liberal-minded deputies, should recognize his achievements. It must be said, however, that the public galleries were rarely sympathetic to him, and far more eager to cheer his critics – especially, of course, Garibaldi.

. . .

THE ROMAN QUESTION: CAVOUR'S LAST POLITICAL BATTLE

In the first debates in the new parliament in March 1861, Cavour was attacked by the Party of Action for not immediately occupying Rome – which would have been a dubious proposition in view of the presence of the French army there. Cavour had said publicly – to many people's surprise – that Rome must one day be the capital of Italy. The parliamentary Right tended to blame him for making so radical a statement. But Cavour had no intention of challenging the French position in Rome. He wanted to secure Rome by negotiation with the pope, as the prelude to introducing his policy of 'a free Church in a free State'.

A fine Italian historian described his attempt to solve the Roman Question as 'the last political battle of Cavour'.[7] A battle it certainly was, though not the kind fought with guns, and its aims were honourable and intelligent. That Cavour lost was not his fault, but rather the fault of Pio Nono, who certainly did not win any battle, either for himself or for the Catholic Church. Both sides were the losers.

With the establishment of the Kingdom of Italy, unification was still, in the geographical sense, incomplete. Rome and Venice, geographically and ethnically part of Italy, were still unredeemed politically. Already in a meeting of parliament in Turin on 11 October 1860 Cavour had undertaken to remember this fact. He knew, however, that Venice could not be secured at that time. There was still a large Austrian army in the Veneto. Although Cavour had been in touch with Hungarian revolutionary leaders during the war of 1859, he no longer had any intention of stirring up revolution in the Habsburg Monarchy. He believed, however, that the Roman Question might prove easier to solve, so it was on the Roman Question that he spent these last few months of his life – unsuccessfully, but time was short.

He knew that he could not open negotiations with the pope directly, but Cavour had often been skilful at using intermediaries. He had done so with Napoleon III, and – less successfully – with Garibaldi. The pope was now the temporal ruler only of Lazio – the region around Rome, a small portion of his former principality. The problem, therefore, was to persuade him to give up this piece of his territory, which really no longer gave him any guarantee of independence and remained under his sovereignty only because of the presence of French forces. In return for this diminutive slice of territory, as Cavour saw it, the pope would be given full liberty as head of the Church in Italy. Cavour hoped that he could evolve out of these rather vague ideas a settlement which would satisfy Napoleon III. What made him hopeful about the outcome of these negotiations was the knowledge that Napoleon wanted to withdraw from Rome. The papal government knew that Napoleon had given his blessing to the Piedmontese expedition through the Papal States, and to the annexation of the Marche and Umbria. Some high-ranking figures in the papal government believed that it would be a mistake to antagonize the new Italian government. But the Secretary of State in Rome was Cardinal Antonelli, and in agreement with the Jesuits, he believed that no concessions should be offered to Italy, and that, anyhow, the new Kingdom would soon be torn apart by internal dissension.

The two intermediaries used by Cavour in his attempt to solve the Roman Question were a medical doctor, Diomede Pantaleoni, and a priest, Carlo Passaglia. Pantaleoni had been a conspirator in his young days, but later, like so many Mazzinians, had become a moderate, sympathizing with Piedmont. In 1848 he had been a deputy in the parliament in Rome, but had refused to stand for election to the assembly of the Roman Republic in 1849, and had stayed in Rome during the papal restoration. The police watched him, but since he was a respected medical doctor, he had many contacts with the aristocracy and prelates in Rome. He was a talkative and emotional man, not well suited to a delicate diplomatic mission but he had a clear understanding of the Roman Question, and Cavour valued his opinion. Cavour's second intermediary, Father Passaglia, had been a Jesuit, and was an eminent theologian. He had been one of Pio Nono's principal advisers when the pope was drawing up the dogma of the Immaculate Conception in 1854. In 1858 he had left the Jesuits, but had remained on good terms with the pope. Unfortunately, he was no better a diplomat than Pantaleoni, so that, although the two men through whom Cavour was to work seemed to have the right backgrounds for the job, their personalities made them less suitable.

On 18 October Cavour wrote to Pantaleoni asking him if the pope could be persuaded that there were better ways of guaranteeing his independence than depending on foreign arms. The question sounded simple, but it begged a more difficult one: what were 'foreign' arms for the papacy? It may have seemed to Cavour that Italian arms were not 'foreign' in Rome, but to the pope they seemed more 'foreign' than any other. Pantaleoni indeed replied that this might not be the moment to approach the pope, given his state of mind. Pio Nono was hoping that his fortunes would improve. A meeting had taken place in Warsaw between the czar, Alexander II, Francis Joseph, and William, the Prince Regent of Prussia, soon to be king. The result of the meeting was not yet known, but it was ominous for Italy that the Austrians were sending fresh forces into Venetia. Pantaleoni believed that the pope might become more pliable if the Warsaw meeting produced no results, if he had to give up hope of help from the Central and Eastern Powers, and if the resistance of the Bourbons ended completely. Pantaleoni further suggested that Cavour might make broad and generous offers to the pope, and then make them public if the pope rejected them. An element of hypocrisy and deception thus entered the negotiations even before they got under way, but Cavour was not averse to such methods if they suited his purpose. Pantaleoni's proposal could get him the good will of Europe by exposing the greed of the papacy, but Cavour would nevertheless have liked to reach agreement with the pope if it proved possible. Pantaleoni now contacted Father Passaglia, who had had discussions with Vittorio Emanuele, who had encouraged him to approach the pope. Even Farini, who hated the papacy almost as much as he hated the Mazzinians (he was strong on hatred), felt that the pope should be approached. Pantaleoni and Passaglia now worked together to get the support of a Cardinal – Sanducci, who was a regular adviser of Pio Nono. Sanducci succeeded in getting the pope to agree to consider proposals for a reconciliation.

Napoleon III then entered the discussion. He presented a project to the Piedmontese, whereby the Marche and Umbria would be restored to the pope, who would also be given the Abruzzi, which had been part of the Kingdom of Naples, but in return Italian troops would replace French troops in and around Rome. The project, although imaginative, was acceptable neither to Cavour nor to Pio Nono. Negotiations, however, continued throughout January, February and March of 1861. Eventually Pantaleoni was thrown out of Rome. Cavour's 'last political battle' had been lost, but in speeches to parliament on 25 and 27 March he made his position clear. Only Rome, he said, could in the end be the capital of Italy, 'but we must go to Rome only on two conditions. We must go in agreement with France. And we must do so only if we can avoid harming the Pope's spiritual power'.[8] It was his theme of 'a free Church in a free State'. The pope had to be convinced that his independence as spiritual head of the Church would not be lessened by the loss of his temporal power. Pio Nono never was to be so convinced. Yet the future was to prove Cavour right. In the long run the spiritual prestige of the Catholic Church increased after the pope had lost the last shred of his temporal power in 1870.

. . .

THE DEATH OF CAVOUR

Cavour died on 6 June 1861, aged only fifty years and ten months. He was said to have died of 'a fever'. He had been ill at Christmas, but had recovered, apart from suffering fits of insomnia. He had been at Leri on 18 May, but returned to Turin on the 19th. He was taken ill on 29 May, and was bled. On the morning of the 31st he appeared cured. He continued to work, seeing Nigra and other colleagues, but at midday was feverish and even delirious. He was again bled several times, and given quinine. Three doctors, including Senator Riberi, the king's doctor, treated him. With the knowledge of twentieth-century medical science we can say that he probably died of malaria, contracted on the rice fields of Leri. Cavour himself insisted on the bleedings, which almost certainly did more harm than good. Crowds gathered, at times threateningly, fearing that the priests would refuse Cavour the sacraments. On June 5 the king visited him. In a semi-delirious state Cavour asked him if a letter had arrived from Paris announcing Napoleon's recognition of the Kingdom of Italy. A friar, a friend of Cavour, was called on the same day. Cavour was probably too ill to make any confession, even if he had intended to do so, which seems unlikely, but at 5 p.m. on 6 June he was given extreme unction. In the nineteenth century great store was laid by a dying person's last words. Cavour, according to the traditional account, suddenly spoke so loudly that he could be heard in an adjoining room. He imagined, perhaps, that he was speaking in parliament on the Southern Question. The Neapolitans, he said, were very intelligent, but corrupt. It was necessary to 'wash' them. But they must not be governed by martial law. They must be treated with honesty, and their young must be educated with the principle of a 'free Church in a free State'. Michelangelo Castelli, one of Cavour's oldest friends, recorded his delirious chattering, and noted:

> No one heard him pronounce a word of hatred, or of rancour; all his feelings were of friendship, respect, compassion, hope . . . He died without agony.[9]

It was just before 7 a.m. on June 6.

Two Englishwomen reacted strongly to Cavour's death. Jessie White Mario, the friend of Garibaldi and Mazzini, considered it:

> a national disaster, since he alone in Europe knew how to impose his will on the emperor of the French and frustrate his plans.[10]

It was a tribute from a revolutionary who had always been on the opposite side of the barricades from Cavour. More profoundly moved was Elizabeth Barrett Browning. The day after Cavour's death she wrote from her home in Florence to her sister-in-law:

> I can scarcely command voice or hand to name 'Cavour'. That great soul which meditated and made Italy has gone to the diviner Country. If tears or blood could have saved him to us, he should have had mine.[11]

She herself died on 29 June, less than a month later. Her friend, the American sculptor, William Wetmore Story, noted that she left a half-finished letter to Jessie Mario, and commented:

> . . . it was for Italy that her last words were written; for her dear Italy were her last aspirations. The death of Cavour had greatly affected her . . . and it was perhaps the last feather that broke her down.[12]

Vast crowds attended Cavour's funeral, in the rain. He was buried at Santena in the chapel of the Castello Cavour, beside his nephew Augusto, who had been killed in the war of 1848. The sad truth was that he had not been close to the other relatives on his father's side, although a great number of people all over Western Europe had enjoyed the company of this remarkable man, and had felt real affection for him.[13]

. . .

NOTES AND REFERENCES

1. Giuseppe Massari, *Diario dalle cento voci 1858–1860*, edited by Emilia Morelli (Cappelli, Bologna, 1959), p. 469. Entry for 16 January 1860.
2. Romeo, vol. III, p. 677.
3. *Cavour-Nigra*, vol. 3, p. 294.
4. *ibid*, vol. 4, p. 122.
5. *ibid*, p. 145.
6. *ibid*, p. 183.
7. E. Passerin d'Entrèves, *L'ultima battaglia politica di Cavour* (Ilte, Turin, 1956).
8. Giorgio Candeloro, *Storia dell'Italia moderna*, vol. V (Feltrinelli, Milan, 1968).
9. Romeo, vol. III, p. 936.
10. Quoted by Carlo Tivaroni, *Storia critica del Risorgimento*, 9 vols., (Roux and Frassati, Turin), vol. 8, p. 400.
11. Joanna Richardson, *The Brownings*, (The Folio Society, London, 1986), p. 182.
12. *ibid*, p. 184.
13. For medical knowledge relating to the illness and death of Cavour, I am indebted to my friend, Dr Edwin Rosen.

Chapter 8

CAVOUR AND THE HISTORIANS

Cavour, like many political leaders of the nineteenth century, but in contrast with Bismarck, left no autobiography or reminiscences. This was perhaps not surprising in view of his sudden, and comparatively early death. But what Bismarck accomplished for himself, by his eloquent, if misleading memoirs, Cavour's friends and colleagues performed for him after his death. Consequently the first writings on Cavour are respectful, affectionate and almost invariably sympathetic. His friends and immediate successors published biographies, collections of letters and diaries giving a flattering picture of Cavour's genius, his success and his liberalism.

.   .   .

BEFORE 1914

An early historian who lived through the period of Cavour's achievements was Luigi Zini. Born in Modena in 1821, Zini published a *Storia d'Italia dal 1850 al 1866* in four volumes in 1866.[1] He was perhaps the first historian fully to analyse the position of Cavour, and if he was full of admiration for the Piedmontese statesman, Zini was also prepared to consider his failings. After pointing out that Massimo d'Azeglio, for all his virtues, was too closed in his mind to consider any further reduction in the prerogatives of the Crown beyond those secured in 1848, Zini contrasted Azeglio and Cavour. From the 'sterility of concepts' from which Azeglio suffered to the 'vivacity and feverish activity which characterized Cavour' the change was little less than an 'upheaval of state'.[2]

Zini recognized however – what some historians are only

getting around to realizing now – that the idea of uniting Italy came to Cavour very late in the day. Probably, according to Zini, Cavour always had a vague idea that one day Italy could be united, simply through the traditional policy of the Savoy dynasty, but this was as far as Cavour's thought went in 1852. However, as Zini pointed out, this was in full conformity with the practical, gradualist nature of Cavour's ideas. It was to Cavour's credit that, when the opportunity arose, he could look far beyond his original horizons, and aim at results which a few years before would have seemed madness to hope for.[3]

A charge made against Cavour in his own day was firmly refuted by Zini. This was that Cavour had forgotten the dictates of Machiavelli in the famous last chapter of the *Principe*, and had called a foreign power, with its great armies, into Italy, rather as Ludovico Sforza had done in 1494. Of course, Cavour's policy in 1859 was triumphantly successful for Italy, while Sforza's policy in 1494 was disastrous, and it could well have been argued that if Machiavelli had lived for another four or five centuries he would probably have admired Cavour's policy. Zini made the point firmly that the French arrival in Italy in 1859 led to great results for Italy, did not lead to Piedmont being subjected to French domination, and that it had clearly been necessary, since so many popular Italian movements, without the help of a great power, had failed in the past.

Zini also stressed Cavour's use of pungent irony in his parliamentary speeches, an irony which was not intended to raise personal resentments, and – perhaps surprisingly – rarely did so. Indeed, Cavour often seemed to regret the hilarity which his ironic remarks raised in the chamber. Although he had defeated his opponent by ridiculing him, he quickly tried to minimize the damage done, by some genuinely felt apology. Zini was probably right in saying that Cavour's sarcasms were rarely malicious, but were simply the products of clear argument and a rather too lively mind.

Zini was by no means always in agreement with Cavour's policy, however. He saw Cavour's commercial treaty with France as simply an act of deference by a small weak country to a powerful neighbour, unconvincingly disguised as a splendid assertion of the doctrine of free trade. He also stressed the modest role Cavour played in the Congress of Paris in 1856, and realized – as some historians have done only recently – that Lord Clarendon's apparent conversion to sympathy and support for Piedmont and Italy at the Congress was soon dispelled when Clarendon returned to London and came under the influence of Palmerston, whose Italian policy was much more cautious at that point.

Zini concluded that Cavour had perhaps died at the right moment so far as his reputation was concerned. Both Heinrich von Treitschke and Benedetto Croce repeated this conviction later, but whereas they were to provide explanations for their judgements, Zini merely added that while Cavour was precisely the right man for the right moment, if he had lived any longer he might have fallen into a fatal period of declining success. It is worth mentioning that Zini took some pleasure in pointing out the failings of his contemporaries, Farini, Ricasoli, Lamarmora and Minghetti among them. Only Zini himself emerges from his history wholly free from blame. He was an admirer of Cavour, but a critical admirer.

Another historian of the moderate school – a rather more influential one than Luigi Zini – was Nicomede Bianchi. A Piedmontese, born in 1818, Bianchi published a study of Cavour only two years after the statesman's death, but the work for which he is best known, and which was still regarded as a standard text in the 1950s, was his *Storia documentata della diplomazia europea in Italia dall'anno 1814 all'anno 1861*, published in eight volumes from 1865 to 1872.[4] The work was considered indiscreet in its day, because it used confidential documents written by people who had only recently died, or in some cases were still alive. To this charge Bianchi replied that 'true friends of the fatherland' would not want to hide anything they had written during these important years of Italian history. There is little doubt that Bianchi's work did a great deal for the reputation of Cavour, but it did it by the selection of favourable documents and the omission of less favourable ones. Also, Bianchi's documents were translations from French into Italian – and very often mistranslations. Alessandro Luzio – of whom more in a moment – writing in the 1930s, charged Bianchi's interpretation, according to which Cavour's genius was the main factor in the unification of Italy, as being based on false evidence. This was going too far, and even Luzio recognized that Bianchi was the first historian to demonstrate that the unification of Italy depended on European factors. Just as Cavour had 'Europeanized' the Italian Question, so Bianchi had Europeanized the historiography of the Italian question.

Writing very much in the tradition started by Bianchi was another Piedmontese historian, Luigi Chiala. Born in 1834, and so belonging to a younger generation than Cavour, Chiala was nevertheless editing an important journal, the *Rivista Contemporanea*, from 1853 to 1857, during the formative years of Cavour's foreign policy, and fought in the war of 1859. Chiala continued the Piedmontese tradition of playing down the role of the democrats in the *risorgimento*, and making Cavour the central and most successful figure. Like Bianchi, he published documents, and omitted passages which did not fit his interpretation, though he was less malicious towards the democrats than Bianchi had been. Like Bianchi, he was, of course, a moderate. His main contribution was *Le lettere edite e inedite di Cavour*, published in six volumes, plus a volume of index, from 1884 to 1887.[5] This has for many years been regarded as the standard collection of Cavour's letters, and it is only now being replaced by a national collection, the *Epistolario*.[6] Chiala's original publication is more than a collection of letters, since half of the work is introductory in theory, but contains long extracts from Cavour's speeches in parliament, and in practice constitutes a full biography.

The third of the three pro-moderate, pro-Cavour historians who wrote soon after Cavour's death was not a Piedmontese, but a Neapolitan, who had found political refuge in Piedmont – Giuseppe Massari. Born in 1824, Massari wrote sooner than Chiala, and his large biography of Cavour, *Il Conte di Cavour, Ricordi biografici*, was published in 1873.[7] His more important work was, however, his life of Vittorio Emanuele, published in 1878.[8] Both of them give extravagant praise to the Piedmontese prime minister and king. Massari was a close friend of Cavour, and his diary[9] is an immensely important source for historians today, but he wrote his biographies for immediate consumption. They are romances rather than history. He puts into direct speech dialogues, for example, between Cavour and the king, on imaginary occasions when Massari was not present. Yet subsequent historians have often accepted Massari's account without question, simply because it is known that Massari was a close friend of Cavour. Perhaps it is important to realize that fiction is always fiction, even when written by someone who was a protagonist of the events. The diary, however, falls into a different category from the biographies, because it is a straightforward record of the events day by day, and was not written to impress anyone.

A classic example of the interpretation of the unification of Italy as an epic history, a glorious synthesis of revolutions, wars and international power politics, was given by Carlo Tivaroni, who published a nine-volume work, the *Storia critica del risorgimento*, between 1888 and 1897.[10] He regarded the historian as a conciliator, someone who could show that the work of Mazzini, Garibaldi and Cavour was all needed if Italy was to be united. In a significant passage, Tivaroni wrote:

In this lies the greatness of the unitarians, and of Mazzini more than anyone: that they maintained intact their faith in unity, when it appeared to be madness to everyone who considered himself wise. Here lies the glory of Mazzini and Garibaldi: that they constrained the House of Savoy to accept unity. Without doubt however, if the king had made a premature proclamation of unity [in 1859], when Mazzini wanted him to do so, it would have turned all the other Italian princes into open enemies; instead of remaining neutral they would have sent their armies to help Austria. So the prudence of Cavour and Vittorio Emanuele played their part, just as did the constancy of Mazzini and the audacity of Garibaldi. Without these four men, each one in his own sphere of action, what would have happened to Italy if any one of them had been lacking? How, with only Mazzini, or with only Garibaldi, could Austria ever have been defeated? And how, with only Cavour and with only Vittorio Emanuele could anyone have thought of overcoming the grave obstacles presented by Rome and Naples? And without Naples and Rome would the Kingdom of Italy not have remained always under the tutelage of France?[11]

The rhetorical questions are appealing, but if this kind of argument – valid though it is – is stressed too often or too forcefully, it is easily forgotten that the liberal or moderate forces, on the one hand, and the republican and democratic forces on the other, were not just rivals: they were bitter enemies. Tivaroni is a little misleading when he says: 'Mazzini was the goad, Cavour the brake, Garibaldi the courage accompanied by a practical sense'. Was Cavour never more than a brake? But when Tivaroni adds: 'in the midst of their struggles, their contradictions and recriminations, Italy was made', it is difficult to refute his conclusion.[12]

Specifically on Cavour, Tivaroni believed that one of his great achievements was the introduction of parliamentary government into Italy. Tivaroni stressed, too, that Cavour became an Italian nationalist very late in the day. As we have seen, Zini had already been aware of the fact, but Tivaroni takes Nicomede Bianchi to task for concealing this aspect of Cavour's aims. Tivaroni quotes Mazzini's comment on Cavour – a comment perhaps not familiar to many: 'The only statesman of the monarchy, a man without creative genius, but rich in the ability to profit from the genius of others', and gives an example of how Cavour adopted the inspiration of others. When Palermo and Naples had been annexed to the emerging Italian state, Cavour had enough courage to say in parliament that Rome must one day be the capital of Italy. At the time it seemed an uncharacteristically radical statement for Cavour to make – a surprising theft of an idea which only the Mazzinis and the Garibaldis had expressed in the past.

A great literary scholar, Francesco De Sanctis, had an interesting observation to make on Cavour. De Sanctis is best known as the author of the classic *Storia della letteratura italiana*,[13] but his reference to Cavour comes in *Mazzini e la scuola democratica*, which is volume 1 of *La letteratura italiana nel secolo XIX*.[14] Cavour made him minister of education in his first Italian government. De Sanctis's comment contributed to the creation of the myth that the unification of Italy needed all kinds of political creeds, movements and skills to achieve success, and that they all complemented each other. As Mussolini put it, very succinctly, *C'è di tutto* – 'There is everything in it'. But De Sanctis at least realized that it was not simply a question of elements complementing each other. He was aware of the struggle and conflict between what he called 'the liberal and democratic schools':

It might seem that the attrition between these two schools must have led to chaos, not to national unity. In fact in Italian history many failures and reactions resulted from the internal struggles between these two. That they might function together at the supreme moment, the liberal school needed a man of genius, capable of scorning the system, and who, although a conservative, might drive himself into action. And there was a need, on the other hand, of a man of elevated spirit, who, seeing that the undertaking was nearly completed by the hated monarchy, and that the power which every party needed was snatched away from the democrats, would hold out his hand to his rivals. Italy was fortunate in that the genius of Cavour and the patriotism of Garibaldi worked together. This is why these two men, who had fought each other in their lifetimes, were put on the same pedestal by new generations, and considered complementary to each other, both necessary factors in the national *risorgimento*.[15]

In considering what the adult world of scholarship thought of Cavour in the nineteenth century, it is interesting to discover what was taught to children about him. Fortunately we have *Cuore*, by Edmondo De Amicis, an immensely popular and successful book, published in 1886. De Amicis was born in 1846, and fought in the battle of Custozza in 1866. His frank intention in writing *Cuore* was to teach schoolchildren the simple virtues of selflessness and respect for parents and homeland. The passage on Cavour provides a direct statement of the great statesman as father of the fatherland. It takes the form of advice from a father to his small son:

Who Cavour was you cannot understand at the moment. For now you need know only this: he was for many years the prime minister of Piedmont: it was he who sent the Piedmontese army to the Crimea, so that, by the victory of the Cernaia, they might increase our military glory, which had collapsed with the defeat of Novara; it was he who made a hundred and forty thousand Frenchmen descend from the Alps to chase the Austrians from Lombardy; it was he who governed Italy in the most solemn period of our revolution, who gave in those years the most powerful impulse to the sacred task of the unification of our country, with his shining genius, his invincible constancy, with his more than human industry. Many generals passed terrible hours on the field of battle, but he passed more terrible ones in his study, when his enormous work could have been ruined from one moment to the next, like a fragile building by an earthquake: he passed hours, nights of struggle and anguish, from which he emerged with his reason disturbed or with death in his heart. And it was this gigantic and tempestuous work which shortened his life by twenty years.[16]

The first article in English by an historian was Lord Acton's appreciation in *The Rambler* in July 1861, on Cavour's death. Acton, always preoccupied with liberty, wrote of Cavour: 'His policy was directed to the greatness of the State, not to the liberty of the people'.[17] The first full study of Cavour in English was H. Bolton King's *History of Italian Unity*, published in 1899. Oddly enough, the book did not attract much attention until Alcan in Paris published a French translation in 1901. From Balliol College, Oxford, Bolton King had moved to Toynbee Hall, which had been founded in 1885. Today it may seem strange that a work dealing with the political history of Italy should emerge from an institution in the East End of London which was concerned with the enlightenment of the poor. It must be remembered, though, that the British working classes in the nineteenth century were always concerned for the struggles for freedom in Europe, whether in Poland, Bulgaria or Italy.

Bolton King's book was to remain standard reading for British students for many years, although it was not based on archives, but rather on secondary works in the British Museum, and since only a few volumes of the Piedmontese parliamentary debates were available in the British Museum, Bolton King remained ignorant of an important part of Cavour's work. On the other hand, a great merit of his study was his recognition of the economic problem posed by the poverty of the South. It had perhaps never been quite so fully realized – even by Italian historians – that the South was so very much poorer than the rest of Italy. Cavour himself, of course, had seen the enormity of the problem, and Bolton King quoted Cavour's remark: 'to harmonize the North with the South is more difficult than to fight Austria or struggle with Rome'. It had been precisely because the South was so desperately poor, so corrupt and so priest-ridden, that Cavour had assumed in 1859 that Italy was not ready for unification, and in 1860 he had accepted it only because Garibaldi had thrust it upon him. Bolton King showed that Cavour quickly adjusted himself to the *fait accompli*, and decided that, since Naples had to be part of Italy, its material conditions must be improved as rapidly as possible. He quoted Cavour's formula: '*Unificare per migliorare, migliorare per consolidare*' ('Unite to improve, improve to consolidate'), although Cavour added that it would take at least ten years.[18] Sadly we might add that 140 years have not been enough.

Like other historians, Bolton King felt obliged to compare and contrast Cavour and Bismarck. 'Cavour', he wrote, 'was often compared with Bismarck, but, notwithstanding the similarity of their work, their methods had nothing in common, except a common disposition to lie, when lying served their purposes. But while the lies of Cavour arrived one by one, those of Bismarck arrived in avalanches'.[19]

A historian writing before 1914, one of the finest to write on Cavour, was Francesco Ruffini, who was born in 1863, and published his *La giovinezza del Conte di Cavour* in 1912.[20] He made one observation on Cavour that had not been made before. Cavour's famous formula 'a free Church in a free State' was greeted by radicals with enthusiasm, but many people whose background was closer to Cavour's must have been puzzled by it. How could someone who had grown up in the devoutly Catholic city of Turin ever have conceived the separation of Church and State as an ideal for Italy? Ruffini offered an explanation – it was an idea Cavour had acquired in Switzerland, from Protestant sources. Indeed, Ruffini was perhaps more interested in the history of religion than in the history of the *risorgimento*, and his *Religious Liberty* was published in an English translation in 1912, with a preface by J.B. Bury, who was enthusing over the separation of church and state which had been introduced into France in 1905. What Ruffini achieved in his study of Cavour was an interpretation of the political philosophy of his subject, an interpretation which showed Cavour's thought to be far more complex and sophisticated – and radical – than had previously been realized.

. . .

BETWEEN THE WARS

Bridging the gap between the pre-1914 and the inter-war periods was Alfredo Oriani's *La lotta politica in Italia*.[21] Although published in 1892, it made its biggest impact after the war, appealing to both liberals and Fascists, for different reasons. A nationalist and an imperialist, Oriani painted his *risorgimento* in vivid colours, and it was the extravagance of his language, rather than his historical interpretation, that appealed to the Fascists. But Benedetto Croce also praised the work for taking the grand overall view of Italian history, a view which Croce considered Hegelian in its approach.

Oriani gave a glowing impression of Cavour. Comparing political leaders in other countries with the heroes of the *risorgimento*, he argued that

> no modern hero was the equal of Garibaldi; no apostle of politics had a soul more tragic than Mazzini, words more evocative, a patience more unconquered; between Cavour and Bismarck the difference is one of national background; the former was the master of dexterity and the latter of rigidity: rubber and granite, both unbreakable . . . Bismarck's idea was a projectile which drills through and ruins all obstacles, Cavour's was a vortex which attracted, encircled, condensed and formed a fatherland: Cavour often had to be humble, sometimes abject, but he resolved more difficult problems than his rival.

Fascist historians were not so enthusiastic about Cavour as Oriani had been. They were bound to feel ambivalent towards a parliamentarian who was averse to dictatorship.

A sharp criticism of Cavour came from an unexpected source – in that it was a severely academic one, and followed a rather surprising line of argument, Alessandro Luzio, who was born in 1857, but lived through the Fascist period to 1942, did great services for Italian historiography, always working from primary sources, and publishing important documents. Yet his political judgement was far from sound. Not only did he stay in Italy under Mussolini (which most academics were obliged, by circumstances, to do), but in his last year, as an old man, he gave his support to the racist and extreme right-wing Republic of Salò. In his writings on the *risorgimento* he praised both of the Piedmontese kings, Carlo Alberto and Vittorio Emanuele II, and attacked Cavour for refusing to serve Carlo Alberto. Cavour, Luzio believed, was egocentric in preferring to grow cabbages and vines instead of playing a role in government under Carlo Alberto. However, in attacking Cavour along these lines Luzio was perhaps unconsciously seeing an analogy with his own age, when some of his contemporaries and colleagues went into exile rather than work under Mussolini and Vittorio Emanuele III, while Luzio kept his professional post in Italy, and worked on official committees.

The positive value of Luzio's work, however, was his immense respect for documentary evidence: some documents in the Helfert collection in Vienna, he said, 'made his mouth water'. He thought of the historian as a judge (and here he approached the attitude of Acton), a judge who must listen to all the evidence, sum it up for the benefit of the jury (or, in the case of the historian, of his readers), and, while he must have his own convictions, he must hint at them only very discreetly. It was his contribution to the editing of documents that made Luzio immensely valuable to a study of Cavour's role in history. He sat on the commission chaired by Paolo Boselli, which edited the important collection of documents, *Il carteggio Cavour-Nigra dal 1858 al 1861*. The documents brought to light by this collection showed that the edition of Cavour's letters by Chiala was not always reliable.

One French historian of the inter-war years deserves mention. Maurice Paléologue, the French ambassador in Rome, pointed out in his work, *Un grand réaliste, Cavour*, published in 1926, an aspect of the statesman which is sometimes forgotten: that he had started his political career from the unpromising base of 'a little kingdom which had been conquered, invaded, carved up, ruined – which was ashamed of itself, and ridiculed in the outside world for the mad temerity of its recent adventure'.[22] It was on such a base that Cavour's achievements had to be built.

The Italians were grateful for the sympathetic interpretations of foreign historians. When the American historian, William Roscoe Thayer, published his *Life and Times of Cavour*,[23] which gave extravagant praise to its subject, a liberal Italian senator, Raffaele De Cesare, suggested that the Italian state should pay for an Italian translation and edition. The minister of education accepted the proposition, but suggested that Trevelyan's *Garibaldi and the Making of Italy*[24] should have similar treatment. These were the days of Giolitti and democracy – June 1912. The darkness of Fascism still lay beneath the horizon.

A changed attitude was bound to come with Fascism. Italy was still a monarchy under the House of Savoy when she became involved in war against Britain and the U.S.A. in the 1940s.

· · ·

SINCE 1945

One of the most penetrating studies of Cavour was made by the Sicilian historian, Adolfo Omodeo. Born in 1889, Omodeo published first in the Fascist period, but his real impact came after 1945. He had started his career with the study of early Christianity, and in particular of St Paul. In no sense, however, did he belong to a clerical school of historians, but what did remain with him from his earlier studies was a fascination with the individuals who have influenced history – not necessarily 'great men', but men who played a significant role, either through the accident of being in a particular place at a particular moment, or through their own ability.

Omodeo's great work, the *Opera politica del conte di Cavour*, Part I, *1848–1857* was published in 1940, and Part II was never written. He had always been opposed to Fascism, although he had remained in Italy under the regime, as Professor of the History of the Church in Naples University. He joined the *Partito d'Azione*, as did so many intellectuals, in 1944, and was briefly minister of education in the coalition government of that year. He died in 1946. A collection of several of his writings, published posthumously in 1951, under the title *Difesa del Risorgimento*, covers the period of Cavour's career from Plombières to his death.

Much writing on Cavour before Omodeo had depicted the statesman as an idealistic liberal. Even Ruffini, in a very sophisticated way, had put across this line, as had Thayer. It was still present in writings in English when A.J. Whyte published his *Early Life and Letters of Cavour* in 1925[25] and *Political Life and Letters of Cavour* in 1930.[26] The interpretation of Cavour as a *Realpolitiker*, rather than an idealist, was perhaps inaugurated by the German nationalist historian, Heinrich von Treitschke, who had written an essay on Cavour as early as 1869. Translations of Treitschke's work reached Italy only in 1921, just in time for a generation of Fascist historians, who, in so far as they admired Cavour at all, liked to see him as a *Realpolitiker* in the tradition of Machiavelli. The Fascist novelist and writer of fantasies, Alfredo Panzini, published his *Conte di Cavour*[27] in 1931, a highly popular work which was in fact plagiarized from the writings of Treitschke. Oddly enough, today most historians of nineteenth-century Europe are more inclined to accept the *Realpolitiker* interpretation than the liberal idealist one. It may be, indeed, that we have now gone too far in that direction. Cavour's was an immensely complex personality. Although his education had been a somewhat patchy one, spent in an institution to which he had felt hostile, he was a highly educated man, having read and thought a great deal. There was room in that remarkable statesman for high ideals and *Realpolitik*, for Rousseau and Machiavelli, for Immanuel Kant and Jeremy Bentham.

Omodeo had studied first under Giovanni Gentile, the idealist philosopher who had gone over to Fascism, become a senator, and written the famous article on Fascism, with Mussolini, in the *Enciclopedia Italiana*. Omodeo took issue with his former mentor when Gentile argued, following Treitschke, that Cavour was always prepared to throw aside his high idealism if *raison d'état* demanded. Gentile had written:

For this Fatherland of his, he [Cavour] was ready, as are all great statesmen and founders of nations, to sell his soul; on the altar of this Fatherland of his he would not have hesitated for a single moment to burn all his sentiments, all his interests, all his preconceived ideas, even the Statuto, if it had been necessary, even religion, if it had been shown to be incompatible with the State in which the Fatherland was incarnate.[28]

Omodeo certainly did not deny that Cavour was an opportunist in the sense that he chose the right moment for his political moves, in a classically Machiavellian sense, but all this opportunism was in the pursuit of a liberal ideal, an ideal first for Piedmont, and then for Italy – and it had nothing to do with the statism with which Gentile was besotted. If, Omodeo argued, Cavour had been prepared to forget his ideals entirely in an opportunistic manner, he would have served under Carlo Alberto, instead of growing rice and caring for cattle at Leri.

Omodeo recognized, however, that Cavour had moments of uncertainty, of indecision, of improvisation, and sometimes made mistakes, precisely on his own political, diplomatic ground. It was this refinement of interpretation on Omodeo's part that distinguished him from the earlier supporters of Cavour – from Chiala, Bianchi and Massari, writers who refused to admit that Cavour could ever take a false step.

Omodeo stressed the point that Cavour established a parliamentary regime in Piedmont, and that he did so in the teeth of opposition from the king, the senate and the Church. He was also the first historian to put across the more sophisticated interpretation of Cavour's role in the intervention of Piedmont in the Crimean War. If those of us who have written since have given slightly different emphases, here and there, to the interpretation, it was Omodeo who drew the broad lines in a manner that does not differ basically from that given in Chapter 3 of this book.

For Alessandro Luzio, Mazzini had been the great prophet of Italian unity, and Cavour had adopted the idea and exploited it at the last moment, in 1860. Their achievements were thus, in Luzio's interpretation, complementary. Omodeo, on the other hand, saw the interplay between the two men and their ideas as a dialectic, which started as a confrontation between a thesis and an antithesis, but ended as a synthesis, without their intending this to happen, or even realizing that it was happening. Cavour had once said that he would be prepared to use the bodies of republican revolutionaries as manure on his farm, and at heart never changed his attitude on the point, while Mazzini never recognized Cavour's 1861 Kingdom of Italy as being in any sense 'Italy' at all. There are, then, difficulties in regarding their achievements as complementary except in Omodeo's sense that the two men represented contrasting energies and aims which were both present in the complex pattern of Italian opinion.

Omodeo was also perhaps the first historian to recognize a fact that Denis Mack Smith's work was firmly to establish: that Cavour lost the initiative to Garibaldi in the spring of 1860, and there was then a hiatus in the development of Cavour's policy until the autumn.

On Cavour's policy towards the Church, Omodeo differed rather from Ruffini's interpretation. While Ruffini had detected a Swiss, if not a Protestant, origin in Cavour's 'free Church in a free State', Omodeo believed that the formula was the result of much discussion in Turin, within Cavour's own cabinet, and with Catholic priests as well as his own colleagues, Costantino Nigra, Marco Minghetti, and others. Omodeo treated the formula as if it were a novel, Italian, creation, whereas really, of course, the separation of church and state had been adopted in Belgium, with its Catholic population, in the 1830s, and also in the U.S.A. Cavour was certainly not unaware of these precedents.

Luigi Salvatorelli realized, perhaps more clearly than Omodeo, the conflict between Cavour's ideas and those of Mazzini. Born in Umbria in 1866, Salvatorelli was three years older than Omodeo, and yet in some ways seemed closer to historians of the later generation. Graduating at the age of twenty – an achievement even less common in Italy than in Britain – Salvatorelli, like Omodeo, started his historical studies by writing on early Christianity, but more quickly developed an interest in the contemporary political scene. Having to choose between a Chair at the University of Naples or a career in journalism, he chose the latter and became editor of La Stampa. This was before Mussolini came to power. In 1925 Salvatorelli was forced to leave La Stampa, and then, wisely, returned to Christian studies with lives of St Francis of Assisi and St Benedict. More courageously, he then studied the history of political thought, and published Il pensiero politico italiano dal 1700 al 1870 in 1935.[29] Salvatorelli was thus writing about Cavour at the time when Mussolini was at the peak of his power, but there is no concession in his work to the political ideas fashionable at that moment.

Salvatorelli saw the flaw in Omodeo's concept of Cavour and Mazzini as parts of a dialectic which would lead to a concrete historical conclusion. Already in an essay written in 1934, but not published until 1948, he had written:

> It would not be exact to say that Mazzini and Cavour had co-operated . . . to reach a result, which, uniting their work, transcended them both. It would be a beautiful construction of historical mediation, but an arbitrary one: a little poem, a pastoral eclogue, not history. In reality there was in the struggle a winner and a loser; Cavour the winner, Mazzini the loser.[30]

However, in a later work, *Pensiero e azione del Risorgimento*, published in 1943, Salvatorelli suggested that there was one sense in which the activities of the two men could be regarded as complementary – the sense in which Mazzini was concerned only with ends, while Cavour was concerned with means, with the continual political struggle. It could, of course, be argued that Mazzini attempted his own means to an end, but that they never achieved any end at all. And it must be said that Mazzini seemed almost not to care if his revolutionary attempts succeeded or failed. The main thing was to carry out one's duty, to struggle endlessly, desperately, for an ideal end. The more serious objection to this part of Salvatorelli's argument is, of course, that the two men had quite different aims, and whereas Cavour achieved his, after several failures and changes of policy, Mazzini never achieved his, except for a very brief moment when he was ruling the Roman Republic in 1849. That was a very ephemeral victory, and – typically for Mazzini – more a moral victory than a political one.

One specific achievement of Cavour that Salvatorelli stressed was his blocking of attempts by Vittorio Emanuele to assert his personal power. Denis Mack Smith's book, *Italy and its Monarchy*,[31] makes it clear that after Cavour's death, the king, and his successor, Umberto I, once again secured more power than a constitutional monarch should be allowed, though they secured it only in a haphazard manner, from time to time.

A fine Jesuit historian, Pietro Pirri, in his *Pio IX, Vittorio Emanuele dal loro carteggio privato*,[32] gave an interpretation of the history of Italy after 1856, which has little good to say of Napoleon III or of Vittorio Emanuele, but, surprisingly, perhaps, puts Cavour's stated policy in a not unfavourable light. For Father Pirri, Napoleon III was the powerful emperor who allowed the pope to be deprived of all his territory except Lazio; Vittorio Emanuele was the monarch who accepted all the loot while trying to place the blame for his actions on Napoleon or on Cavour. In contrast to these two hypocrites Cavour at least stated his policy frankly, in his two famous speeches of 25 and 27 March 1861 on the Roman Question, when he said that Rome must ultimately be the capital of Italy.

After the second world war Italian scholarship of the *risorgimento* was injected with new arguments and creative ideas by the writings of Gramsci. One of the founders of the Italian Communist Party, Antonio Gramsci was also one of the two or three most interesting Marxist theorists of the twentieth century. He was born in Sardinia in 1891, was arrested by the Fascists in 1926 and lived until 1937 in prison, dying that year soon after his removal to a hospital. His writings on the *risorgimento* consist of brief snippets, collected together after the war and published as *Il Risorgimento*.[33] So far as the role of Cavour is concerned, the effect of Gramsci's writings was to play down the contrasts and confrontations of Cavour and the moderates on the one hand, and Mazzini and the democrats on the other. Gramsci argued that the Italian middle classes in fact formed a homogeneous group, because the Party of Action – the Mazzinians – were not identified with any working-class or peasant group: their interests were really the same as those of the moderates – in the last resort the same as those of Cavour. Thus when Vittorio Emanuele said that he had the Party of Action 'in his pocket', he was stating more than the simple fact that he had secured the personal loyalty of Garibaldi. He was saying in effect that the Party of Action was ' "directed" indirectly' (the phrase is Gramsci's) 'by Cavour and the King'.[34] Francesco Crispi had said that Cavour had merely 'diplomatized the revolution', to which Gramsci commented: 'Cavour was not only a diplomat, but essentially a political "creator", only that his method of "creating" was not that of a revolutionary, but of a conservative: and in the last analysis it was not the programme of Mazzini and Garibaldi that triumphed, but that of Cavour'.[35] To call Cavour a 'conservative' is clearly unsatisfactory in many respects, since he did so much more than 'conserve', but equally, in many other respects, the term 'liberal' is not entirely satisfactory. The concept of the 'creator' in history has a distinctly Hegelian ring about it, and reminds us that Gramsci started his career as an idealist, a student of Croce, and only subsequently revolted against Croce, as Marx had revolted against Hegel. However, although Gramsci saw Cavour as a 'creator', and, ultimately, as a creator of Italian unity, he had no illusions about the nature of Cavour's creation: Cavour 'conceived unity as an increasing of the Piedmontese state and of the patrimony of the dynasty, not at base a national movement, but a royal conquest'.[36] It can, of course, be argued that the unification of Italy, far from being a royal conquest by the House of Savoy, can be seen as the extension of free institutions (not democratic, but nevertheless free, institutions) from Turin to the rest of Italy.

In Gramsci's eyes the ideas of Vincenzo Gioberti and Giuseppe Mazzini were doomed to failure because of existing realities in Europe, whereas the political realism and empiricism of Cavour were more likely to succeed. The ideas of the French Revolution had been able to reach Western, Central and some of Eastern Europe simply because France had existed for several centuries as a major power in Europe. Gioberti's belief in 1843 (which he later abandoned) that a democratic Catholicism could be spread by Italians throughout Europe, and Mazzini's conviction that from Rome could be spread a pure democracy, were destined to be disappointed, because Italy simply did not exist in political terms. Cavour, on the other hand, with realistic, if limited, aims, could seize the initiative, and actually utilize French power for his own ends.

Gramsci believed, of course, that a popular revolution would have been possible in nineteenth-century Italy if there had been a middle class which was prepared to listen to the wishes of the peasants and the people as a whole, as the men of France had been in 1789, at least briefly. The Italian *risorgimento*, in Gramsci's eyes was an agrarian revolution *manqué*, but he realized, of course, that there was no question of Cavour leading such a revolution, nor, indeed, of Mazzini doing so.

A socialist historian who wrote perhaps the best detailed narrative history of modern Italy was Giorgio Candeloro. His account ran into eleven volumes, of which Volume IV is the relevant one for Cavour.[37] There is little overt Marxist character in Candeloro's balanced and dispassionate account, but Gramsci's interpretation is never rejected or queried. Cavour's love of the *juste-milieu* is closely analysed, Candeloro points out that there was 'a notable dose of conservatism' in it, but

> Cavour all the same did not want to conserve what was left of the old aristocratic structure: he wanted, on the contrary, to eliminate every remnant of feudal privilege; he laughed at the illusions and the petty caste spirit of the reactionary nobles and judged that the absolute monarchy had passed its sell-by date.[38]

An English historian who has written in a radical, rather than a socialist tradition is Denis Mack Smith. When Mack Smith published his *Cavour and Garibaldi 1860. A study in political conflict* in 1954,[39] it created a considerable stir in Italy, and for many years Italian historians were eager to dispute points with him, and to challenge his conclusions. They have always respected Mack Smith's historical erudition, and his immense familiarity with the primary sources, both printed and manuscript, but they have found it difficult to forgive the severity of his condemnation of Cavour. Mack Smith was taught in Cambridge by G.M. Trevelyan, and his *Cavour and Garibaldi 1860* is dedicated to G.M. and Janet Trevelyan. For Trevelyan, Garibaldi had been the great hero, the centre of an astonishing epic, but Trevelyan had never attacked Cavour for his treatment of Garibaldi. This Mack Smith proceeded to do in no uncertain manner.

He was surely justified in underlining the shabby treatment Cavour gave Garibaldi in 1860. His argument that Garibaldi would probably have done better as a governor of the South than the Piedmontese generals did is a convincing one, but his belief that Garibaldi might have got away with the taking of Rome in 1860 was bound to raise a storm of protest from Italian historians. Such arguments are, of course, speculations on both sides, but historians have perhaps been – and still are – too ready to accept the idea that a Garibaldian march on Rome in 1860 would have led to a clash with the French. Napoleon III's force in Rome was much smaller than Garibaldi's, which, by September 1860, numbered over 20,000, rather than the original Thousand. It is quite conceivable that Napoleon would have withdrawn his small force, rather than face defeat, and would then have depended on diplomacy, and perhaps an international congress, to resolve the Roman Question. However, this all presupposes inactivity on Cavour's part, and, as we know, Cavour in the event took the colossal gamble of invading the Papal States and confronting Garibaldi with a Piedmontese army. For this act, also, Mack Smith condemned him.

Mack Smith continued his criticisms of Cavour in subsequent articles, but in the preface to his biography of Cavour, published in 1985, he puts his subject in a far more favourable light, by saying that although Cavour 'sometimes made what by his own judgement were serious mistakes of judgement and employed methods which he thought would be discreditable . . . his ability can be appreciated only after tracing not only his successes . . . but the difficulties, the uncertainties, the errors', and he concludes: 'No politician of the century . . . made so much out of so little.' It must be said that the mistakes and the errors of Cavour are rather more in evidence in Mack Smith's book than the successes are, and yet a fair picture emerges in the end.[40]

A short study in English has been made by an American Catholic historian, Frank Coppa.[41] A balanced and impartial study, it shows no trace of religious prejudice, and is agreeably free of the powerful influences of previous historians discussed in this chapter. If Coppa dealt rather more with Cavour's domestic achievements than with those of his foreign policy, he has effectively redressed the balance with his fine study of *The Origins of the Wars of Italian Independence*.[42]

The attempt to write 'definitive' history is always a vain one. Something more will always remain to be said, whether the subject is the rise or fall of a civilization or the life of one person. Also, as the spirit of the times changes, so new interpretations will have to be made. But in so far as there has been a definitive life of Cavour, it is Rosario Romeo's massive study, *Cavour e il suo tempo*, which runs to three volumes.[43]

Romeo, a Sicilian, born in 1924, published his *Il Risorgimento in Sicilia* in 1950,[44] but became better known with the publication of two essays, *Risorgimento e Capitalismo* in 1959.[45] Primarily an attack on Gramsci, *Risorgimento e Capitalismo* was the work of a passionate anti-communist, and with those of us who had to withstand his letters he did not restrain the strength of his political feelings. Yet his fine work on Cavour is brilliantly objective, and interprets the statesman in a depth which goes almost beyond the point at which judgements can be made. Lord Acton believed that it was the main function of a historian to make value judgements of the figures of history who had escaped punishment in their own day. However, every historian who has studied any figure in depth knows that such a task becomes more difficult the more familiar the figure becomes. With Cavour final judgement is difficult, but fortunately historians have never given up trying to reach it. It is unlikely that they ever will.

. . .

NOTES AND REFERENCES

1. L. Zini, *Storia d'Italia dal 1850 al 1866*, 4 vols., (Treves, Milan, 1866).
2. *ibid.*
3. *ibid.*
4. N. Bianchi, *Storia documentata della diplomazia europea in Italia dall'anno 1814 all'anno 1861*, 8 vols., (Unione Tipografica, Turin 1865–72).
5. L. Chiala, *Le Lettere edite e inedite di Cavour*, 6 vols. (Roux, Turin, 1884–87).
6. National Commission for the publication of the correspondence of the Count of Cavour, 12 volumes (Zanichelli, Bologna, 1962–1990).
7. G. Massari, *Il Conte di Cavour, Ricordi Biografici* (Botta, Turin, 1873).
8. G. Massari, *La vita e il regno di Vittorio Emanuele II, primo re d'Italia* (Treves, Milan, 1878).
9. G. Massari, *Diario dalle cento voci, 1858–1860*, edited by Emilia Morelli (Cappelli, Bologna, 1959).
10. C. Tivaroni, *Storia critica del risorgimento*, 9 vols. (Roux e Frascati, Turin, 1888–97).
11. *ibid*, vol. ix, pp. 202–3.

12. *ibid*, p. 201.
13. F. De Sanctis, *Storia della letteratura italiana*, edited by N. Gallo, in the *Opere* of De Sanctis (Einaudi, Turin, 1958).
14. F. De Sanctis, *La letteratura italiania nel secolo XIX*, vol 1, edited by Giorgio Candeloro and Carlo Mascetta (Einaudi, Turin, 1953).
15. *ibid*, pp. 22–23.
16. Edmondo De Amicis, *Cuore* (Garzanti, Milan, 1943 edition), pp. 164–65.
17. Republished in *Historical Essays and Studies*, by John Emerich Edward Dalberg-Acton, First Baron Acton, edited by John Neville Figgis and Reginald Vere Lawrence (Macmillan, London, 1926), p. 182.
18. H. Bolton King, *History of Italian Unity*, Italian edition (Treves, Milan, 1909–10), vol. II, pp. 199–203.
19. *ibid*, p. 238.
20. F. Ruffini, *La giovinezza del Conte di Cavour* (Bocca, Turin, 1912).
21. A. Oriani, *La lotta politica in Italia* (Roux and Frassati, Turin, 1892).
22. M. Paléologue, *Un grand réaliste. Cavour* (Plon, Paris, 1926) p. 52.
23. W.R. Thayer, *Life and times of Cavour* (Houghton Mifflin, Boston, 1911).
24. G.M. Trevelyan, *Garibaldi and the Making of Italy* (Nelson, London, 1911).
25. A.J. Whyte, *Early Life and Letters of Cavour* (Oxford University Press, 1925).
26. A.J. Whyte, *Political Life and Letters of Cavour* (Oxford University Press, 1930).
27. A. Panzini, *Conte di Cavour* (Mondadori, Milan, 1931).
28. Gentile's preface to Cavour, *Scritti politici* (Anonima Romana Editoriale, Rome, 1925), p. xix.
29. L. Salvatorelli, *Il pensiero politico italiano dal 1700 al 1870* (Einaudi, Turin, 1935).
30. L. Salvatorelli, in *Prima e dopo il Quarantotto* (De Silva, Turin, 1948) p. 189.
31. D. Mack Smith, *Italy and its Monarchy* (Yale University Press, 1989).
32. P. Pirri, *Pio IX, Vittorio Emanuele dal loro carteggio privato* (Pontificia Università Gregoriana, Rome, 1954).

33. A. Gramsci, *Il Risorgimento* (Einaudi, Turin, 1949).
34. *ibid*, pp. 69–70.
35. *ibid*, p. 149.
36. *ibid*, p. 46.
37. G. Candeloro, *Storia dell'Italia Moderna* (Feltrinelli, Milan, 1956–86).
38. *ibid*, vol. iv, p. 128.
39. D. Mack Smith, *Cavour and Garibaldi 1860. A study in political conflict* (Cambridge University Press, 1954).
40. D. Mack Smith, *Cavour* (Weidenfeld & Nicolson, London, 1985).
41. F. Coppa, *Camillo di Cavour* (Twayne, New York, 1973).
42. F. Coppa, *The Origins of The Wars of Italian Independence* (Longman, Harlow, 1992).
43. R. Romeo, *Cavour e il suo tempo* (Laterza, Bari, 1969–84).
44. R. Romeo, *Il Risorgimento in Sicilia* (Laterza, Bari, 1950).
45. R. Romeo, *Risorgimento e capitalismo* (Laterza, Bari, 1959).

Chapter 9

SEQUEL AND CONCLUSION

The dramatic phase of Italian history, from 1830 to 1861, which culminated in the establishment of the Kingdom of Italy, has traditionally been associated with the three figures of Mazzini, Cavour and Garibaldi. Even the most austere of academic historians would find it hard to deny that there was an element of glamour in that period of history, or that each of those three men must have had his own kind of charisma. After 1861 most students of European history find less to interest them in Italy, and turn their attention to Germany, where Bismarck was beginning his remarkable career. In Italy the narrative of the years after 1861 is bound to seem like an anticlimax. Benedetto Croce argued – not altogether convincingly – that the people who had to cope with political and social developments in Italy after the creation of the Kingdom had an even harder task than Cavour had faced. To attempt such a comparison would perhaps be pointless, but it must at least be said that Cavour left immense problems for his successors.

.   .   .

CAVOUR'S IMMEDIATE SUCCESSORS

Cavour's party, the Party of the Right, or the *Destra*, retained power, through a parliamentary majority, until 1876. They inherited a bitter struggle in the South, which had some, though not all, of the characteristics of a civil war. They also inherited a considerable debt in the purely financial sense. The wars of 1854 and 1859 had been costly for a small state like Piedmont, and even the campaign of 1860 in the Papal States had involved some expenditure. Although

Cavour had never let finances get out of control, he had assumed that the cost of the struggle for independence and unity would have to be partly met in the future. The Party of the Right thus had to concentrate on attempts to balance the budget, attempts which never completely succeeded. A policy of retrenchment and austerity is neither popular at the time, nor exciting as the subject of historical narrative. The men of the *Destra* who followed Cavour are often seen as unimaginative and ultra-conservative, though Croce pointed out that there is no evidence in these years of the kind of corruption that characterized the post-1876 period. The prime ministers of the years 1861 to 1876 made no brilliant achievements, but at least they held the Kingdom together at a time when many people outside Italy – among them Pius IX – believed that a united Italian state could not survive.

The social policy of the Right, however, was lacking in humanitarian concern for the poor, or compassion for the peasants of the South. They imposed crushing taxes on the least fortunate subjects of the recently proclaimed King of Italy. The taxes led to civil disorders, and the extreme poverty of the peasants prevented the birth of a domestic market for industrial products. Cavour had not been the most compassionate of men, and, although he had been a good landlord on his own estates, it is likely that he would have been less concerned with the social deprivation of many Neapolitans than with the stifling of the growth of industry in the country at large. Speculation as to what Cavour's fiscal policy might have been is perhaps unrewarding, but it can safely be assumed that it is unlikely to have been less imaginative than that of his successors.

Cavour's immediate successor as prime minister of Italy was the Baron Bettino Ricasoli. Vittorio Emanuele disliked Ricasoli even more than he had disliked Cavour. Ricasoli was a puritan, and did not conceal his distaste for the king's irregular private life. That he became prime minister is thus an illustration of the fact that Cavour had created a parliamentary state, not a monarchical one. Equally important was the fact that Ricasoli was a Tuscan. The king would have preferred to appoint a Piedmontese minister, but that Cavour's immediate successor was a Tuscan is one of several points that undermine the facile argument that the unification of Italy was nothing more than a process of

Piedmontization. This rich, conservative, Tuscan landowner had pressed for the annexation of Tuscany to Piedmont, when Cavour himself had been inclined to move more slowly. It is difficult to place Ricasoli in the political spectrum. His extreme Italian nationalism seems to place him to the left – towards Mazzini, yet he was a patriarchal landowner, with a horror of republican democracy, and it was for this reason that the Party of the Right were prepared to have him as their leader.

Ricasoli lasted only until March, 1862 – a little less than a year. If his appointment had indicated the parliamentary nature of the regime, his resignation showed that the king still had more influence than should have been acceptable in a constitutional monarchy. The influence of the crown in a newly created state is bound to depend upon the strengths of personalities. Vittorio Emanuele was far from being a retiring, passive, king, but the force of his personality fortunately varied from one moment to the next. He did not consistently strive for power. His political aims, like his intelligence, were, after all, limited. He had not vetoed the appointment of Ricasoli, but the poor relations between the two men made it impossible for Ricasoli, with his pride and his rectitude, to continue in office.

Ricasoli was followed as prime minister by Urbano Rattazzi, the one-time leader of the Centre Left in the old Piedmontese parliament. Precisely because he was Piedmontese, and had been long familiar with the workings of the Piedmontese parliament, he was more acceptable to Vittorio Emanuele. Both Ricasoli and Rattazzi had experienced close political relations with Cavour, yet neither of them was his obvious successor. Rattazzi was in office for the first time for only nine months, after which he was replaced by Luigi Carlo Farini, who had been more fully a creature of Cavour than either Ricasoli or Rattazzi. Farini had originally been a subject of the pope, so that once again it could be said that the highest office of state was not preserved for the Piedmontese. Farini was a disaster as prime minister, however. He had always been an excitable man, and during his premiership experienced a complete mental breakdown. In an interview with the king he insisted that Italy should declare war on Russia, and when Vittorio Emanuele – understandably – rejected the idea, Farini threatened him with a knife. Drawing a knife on the monarch is unusual behaviour for a prime minister, and it was not surprising that Farini was now relieved of his office.

Perhaps the most worthy successor to Cavour among the leaders of the Right was Marco Minghetti, arguably the most intelligent man to hold power in Italy in the last 132 years. He was prime minister in 1863–64, and, again in 1873–76, after the acquisition of Rome. A scholar of literature and economics, he was remarkably free of ideological or party commitments, and believed that the needs of the country should be studied in a scientific manner. Again, he was not Piedmontese, but, like Farini, had originally been a subject of the pope.

.   .   .

THE SUBSEQUENT HISTORY OF GARIBALDI

Although Cavour had always regarded Garibaldi as a dangerous rival, and at times as a personal enemy, by a strange paradox Garibaldi, after Cavour's death, never again reached the heights of achievement he had reached in 1860. There was, of course, no causal connection between the disappearance of Cavour from the scene and the ending of Garibaldi's triumphs. It was during two periods when Rattazzi was prime minister that Garibaldi attempted to take Rome for Vittorio Emanuele. On both occasions Rattazzi seemed to be encouraging Garibaldi to lead an irregular force against the pope and the French army protecting him; but on both occasions, too, Rattazzi withdrew support after Garibaldi had started his attempt.

In 1862 Garibaldi was allowed by Rattazzi's government to assemble a volunteer force in Sicily, and even to secure ships to transport them to the mainland. Only then did the Italian authorities decide to halt Garibaldi. At Aspromonte, on the very tip of Italy's toe, a royal force fired on the Garibaldians, and a brief skirmish took place. Garibaldi was quite severely wounded in the ankle. The wound probably exacerbated, if it did not cause, his arthritis, and he was never to be so fit again. At least Cavour had never ordered Italian troops to fire on Garibaldi, though he had sometimes come close to doing so.

The second of Garibaldi's attempts on Rome, again at first

encouraged by Rattazzi, but then abandoned by him, was on a rather larger scale. Rattazzi became prime minister for the second time in April 1867. By an agreement with Italy, Napoleon III had withdrawn his troops from Rome in 1866. In the autumn of 1867 Garibaldi seized the opportunity to raise another irregular army for the occupation of Rome, and, again, Rattazzi did nothing to dissuade him. On this occasion, however, Garibaldi had to fight, not a small Italian force, but a considerable, newly equipped, French force, which Napoleon despatched to the Papal States. Garibaldi was defeated at the battle of Mentana.

It should be said, though, that Garibaldi had fought effectively with a volunteer force, under the general Italian command, in the war of 1866. In the Franco-Prussian War in 1870 he led another volunteer force in defence of the French Republic, and in that, the last fight of his career, his men captured a Prussian standard. He died in 1878, after a lifetime of struggle for Italian independence and unity, and, ultimately, for democracy. Unlike Mazzini, Garibaldi had recognized the Kingdom of Italy, to the creation of which he and Cavour had contributed so much, and he had accepted election as a deputy in its parliament. He would, nevertheless, have preferred Italy to have been a more democratic country, and he never forgave Cavour for failing adequately to reward his red-shirts. Yet Cavour had never deceived and betrayed him as Rattazzi had done.

.   .   .

THE COMPLETION OF ITALIAN UNITY

In one sense the task of creating the nation-state had been completed when the Kingdom of Italy had been proclaimed and the majority of world powers had extended diplomatic recognition to it. In another sense the task was, at that stage, far from complete, since the institutions of the former sovereign states – the Kingdoms of Piedmont and Naples, the Austrian provinces, the territories formerly ruled by the pope, the Grand Duchy of Tuscany and the Duchies of Parma and Modena – still had to be integrated as the institutions of the Kingdom of Italy. This was perhaps the most important task left by Cavour to his immediate successors.

At least one part of the task had been accomplished by

Cavour before his death. A parliament of united Italy was quickly elected, according to the model laid down back in 1848 by Carlo Alberto's *statuto*. This part of the process of integration was undeniably one of 'Piedmontization'. The first parliaments met in Turin, which must have seemed a very remote place to which to travel for deputies from Palermo or Naples.

The parliamentary life of Piedmont, and now of Italy, was based very much on the Westminster model, of which Cavour had been a great admirer. The administrative system, on the other hand, was based on that of France, partly because this was the system that Napoleon I had exported to Italy, and which even the restored regimes of 1815 had maintained, simply because it seemed to work efficiently. It involved rigid centralization, with prefects and sub-prefects sent out from Turin.

To integrate the armed forces was an enormous task. The Piedmontese and Neapolitan armies, and the 'Army of the South', as Garibaldi's force had come to be called, together with the much smaller armies of the Grand Duke of Tuscany and the Duchies of Parma and Modena, had to be turned into a single national army. The operation was not carried out without friction. Two navies, of which the Neapolitan was appreciably larger than the Piedmontese, were not merged for some years, although, of course, they were placed under a single command. That Italy's naval record in the 1866 war was so abysmal is therefore not altogether surprising.

What is surprising, on the other hand, is that the process of integrating institutions was carried out without bloodshed. The educational systems, for example, were bound to be difficult to merge. The Universities of Bologna, Ferrara and Naples were far more ancient and internationally famous than the University of Turin, but universities and schools were all to be united under a Ministry of Education in Turin. Before his death, Cavour took the sensible step of appointing an eminent figure from the University of Naples, the great literary critic, Francesco De Sanctis, as minister of education. De Sanctis handled a delicate question with great tact, centralizing the system, but instructing the bureaucrats in Turin to exercise their powers with as light a touch as possible.

In 1861 the unification of Italy remained to be completed in a more obvious sense than that of integrating institutions: Venice and Rome were still outside the Kingdom. As we have seen in Chapter 7, Cavour's attempts to secure Rome by peaceful negotiation with Pius IX and Napoleon had failed. For the acquisition of Venice he had been prepared to wait, but he had not removed it from his agenda. In the event Venice was to be acquired only after a Third War of Independence in 1866. For Italy the war was a moral defeat of a kind that Cavour had never had to suffer. The Italians were badly defeated on land and sea. That the Austrians were defeated was entirely due to Italy's ally, Prussia, and more specifically to the genius of Von Moltke and his creation of a modern-type general staff for his army. Bismarck had secured the alliance with Italy in order to burden Austria with a war on two fronts, and although the Italian contribution to the war was a pathetic one, both Prussia and Italy gained from the Austrian defeat. Napoleon III remained neutral in the war, but his diplomacy also played a part in Italy's acquisition of Venice.

The acquisition of Rome was also due to events outside Italy, but, unlike that of Venice, it did not involve the fighting of a bloody and humiliating war. After Garibaldi's defeat at Mentana, Napoleon left his troops in Rome, to deter any future attack. For a few years the capital was moved from Turin to Florence, partly to satisfy Napoleon, who, by some curious reasoning, believed that if the Italians had moved their capital once they would not do so again, and partly because the line of the Appenines made Florence a more defensible capital against Austrian attack than Turin had ever been. Nevertheless, one of Cavour's more sensational statements before his death had been that Rome must one day be the capital of Italy, and his successors had never given up the idea, which had, not so many years before, been a wild Mazzinian dream.

When the Franco-Prussian war broke out in 1870, Napoleon III, even before he had suffered any defeats, brought his troops home from Rome. The Italian government of Giovanni Lanza cautiously waited to see the results of the first battles, but after Napoleon's defeat at Sedan, an Italian force was sent to Rome. It was briefly resisted by a papal force at the Porta Pia, and a few lives were lost, but eventually the pope was ejected from his palace of the Quirinale, and forced to become – as he saw it – 'the prisoner of the Vatican'.

. . .

CAVOUR'S PLACE IN HISTORY

Several questions can be asked about Cavour's role in the creation of Italy. Some have already been hinted at, and tentative answers given: Did he die at the right moment – before the terrible 'Brigands' War' illustrated some serious flaws in the unitary Kingdom? Was it wise to force a tightly united, integrated, state on to an Italy where the differences between North and South, and between one city and another, were so marked? Would it not have been better to have some kind of federal structure, which would have allowed the regions to have an element of autonomy?

In answer to the first of these rhetorical questions, it must be pointed out that the 'Brigands' War' was not of Cavour's making. Civil wars are usually more bitter and brutal than international wars, and, in so far as this was a civil war, it was a peculiarly ferocious one. It has sometimes been said that more people died in it than in all the wars of the *risorgimento*. The relevant statistics – especially those for the 'Brigands' War' – are not too reliable, but it can safely be said that the death toll was appalling. The people who fought the 'Brigands' War' against the authorities of the new Kingdom of Italy were a strange alliance of genuine brigands, disbanded soldiers and deserters from the Neapolitan army, with a sprinkling of genuine supporters of the old Bourbon regime.

Horrific atrocities were committed in this war: prisoners were burnt to death or crucified by the insurgents, but the Italian authorities were not slow to shoot anyone with arms, or to burn down villages which harboured 'brigands'. It was more than a 'brigands' war', and yet it was less than a civil war. It lasted for some four or five years, and in Sicily for rather longer. Even when the 'brigands' were defeated, criminal groups, of which the *mafia* survived the longest, kept the agony of organized crime alive.

Part of the bitterness of the war was probably due to the immediate application of martial law by the Italian royal authorities. In his last days Cavour had warned against the introduction of martial law. Whether he could have handled the crisis by other means can never be known.

To the second of the three rhetorical questions it must be answered that in practical terms Cavour had no alternative but to impose a unitary state on Italy, since no authority was available for running the South in a liberal and responsible manner, except the existing authority in Turin. Even Garibaldi had asked only that he could remain dictator of the South for a year, after which he assumed that a centralized Italian government would take over. It would perhaps not have been so impossible for Cavour to have granted Garibaldi's request, but there would have been the danger that Garibaldi would have used his year's dictatorship to prepare a larger army with which to march on Rome.

So far as rivalries between Italian cities are concerned, it is true that Italy is essentially an urban civilization, and individual cities have a stronger sense of identity than do those of most other countries. Yet, as we have seen, the centralization of Italian institutions was in the event carried through without bloodshed. The citizens of Turin, Milan, Bologna, Florence, Rome and Naples did not make war on each other, and their educated classes had, after all, been sharing the same literature since the age of Dante. The existence of different dialects should not be allowed to obscure the fact that they were all dialects of Italian.

The third of the three rhetorical questions can be taken to imply that, even if a single authority for Italy had to be enforced for the time being, a federal structure should subsequently have been allowed to evolve. Although neither Cavour, nor democrats like Mazzini and Garibaldi, were in sympathy with the federal idea, there were serious-minded and far-thinking theorists who recommended a federation. Chief among them were Giuseppe Ferrari and Carlo Cattaneo. Both were democrats and republicans, but both believed that Mazzini was mistaken in working for a unitary state, because the fragmentation of Italy historically made a federation the obvious solution.

It was essentially an academic argument. In the event the unitary state survived, and developed into a democracy before 1914, and the lack of a federal structure can hardly be blamed for the Fascist period after the first world war. The system of regionalism allowed for in the 1948 constitution, and slowly adopted in the 1960s and 1970s, was successful. In the 1990s the movement of the *Leghe* in the North aimed at federalism, but only to escape from the criminality and corruption of the South, and once it became apparent that the northern cities were also riddled with corruption, the appeal of the *Leghe* was bound to suffer.

To blame Cavour, or the *risorgimento*, for the negative features in subsequent Italian history, while overlooking the positive features, would clearly be absurd. Cavour was essentially a man of his day, a man who appreciated the dynamic forces at work in Europe. His belief in individual freedom, in a future fuelled by science, and in a steady progress towards human well-being, distinguishes him from so many contemporaries who were still prisoners of the traditions and superstitions of the past. His own contribution to progress, to the securing of the independence and the unity of Italy, marks him out as one of the major figures of the nineteenth century.

CHRONOLOGY

1810   Birth of Cavour, 10 August.

1820   Goes to school at the Royal Military Academy in Turin.

1824   Made a page of Carlo Alberto.

1826   Given a commission in the Piedmontese Royal Engineers.

1828   Sent to Ventimiglia and other garrison posts in connection with the building of fortifications.
Starts reading economics and political science.

1830   Meets Anna Giustiniani. Posted to Genoa.

1831   Leaves the army – suspected of subversive opinions.

1835   Travels in France and Britain for the first time.
Returns to take over his father's estates.

1841   Suicide of Anna Giustiniani.

1846   His review article on the railways published.
Election of Pius IX.

1847   Relaxation of the press censorship in Piedmont.
With Cesare Balbo Cavour founds *Il Risorgimento*.

1848   Carlo Alberto grants the *Statuto*, 4 March.
Rising in Milan against the Austrians, 17 March.
Carlo Alberto declares war on Austria, 23 March.
Piedmontese defeat the Austrians in the battle of Goito, in which Cavour's nephew is killed, 30 May.
Cavour elected to parliament for the first time.
Cavour's first speech to parliament, 26 June.
Austrians defeat the Piedmontese at the battle of Custozza, 24 July.

1848   Piedmontese renew war with Austria, but are defeated at the battle of Novara, March.
Abdication of Carlo Alberto, and accession of Vittorio Emanuele II.

1850   Cavour made minister for trade, agriculture and the navy, October.

1851   Cavour made minister of finance, 26 February.
Cavour negotiates the *connubio* with the Centre Left, February–March.

1852   Cavour prime minister.
Proclamation of the Second Empire in Paris, 1 December.

1853   Mazzinian rising in Milan fails, February.
Cavour arrests Crispi and other Mazzinians, but protests to Austria at the sequestrations of the property of Piedmontese subjects.
Russia declares war on Turkey, 1 November.

1854   Britain and France declare war on Russia, and sign treaty of alliance on 10 April, 28 March.

1855   Piedmont accedes to Anglo-French treaty of 10 April 1854, 10 January.
Cavour signs military convention for intervention in the war, 26 January.
Palmerston becomes prime minister in London, February.
Piedmont declares war on Russia, 4 March.
Napoleon asks Cavour: 'What can I do for Italy?', 7 December.

1856   Cavour replies to Napoleon's question, 21 January.
Congress of Paris, 25 February-16 April.
Clarendon addresses the Congress on Italian affairs, 8 April.
Britain and France break off diplomatic relations with Naples.
Cavour awarded the 'Anunziata', 29 April.

1857   Pisacane's failed revolution in the Kingdom of Naples.
Case of the *Cagliari*.
Foundation of the National Society, August.

Elections in Piedmont mark a swing to the right, November.

1858   Orsini's bombs fail to kill Napoleon III, 14 January.
Cavour destroys the *Italia e Popolo*, January.
Cavour sends defiant letter to Paris, 9 February.
Cavour explains his policy to parliament, 16 April.
Pact of Plombières between Cavour and Napoleon, July.
Napoleon, at New Year's Eve reception, tells the Austrian ambassador that he regrets bad Franco-Austrian relations, 31 December.
Fall on the world stock markets results.

1859   Franco-Piedmontese Treaty for offensive war against Austria (back-dated to 12 December 1858), January.
Opening of Piedmontese parliament: King's *grido di dolore* speech, January.
Piedmont calls up reserves, 9 March.
Austria mobilizes her army, 7 April.
Austrian ultimatum to Piedmont rejected by Cavour; Austria declares war on Piedmont; France declares war on Austria, 19–23 April.
Austrians invade Piedmont, 29 April.
Revolutions in Tuscany, Parma, Modena and the Papal Romagna.
Ricasoli seizes control in Florence.
Battle of Magenta, 4 June.
Farini takes control of Modena for Piedmont, 19 June.
Battle of Solferino, 24 June.
Napoleon and Francis Joseph sign armistice at Villafranca, 11 July.
Resignation of Cavour.
Lamarmora becomes prime minister of Piedmont.
Assemblies in Tuscany and Modena vote for union with Piedmont, August.
Farini assumes dictatorial powers in Parma, 18 August.
Assembly in Papal Bologna votes end of temporal power of the Pope, and union with Piedmont, 6–7 September.
Assembly in Parma votes for union with Piedmont, 12 September.

Treaty of Zurich confirms most terms of Villafranca, by which Lombardy becomes part of Piedmont, 10 November.

Publication of *Le Pape et le Congrès*, December.

1860   Lord John Russell proposes a policy of non-intervention in Italy. It is accepted, sometimes reluctantly, by the Great Powers, January.

Cavour again prime minister, 21 January.

Plebiscites in Tuscany, Parma, Modena and the Papal Romagna (the last three now linked as 'Emilia') strongly favour unity with Piedmont, 11–15 March.

Treaty ceding Savoy and Nice to France, 12–14 March.

Plebiscites confirm the treaty, April.

Garibaldi sails from Quarto, for Sicily, with the Thousand, 5–6 May.

Garibaldi's first victory with the Thousand, at Calatafimi, 15 May.

Garibaldi takes Palermo, 27 May.

Cavour sends La Farina to represent him with Garibaldi, June.

La Farina arrested and deported from Sicily, 7 July.

Cavour makes contacts in Naples, and sends agents there, in an unsuccessful attempt to start a pro-Piedmontese revolution, July-August.

Garibaldi crosses to the mainland Kingdom of Naples, August.

Piedmontese cabinet accepts Cavour's proposal for an invasion of the Papal States, 26 August.

Garibaldi enters Naples, 7 September.

Piedmontese invasion of the Papal States, 11 September.

Battle of Castelfidardo, 18 September.

Plebiscites in Naples and Sicily favour a united Italy, 21–22 October.

Garibaldi and Vittorio Emanuele, and their armies, meet at Teano, 26 October.

Plebiscites in the Marche and Umbria also favour merging with Italy, 4–5 November.

1861   Elections for Italian parliament give Cavour's party a large majority, 27 January.

Parliament meets in Turin, 18 February.

Vittorio Emanuele II proclaimed King of Italy, 17 March.

Garibaldi denounces Cavour in parliament for the treatment of the officers of the Thousand, and for Cavour's attitude to Garibaldi's campaign, April.

Cavour negotiates, unsuccessfully, with the Papacy for a solution of the Roman Question, January-March.

Cavour, in speeches in parliament, affirms that Rome must one day be the capital of Italy, 25/27 March.

Death of Cavour, 6 June.

BIBLIOGRAPHICAL NOTE

Works which have, in one way or another, become classics, or which deal directly with Cavour, are discussed in Chapter VIII. This note is intended to be supplementary to that chapter.

Some material has been used from the following archives:
Archivio di Stato, Ministero degli Affari Esteri, Rome
Archivio di Stato, Turin
The Bodleian Library, Oxford
Archives du Ministère des Affaires Etrangères, Paris.

PRIMARY PRINTED SOURCES

These are listed roughly in order of importance, rather than alphabetically, or chronologically:

Il carteggio Cavour-Nigra dal 1858 al 1861, 4 vols., (Zanichelli, Bologna, 1929; reprinted 1961)

Carteggio Cavour-Salmour (Zanichelli, Bologna, 1936; reprinted 1961)

La questione romana negli anni 1860–1861, 2 vols., (Zanichelli, Bologna, 1929; reprinted 1961)

Le relazioni diplomatiche fra la Gran Bretagna e il Regno di Sardegna, 1848–1860, edited by Federico Curato and G. Giarizzo, 7 vols., (Rome, 1961–68)

There are two excellent selections of documents translated into English:

Derek Beales, *The Risorgimento and the Unification of Italy, 1796–1866* (Allen & Unwin, London, 1968; new edition, Longman, London, 1988)

Denis Mack Smith, *The Making of Italy, 1796–1866* (Macmillan, London, 1968; new edition 1988)

Discorsi parlamentari, edited by Adolfo Omodeo, L. Russo and A. Saitta, 15 vols., ('La Nuova Italia', Florence, 1932–1973)

A selection of a few of Cavour's more important speeches was made by Delio Cantimori: *Discorsi parlamentari* (Einaudi, Turin, 1962)

Tutti gli scritti di Camillo Cavour, edited by C. Pischedda and G. Talamo, 4 vols., (Centro Studi Piemontesi, Turin, 1975–78). An extraordinary collection of Cavour's jottings.

. . .

SECONDARY WORKS

For the background:

Stuart Woolf, *A History of Italy, 1700–1860* (Methuen, London, 1979)

Harry Hearder, *Italy in the Age of the Risorgimento, 1790–1870* (Longman, Harlow, 1983)

Previous lives of Cavour of importance are mentioned in Chapter VIII. Of these, two need to be repeated here:
Denis Mack Smith, *Cavour* (Weidenfeld & Nicolson, London, 1985)

Rosario Romeo, *Cavour e il suo tempo*, 3 vols., (Laterza, Bari, 1977–1984)

. . .

WORKS DEALING WITH A FEW SPECIFIC THEMES

W.K. Hancock, *Ricasoli and the Risorgimento in Tuscany* (Faber & Gwyer, London, 1926)

Raymond Grew, *A Sterner Plan for Italian Unity* (Princeton University Press, 1963). A study of the National Society.

Derek Beales, *England and Italy, 1859–1860* (Allen & Unwin, London, 1961)

Angelo Tamborra, *Cavour e i Balcani* (Ilte, Turin, 1958)

Ronald Marshall, *Massimo d'Azeglio. An Artist in Politics* (Oxford University Press, 1966)

Arnold Blumberg, *A Carefully Planned Accident. The Italian War of 1859* (Susquehanna University Press, London and Toronto, 1990)

. . . . .

MAP

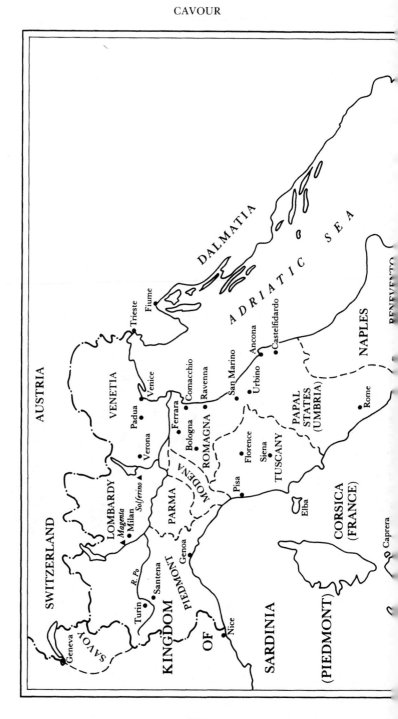

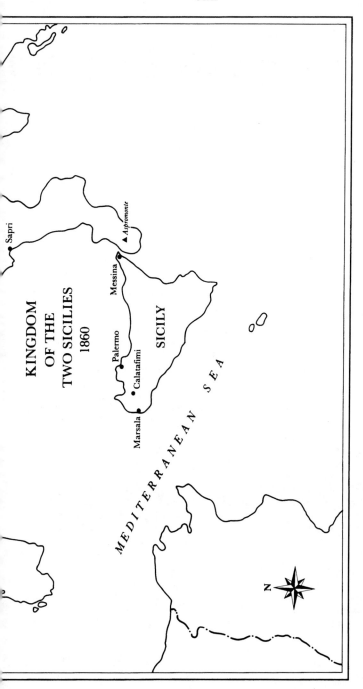

KINGDOM
OF THE
TWO SICILIES
1860

SICILY

Sapri

▲ Aspromonte

Messina

Palermo

Calatafimi

Marsala

MEDITERRANEAN SEA

N

INDEX